Routledge Revivals

ACCOUNTICS
APRIL 1897 TO
AUGUST 1900

ACCOUNTICS
APRIL 1897 TO
AUGUST 1900

Part III
Volume VI, Nos. 1 to 6, January 1900 to June 1900
Volume VII, Nos. 1 to 2, July 1900 to August 1900

Foreword by
Gary John Previts

Routledge
Taylor & Francis Group

First published in 1992 by Garland Publishing, Inc.

This edition first published in 2018 by Routledge
2 Park Square, Milton Park, Abingdon, Oxon, OX14 4RN
and by Routledge
52 Vanderbilt Avenue, New York, NY 10017, USA

Routledge is an imprint of the Taylor & Francis Group, an informa business

Publisher's Note
The publisher has gone to great lengths to ensure the quality of this reprint but points out that some imperfections in the original copies may be apparent.

Disclaimer
The publisher has made every effort to trace copyright holders and welcomes correspondence from those they have been unable to contact.

A Library of Congress record exists under ISBN: 78066608

ISBN 13: 978-0-367-14397-8 (hbk)
ISBN 13: 978-0-429-03184-7 (ebk)

ISSN 1060-1228
Design by Marisel Tavarez

New Works in Accounting History

Richard P. Brief, *Series Editor*

Leonard N. Stern School of Business
New York University

A Garland Series

ACCOUNTICS
APRIL 1897 TO
AUGUST 1900

Part III
Volume VI, Nos. 1 to 6, January 1900 to June 1900
Volume VII, Nos. 1 to 2, July 1900 to August 1900

Foreword by
Gary John Previts

Garland Publishing, Inc.
New York and London 1992

Library of Congress Cataloging-in-Publication Data

Accountics: A monthly magazine for Office Men. Published from April 1897 to August 1900.
This reprint has been classified by the Library of Congress as a serial.

ISBN 0-8153-0683-0 (pt. 3)
ISSN 1060-1228

Printed on acid-free, 250-year-life paper.
Manufactured in the United States of America.

Design by Marisel Tavarez

CONTENTS

Volume VI, Nos. 1 to 6
January 1900 to June 1900

Accountics:—
T.....HE OFFICE MAGAZINE

Volume VI
Number 1

JANUARY, 1900

Monthly, $1 a year
Single Copy, 10 cents

Dissertations on Business Half-Facts

CONDUCTED BY PIERSON PEALE.

"Who are a little wise, the best fools be."—Donne.
"What fools these mortals be."—Puck.

In this department, which is undertaken solely for the purpose of attacking error as I perceive it, and suggesting correc tions and improvements to the limit of my ability, I do not want to seem to call all men fools. Of course, whether or not a man is a fool, turns altogether upon the point of view that is occupied. We are, every one of us, fools in the light of the wisdom of those who have had greater experience than ourselves. By all such comparison our most cherished facts are only half-facts. They are in reality a mixture of truth with obvious error.

What is a business half-fact? I answer something that appears like a fact, but which is only half true. It is an assertion or a rule in which there is an admixture of error.

I might add that there are comparatively few "whole facts" to be met in some lines of business, save as we closely examine those features which are the results of the winnowing and refining of years. Even then, unless we take into most careful account the shifting conditions of the times, we are still very apt to be mislead.

A whole fact of to-day may be a half-fact to-morrow, for evolution in business is working astounding changes.

If there is any one feature of business to-day concerning which there is more misinformation current, than cost accounts in manufacturing I do not know what it is. It would seem that business men in considering the problems of cost prefer to stand in their own light,—that they like to use the short arm of the lever just to show how hard it is to move the weight.

Here, for example, is what a manufacturer of textiles says about the cost of goods: "It may be questioned whether there is any system by which an absolutely correct cost of production may be ascertained. A hundred things will vary cost in a single mill, and different mills will vary according to their equipment. Each individual mill must establish its own cost of the different processes by separate accounts, and every item should be entered, however insignificant, from the raw stock to the commission house, and when all this is accomplished the figures are largely conjectural. And having established a standard of cost at the mill, one cannot foresee breakdowns, strikes, bad work, and many other things beyond control of human effort which increase cost and which may happen in any contract large or small. An approximate cost may be obtained of each process, and not without the expenditure of considerable time and trouble; but once obtained, you have a sort of standard by which to be governed, which must be readjusted in changing from one class of goods to another."

There are several whole-facts in this, as well as half-facts. Let us first give attention to the former:

It is undoubtedly true that each individual mill or factory must establish its own costs, for it is inconceivable that any two concerns will ever show absolutely the same results. That every item must be included in calculating costs is self evident. It is also true that the equipment of the mill exercises a potent influence over costs.

Now for the other class:—The charges for selling have nothing whatever to do with the costs of goods. Therefore, the commission house item should not be included. Manufacturing costs are one thing and commercial expenses quite another. This is so apparent as to need no argument.

A break-down which stops production does not increase the cost of product, for costs, properly considered, cease whenever the factory is closed. A strike, save as it results in the payment of higher wages does not increase cost. A shut-down mill is not making goods, and therefore its costs are not chargeable to goods. They are instead a loss of profits already made, or, in the absence of a surplus to draw upon, a loss of capital.

Instead of an absolutely correct cost of production being a very difficult result to obtain, it is in truth a very easy one. For example, the cost of all the goods made in a given factory during a specified period will be equal to the total of the cost of the materials consumed, the cost of the labor applied, and the general expenses of the factory for that time. Does any one dispute this?

The real difficulty comes in when the effort is made to pro-rate this cost over product in a way to let each lot of goods bear its own proper cost, and no less and no more. The trouble greatly increases whenever the effort is made to show this distribution of costs during operations,— that is, as going results,—the actual costs being declared promptly and correctly as the different lots of goods are finished.

The problems involved in this work, however, are merely clerical in nature. Reduced to their simplest forms they are questions of classification and indexing. The writer whom we have quoted to the contrary notwithstanding, there are those at the present day who are abundantly able to perform the work speedily, efficiently and economically, if only they are afforded the chance. Cost figures established in this way are embodiments of the facts of the situation, and are in no respect conjectural.

"An approximate cost may be obtained of each process." These words do not convey what this author really means. He is thinking of a schedule of rates, a table of constants, by which amounts approximating costs may be calculated. He is reaching after a rule by which to estimate the amount of costs. But costs, as before stated, are facts. They are never estimates, nor yet are they ever approximations.

"Once obtained, you have a sort of standard." Bob Burdette a long time since made a comparison using as the measure a 'tolerably" good egg. No one, he pointed out, would be content with any egg except a "good" egg. "A sort of standard" is arrant nonsense. "A standard" (without qualification or apology) is the only thing a business man can abide and this, in the case under consideration, is the actual facts properly classified and presented. On nothing short of this can business policy and management be safely predicated.

A word about "readjustments:" No two lots of goods in any mill or factory will ever cost the same. But all necessary readjustments will become automatic whenever the actual facts of cost are inspected, instead of guesses as to cost, or the results of emperical rules.

Half-facts always tend to business destruction, and should be shunned like a pestilence.

English as a World Language

The steady progress that English is making as the treaty and commercial language of the world, was evidenced a short time since by the fact that the new commercial treaty between Mexico and China was written in English. The use of the English language in drawing up

International agreements is something unprecedented. French has had the distinction of being the diplomatic language, but the State Department officials now think that the drafting of the Mexican-Chinese treaty marks the beginning of the end of the general use of the French in this particular.

For the past 200 years in a large majority of negotiations looking toward the formation of international agreements, the language of the French people has been widely used by diplomats in official correspondence and in the actual drawing of the treaty itself. This rule, while general, has not been universal, but the few exceptions have only gone to prove the rule. French has been the great social language. Nearly all men of education have been taught it and in the social intercourse of Europe it has been generally spoken. From the fact that the diplomats of the world have been familiar with it, it has crept into diplomatic intercourse to the almost total exclusion of other languages.

The treaty of peace between the United States and Spain was written in French as have also been the majority, of international documents during the past two centuries. . Within recent years a rule has been made in diplomacy by which a diplomatic representative in official correspondence may employ the language of his own country, or that of any other if he chooses. Notwithstanding this rule, the French has been retained in perhaps a majority of instances.

The German Ambassador now uses German in his correspondence with the State Department and England's representative the English. The Swedish, Norwegian, Russian, Belgian, Turkish, Italian and Greek diplomatic representatives all employ the French while those of China and Japan use English.

In a large measure English is supplanting the French both as a social and commercial language. The statistics of the International Postal Union gave the number of letters addressed in English from all parts of the world as being about 75 per cent.

In foreign universities the tongue of the Anglo-Saxon race is taking the place of the French and it is fast becoming the social medium of intercourse. From the general prevalence of the language, it is thought that it will, before a quarter of a century, be the diplomatic language.

Credit Department Methods

The unity of interest between the bank and the borrower is a matter of growing appreciation throughout the business world. The borrower feels more keenly than ever before that in the integrity of the bank lies his safety, and the banker has come to regard the borrower not as one to whom (to use an old and perhaps unfortunate term) accommodation is extended, but as the rightful participant in the benefits which his bank as an agency of the public can extend.

In an address recently delivered by James G. Cannon, Vice-President of the Fourth National Bank of New York, he

described the methods of obtaining credit now in vogue and then proceeded to recommend certain changes in the system. His views from their broad grasp of the relation between the bank and the borrower must commend themselves to all business men. The following extract presents the matter in his own words:

The methods of conducting business have so changed in recent years that merchants now find it necessary to sell their goods largely upon open accounts instead of taking notes in payment of merchandise indebtedness, and having the obligations discounted at bank, hence credit extended to the merchant must be predicated upon his solvency. This being the case, it is essential to have at hand definite knowledge as to the financial responsibility of the applicant for credit; and this information can be secured from no better source than the applicant himself. A third party may give valuable impressions, ideas, and opinions; but the facts which will place the creditor in position to do justice to himself and to the party to whom he loans money or sells on open account, can only be obtained from the credit-seeker.

In order to have this information in such shape that it may be referred to at all times by the party who extends credit, either for money or merchandise, there has been devised the property statement blank which has come into such extensive use during the past ten years. The property statement blank provides for a tabulated balance sheet, with a set of questions so arranged as to clearly reveal to the bank or the seller of merchandise such facts concerning the assets and liabilities of the party seeking credit as will readily indicate the true condition of his affairs. Such information as is provided for by this blank, I contend, is the only true basis for the extension of credit. * * * It is time that banks realized the necessity for insisting on the receipt, at stated intervals, of signed property statements from all their customers who seek accommodation. When a loan without collateral is applied for, it should be established, as a principle of banking and good business usage, that the borrower should make a clear and comprehensive statement of his financial condition. It is our duty, handling as we do, money belonging to our stockholders and depositors, to insist upon such protection for our unsecured loans; and we should have no hesitancy in applying for exhibits.

Credit is based on possessions, but abundant assets are not always requisite for the creation of credit. It is very desirable, however, that the credit given should be proportionate to the actual assets of the borrower. The grantor of credit is a contributor of capital, and becomes, in consequence, interested in the success or failure of the debtor; and as such he is clearly entitled to complete information as to his financial condition at all times.

The making of property statements also has the effect of educating the borrower to higher standards of business methods,

as many applicants for credit fail to realize their own precarious condition until their cases are carefully diagnosed by a painstaking, conscientious bank officer from facts revealed by a detailed statement. By means of these statements, and their careful analysis, unbusinesslike practices are brought to light; and the borrower, if properly advised, is diverted from a dangerous course to one of safety, conservatism and prosperity. When an applicant for credit makes a showing of his affairs and unreservedly discloses his financial condition to his banker, he should then be afforded credit facilities commensurate with his responsibility and the average bank balance maintained. This places the whole matter of borrowing upon a business basis, and favoritism is eliminated. Banks are not private enterprises, but public institutions, whose doors should be wide open, and whose legitimate facilities should be placed at the disposal of worthy depositors. The obtaining of accommodation should not be, as it often is, a matter of partiality, but a right to which every customer is entitled who can show that his financial condition warrants his borrowing.

Good credit contributes largely to a borrower's business success. It gives him greater capital, enables him to carry a larger stock, and increases his sales and profits. It should be understood that a request for a statement does not imply a reflection on the borrower's character, honesty or business ability; but it is made simply to secure such information as will enable the banker intelligently to transact his business with his customer. Some one has well said, "The merchant who desires to serve his own best interests should recognize that his most valuable possession, apart from his actual assets, is a sound, substantial and unquestioned reputation as a credit risk, and that under the prevailing conditions and demands of business the most effective and eminently the best way to prove his basis for credit is to be willing to submit a statement of his financial condition.

The Ledger Sentimentally Considered

By LANCASHIRE PEN.

The business man from his own motion, or by reason of his relation to the great network of activities all over the land, now takes part in that general summing up and examination of accounts that comes at the end of the year. As he studies his ledger he finds many things pleasant to contemplate and some over which he does not care to linger.

Here is a fortunate investment; there a record of a mistake of judgment. Here is the name of a man who faithfully meets his engagements, whose word is as good as his bond, and there the name of one who shirks a duty whenever possible, and whose promises are made only to be broken. Down the page his eye falls upon a name that will never be seen on his ledger again. The friend who started with him in youth—to build up a name and standing in the community has met his final engagement, and settled his last account. There is a vacant place and a face that he will see no more in the busy throng rushing through the crowded streets. He was an honest man, and a true friend. The ledger shows a clean record. There is a tightening of the throat as he turns with a sigh to the next page.

Another name, and with it come memories of misplaced confidence, unfaithful stewardship, a wife's suffering and tears, and homeless children through a father's dishonesty. He shakes his head and hastens to pleasanter reminders. His eye brightens as it falls upon the record of money given to aid a beneficent object, and he stops while he makes a mental calculation of the possibility of increasing the contribution the coming year. Again he pauses as he notices figures that tell of months of work and struggle and weary waiting while heavy interests hung in the balance. His success would be the success of many others and his failure their ruin. There were anxious days and sleepless nights, followed at last by a happy issue, and a reward to the trust imposed.

The old ledger dry? It is eloquent with meaning to him who has the eye to perceive and the heart to understand.

The Trust Fund Doctrine

By B. R. PRICE.

The relation existing between a corporation and its creditors is somewhat analogous to that which exists between a partnership and its creditors. If a partnership becomes insolvent, a court of equity assumes charge of all of its property and effects, and, through its officers, collects and distributes the fund to partnership creditors before any portion of it can be applied either to the partner or his individual creditor. It may be said that the court holds the property in trust for the partnership creditors, or that they have an equitable lien thereon. This means that the partnership creditors simply have an equitable prior right to have their claims satisfied out of the partnership property in the hands of the court belonging to the insolvent partnership before individual creditors can be paid.

So it is with a corporation. Solvent and out of the hands of the court, it holds complete dominion over its property, unfettered by any direct trust or specific lien in favor of either creditor or stockholder. It can deal and be dealt with in relation to its property as effectually as an individual can with his. While the directors and officers stand in a fiduciary relation in respect to its property, and may be called to account by the stockholders for any fraud or mismanagement of its affairs, yet, as between the corporation and its creditors, there exists simply the relationship of debtor and creditor, and the company does not hold its property charged with any direct trust or lien in their favor.

It may be contended that this view is in antagonism to the prevailing and settled opinions of both state courts and text writers upon this subject. Whatever may have been the views of text writers, rati-

fied and supported as they may have been by courts of high state authority, it is sufficient that the Supreme Court of the United States, in a recent decision, has given, in clear and unambiguous language, its latest emphatic expression upon this question, and its opinion is a controlling authority upon other courts.

Justice Brewer, speaking for that court, said: While it is true language has been frequently used to the effect that the assets of a corporation are a trust fund held by a corporation for the benefit of its creditors, this has not been to convey the idea that there is a direct and express trust attached to the property. As has been said by a leading text writer, they are not, in any true and complete sense, trusts, and can only be called so by way of analogy or metaphor. Whatever of trust there is arises from the peculiar and diverse equitable rights of the stockholders as against the corporation in its property, and their conditional liability to its creditors. It is rather a trust in the administration of the assets after possession by a court of equity, than a trust attaching to the property, as such, for the benefit of either creditor or stockholder.

It may be said that to adopt this view is to overturn a settled rule applicable to trust funds, which from the days of Judge Story has grown and become deeply imbedded in our state and national jurisprudence. To say that this will overturn a settled rule is but to confound the destruction of a principle with the time and manner of its application. The principles underlying the trust fund doctrine, as applied to the property and assets of a corporation, are not overturned, but still exist; not, however, in the broad and unlimited degree which some courts of high authority have announced, but in a more limited sense; not in the broad sense that the entire property and assets of a solvent and going corporation are a trust fund, charged with an express trust or specified lien in favor of either stockholder or creditor, but in the sense that when the conditions and circumstances in relation to the business of the corporation arise, when it becomes insolvent and in the custody of the court, then the principles of the trust fund will apply, and will lay hold of the property, and, under the supervision of the court, will be administered to the creditors and stockholders. This view is consonant with both logic and reason.

The trust fund idea had its origin in the early history of our jurisprudence, when the business of the country was confined to narrow limits, when there were comparatively but few organized companies engaged in the transaction of business, and when there were but few, if any, railroad corporations in existence. From a provincial state we have become a great commercial nation, whose vast business interests are largely owned and conducted by artificial persons, in the form of corporate bodies. Probably four-fifths of the capital invested in the commerce and business of the country is controlled and managed in this manner. To declare that this entire property is held by those cor-

porate bodies charged with an express trust in favor of the individual stockholders, or covered by a specific lien in favor of the creditor, is to extend the application of the trust fund idea to a dangerous limit, and to a limit never contemplated by the founders of that doctrine. This is not the abrogation of the rule, nor the destruction of the doctrine, but simply to limit its application to that class of cases where the facts and circumstances will justify the courts in invoking its aid for the relief of creditors and stockholders.

Modern Department Stores

The wonderful development of the mercantile business of this country within the last twenty-five years is illustrated by the following data relating to an enterprise carried on by a simple partnership and which in no sense can be termed a corporation or trust: The combined floor space of the two stores of this firm is equal to twenty-eight acres which, added to the fourteen acres of outside ware-rooms that are occupied, makes the entire surface covered equal to that of a fair-sized farm. Nearly nine thousand persons are employed in the work of the fifty-five departments in each store and 492 horses and 177 wagons are necessary for transportation of goods to or from the stores. The executive ability requisite for the successful management of a business conducted on a scale of such magnitude is not less than is demanded of the head of a department of the National Government. To this must be added a knowledge of detail, which is the result of a familiar acquaintance with the workings of the various lines of the particular business in hand. Only as brains and training are thus combined can a merchant hope to compete with the broad-minded men who tower above their fellows in the successful conduct of large concerns.

Giving Advice

Did you ever give advice? Did you ever ask advice? If you gave advice, did you feel that your friend would be ill-treating you if he did not follow it? If you have asked advice, did you ever feel obliged to proceed exactly as your friend recommended? In giving advice, have you always spoken truthfully or have you sometimes made allowances for the person who sought your counsel? If you have advised him honestly, was he benefited thereby? Did he continue to call you friend? The following lines which appear in a Chicago paper, very pleasantly record the result of one such experiment.

He came to ask me for advice,
  I sat and heard him through;
I gave the matter careful thought,
And then, in candor, told him what
  I deemed it best to do.

A cloud appeared upon his face,
  He tried to talk me down;
I sought to guide him for the best—
He came with friendship in his breast,
  And left me with a frown.

MORAL.
When men go out to seek advice
  Is truth what they demand?
Not if it shows rough ways before,
Or throws the slightest shadows o'er
  The things that they have planned.

The Monthly Statement

The World's Fair, to be held at Paris this year, is attracting considerable attention everywhere, not only by reason of the magnitude of the promised display, but also on account of certain political questions which have been more or less discussed in connection with this enterprise. The daily papers recently contained a list of the congresses which are to be assembled in Paris on different dates during the progress of the exhibition. These congresses, as announced, are upward of one hundred in number, and for their convenience a special building has been prepared, in which several assemblies may meet at the same time. Broadly speaking, there is a congress provided for nearly every branch of science and art, education and labor. With this said, however, we are obliged to admit that the exception proves the rule, for we fail to find in the list anything that relates specifically to accounting. It is true there is an actuarial congress proposed; popular credit is to have attention; commercial high schools are to be considered, and technical, commercial and industrial education each find a place in the list. Stock corporations also come up for attention, and traveling salesmen and commercial agents have a special convocation of their own, but there is nothing directly relating to accounting.

⁂

Are we to infer from this that the activity of the French mind, which has been widely commented upon in view of the long list of congresses proposed, has left out of consideration the vital element of business? Or is it due to the fact that accountants throughout the world have been neglectful of their own interests and have not suggested to the management the propriety of such a gathering? Possibly accountants who have thought of this matter—for we scarcely believe it possible that every one in the profession has forgotten it—have been deterred from suggesting a congress for fear it would fail of respectable attendance. It is well known that the gatherings of accountants, even when their own best interests are at stake and when discussions are in order with respect to means of securing improved conditions, in this country at least, are poorly intended. The proposition of an international organization, which would be a very apropos connection with the World's Fair, has not made any particular progress to date, and perhaps for this reason alone accountants have been deterred from taking any action in the premises.

⁂

Whatever may be the reason for this neglect in the program, it still remains that accounting is the vital element of business. The World's Fair and the congresses which are to be held in connection therewith, could not progress if it were not for accounting. Even though accountants may not be present in a congress assembled in Paris during the continuation of the World's Fair, still if the accounting that is being done day by day were to be withheld for even a very brief period of time, the Paris fair and the various congresses to be assembled in connection therewith would prove to be a babel of confusion. Without accounting it is impossible for any business to progress. The World's Fair is only a gigantic manifestation of business enterprise. It cannot be held save only as those who follow accounting give it their practical aid and assistance.

⁂

But what of the future? There will be other world's fairs. There will be other world's congresses assembled, either in connection with international expositions or upon independent occasions. Are accountants ever to be represented in these world movements, or does the profession feel that ultimate development has been reached and that there is nothing more possible? It would seem, from the way that many conduct themselves and from the expressions to which they give voice from time to time, that this latter opinion prevails in many directions. Close observers, however, are continually made aware of the fact that notwithstanding the apathy and lethargy of professional accountants, accounting is really progressing, that is is developing, and that the accounting world is moving. That it would move more rapidly, that it might develop more intelligently, and that it might be made of greater assistance to the business man at an early date, if the profession were broad enough, intelligent enough and sufficiently liberal-minded to co-operate in the work seems to be very probable. That which has been accomplished in other professions by congresses and assemblies of different kinds could as well be accomplihed in accounting. All that is necessary is the same work and the same effort. Upon the profession itself rests the entire responsibility.

⁂

While discussing these points, another thought obtrudes itself, the presentation of which in this connection is not out of place. The progress which accounting has made in the past has been due to the efforts of those outside of the accounting profession rather than to an intelligent co-operation of those following the profession in an effort to improve the technics and practice of their calling. To every observer it must be evident that conventional double entry, as it has been taught in the past and as it was long practiced in business, has passed away. Few and far between at the present time are regular double entry books. In the place of double entry, as formerly practiced, there has come into use various fragments of advanced systems—a special ledger here, sales sheets in the place of of the sales book there, cash tickets in the place of the cash book in another instance and innovations of various kinds in still others. As a rule, all of these have been devised, not by accountants, but by untrained men, who, seeing the need of modifications of the old ways and the necessity of labor-saving devices, have put into motion methods and adaptations with which accountants from day to day are gradually becoming acquainted. The art of bookkeeping is progressing, the science of accounts is becoming understood, and business is constantly getting the benefit of the changes, even though the accounting profession holds back, frowns upon improvements and innovations, and takes no active part in the world's progress.

⁂

In the discussion of trusts and large corporations which is going on in various directions at the present time, there is much that is presented, pro and con, that is of interest to accountants and there is much more that is of interest to business men and all careful students of the problems of the day. Narrow-minded men and demagogues from one end of the country to the other are crying out against large corporations or so-called "trusts" as though they are the personification of evil and their existence in itself a disadvantage to the people at large. They assume unreasonably that a trust or large corporation is owned by a single interest, entirely overlooking the fact that a trust is only an aggregation of diffused capital. A single individual might have enough wealth to dominate one or several corporations of moderate size, but when it comes to those of very large dimensions it is a necessity to have the combined strength of a multitude of investors. Under such conditions the small investor in the aggregate becomes an important party in interest. For example, one of the most important trunk lines of the United States, which by its geographical location is a monopoly of the first class, and which is ordinarily accredited to a certain family as belonging to them, has as a fact upwards of ten thousand stockholders, and the amount of the capital stock that is actually owned by the family referred to is stated to be considerably less than one-half of the entire investment. To cite another case, the most prominent "industrial" mentioned in the daily reports is credited with having nearly fifteen thousand stockholders, among which are estates, trust funds and a multitude of those who have put into it their small savings.

⁂

A so-called "trust" or large corporation at the outset is usually the combination of several smaller business enterprises. The reason for such combination is to lessen competition. Competition is sometimes described as the life of business. That may have been the case under certain conditions of business development in the past, but as things are at present undue competition means the death of business. Combination as a principle is undoubtedly sound, and under no circumstances can combination be more heartless than competition. Combination increases the economy of production and saves waste of labor and wealth.

There are reasons for combinations and consolidations and for the presence of large amounts of capital in certain industries at the present time that did not exist a short time ago. The country in the interval has grown, and with the growth of the country opportunities for business have also grown, wants have grown, and individual necessities have increased. It would be utterly impossible to supply the present wants of the population of this country upon the old plan. We might as well return to the stage-coach, giving up our limited express trains, with their equipment of palace cars, as to attempt to supply the wants of this country through the small business institutions which formerly existed.

A very prominent man, writing upon this point some time since, asserted that corporations have continued to grow, and at present are growing so fast as to threaten to absorb the entire industrial business of the country, which is capable of being administered by centralized management. This he further declares to be in accordance with the evolution which has taken place within the last half a century, and which may be in accordance with natural law, if there be natural laws involved in the progress of modern civilization.

It is no doubt true that corporate privileges are greatly abused at times, to the disadvantage of the public, but on the other hand individuals in business frequently lie and cheat. The mere degree does not necessarily constitute the sum of guilt. If what is urged as being wrong upon the part of corporations is true, then all business is wrong. If what certain corporations do in the legitimate exercise of their functions is against public policy, then much or all of that which business men and business firms do is likewise against public policy.

These are points for consideration upon the part of accountants who are frequently called upon to assist in the formation of combinations, and also should be carefully considered by business men who are either in competition with large corporations or else are weighing the question of consolidating their business with others, thereby forming a trust, so-called. So far as a political question can be made out of this matter, there are some who will thoughtlessly urge the wrong of corporations in general. There are others who will be apologists for all corporations regardless. The thinking majority of the public we believe, however, will take the ground that corporations are a necessity and that good ones are to be encouraged and evil ones controlled. The question in the course of time is likely to be regulation of corporations, rather than suppression of corporations.

If confidence is a plant of slow growth, credit is one which matures much more slowly.—Beaconsfield.

Making Business

There are many unemployed accountants and bookkeepers, who might, by the exercise of a little ingenuity, supported by tact and energy, find something to do that would pay far better than the kind of work they are ordinarily seeking. What is required is the ability to strike out in new lines, and to fill a want that others have not been bright enough to see, or if they have seen it, have not realized their capacity for the place. Here is the story of a man who has been successful in such an undertaking and who has come to be known as a "business monger for doctors." There are numerous physicians and dentists who pay a certain sum each month to have their bills made out. The men so employed go to their offices for a day or two, write up their books, make out their bills and mail them. Sometimes three or four doctors having offices in the same building will employ one man among them for this purpose. Members of these professions are notoriously poor business men and some of them lose much of what they make owing to that fact.

But this man, asserts one who has investigated his operations, does even more than that. He has taken up the original idea and carried it to its logical conclusion. He has an office of his own, and all bills are made payable at that office. He takes the books of his clients to his own office, makes out the bills and collects the money. Of course, he has to be a man of standing, in whom the profession is all of that and he does just the work a physician needs to have done.

For some reason a doctor's bill is the very last one that most men pay. The average citizen will pay his grocer or his butcher or any other tradesmen with reasonable promptness, but will let his doctor wait. I don't know why this should be so, but it is. Perhaps it is due to the fact that the doctor has been in the habit of letting his bills run. He sends them out, but he doesn't follow them up. If a bill sent out by a business house doesn't receive attention within a reasonable time, a duplicate is mailed, and if that is ignored, a collector calls on the debtor to remind him that it is time to pay up. That is regarded as business and no exception is taken to it. If the debtor doesn't like to have a call from the collector, he knows he can avoid it by paying the bill when he first receives it. The doctor's account, however, does not receive any such attention ordinarily. If the doctor is busy and undertakes to look after his financial affairs himself it may be two or even three months after the services are rendered before the bill is sent, and it may be another two or three months before a duplicate statement is mailed. And by that time it has come pretty close to becoming a bad debt unless put into the hands of a lawyer. It's the old bill that one doesn't like to pay. Every business man realizes that. Now, this young man of whom I am speaking simply conducts the financial part of the doctor's business on business principles. He does just as much as a merchant would do and no more. The

first bill is followed by another, and if that receives no attention, he goes out as a collector and presents the third in person. But, he says, the mere fact of the bills being sent out on time and followed up with reasonable promptness, sometimes with a courteous letter requesting that they receive early attention, has had a wonderful effect in increasing the number that are paid promptly, for, after all, the doctors are largely responsible for their own trouble in getting pay for their services. The young man is not a lawyer and he never sues for the money. He does not pose as a bad debt collector, never writes threatening letters and never resorts to bulldozing tactics. Yet, as I say, he has been most successful, and has proved himself worth far more to his clients than they have to pay for having their business affairs methodically conducted. After he is through, if he has failed to get the money, it rests with the doctor to decide whether he wants the bill put into the hands of a lawyer, and he has the further satisfaction of finding out in a much shorter time than ever before just what bad debts he has on his books.

Ledger Paper

Surprise is sometimes expressed that nearly all ledger paper made in the United States, as well as for the large export trade, should be produced in a comparatively small section of what is generally known as the New England States. In a pamphlet issued by the Byron Weston Company, Dalton, Mass., the statement is made that the dry climate and clear atmosphere of New England, and the abundant springs and artesian wells, enable the American to make such paper as can hardly be produced in other parts of the world. The paper thus produced will stand the test of ages and can be used in records that defy the tooth of time.

In the same circular are presented the following interesting details concerning the history of paper:

Before the invention of paper the writings of the ancients were made on bark, leaves, stones, ivory tablets, metal plates, and soft bricks, stamped and afterward baked. Eighteen hundred years ago papyrus was in common use. This was procured from the papyrus plant, or reed, growing in moist places by river banks. The stalk could be unrolled into sheets, the part next the bark being thick and strong, while that near the center was thin and delicate. Papyrus was still used as late as the twelfth century, but gradually gave way to the use of parchment made of skins.

Paper was first made from fiber in Spain, by the conquering Saracens, in the year A. D. 704, who it is supposed brought the invention from China. Their method was to pound the rags of fibrous material in mortars till reduced to a short fiber pulp, then spread on frames made of reeds.

In the year 1150 the Germans began making paper from rags, and in 1588 a German made such good paper in England that Queen Elizabeth knighted him.

Before 1798 all paper was made by hand; in that year Louis Roberts of France invented the machine now called the Fourdrinier, which made paper in continuous web. About the year 1840 the Cylinder and Fourdrinier machines were perfected to such a degree that the making of paper by hand was almost abandoned, as the machine made more uniform and, in most respects, better paper.

Questions and Answers
Concerning the
BALANCE-SHEET SYSTEM OF ACCOUNTS
Conducted by the
Account Audit and Assurance Co., Ltd.
25 Pine Street, New York

From A. B., L..ton:

Among other questions that I would like to ask concerning this system of accounting is why you call it the "Balance Sheet System"? Does not every adequate method of accounting employ a balance sheet? Are not all systems of accounts balance sheet systems?

ANSWER.—It is hard to conceive of any accounting plan, adapted to the requirements of a commercial or manufacturing enterprise, that does not reach, as its final result, a balance sheet. The balance sheet is what the business man demands of his accountant. In fact, it is asserted that the object of all bookkeeping is to produce a perfect balance sheet. To this extent our correspondent is correct in attributing to all adequate bookkeeping methods a balance sheet as a prominent element therein. Why, then, should a special system of accounts appropriate to itself the name "balance sheet system"? The question in this form is very easy of answer.

With other systems the balance sheet comes last. With this system the balance sheet comes first. The usual plan, as the reader will recognize, is to keep the books in any old way, and then at the end of a fiscal period take an inventory and review the record as presented by the books of accounts, and in the light thereof make up a profit and loss statement and balance sheet, the latter being entirely outside of and distinct from the books.

In the Balance Sheet System of Accounts, however, the reverse is the opera-tion. The form that the balance sheet is to assume, including the profit and loss statement—that is, the particular form that it is expedient for these two showings to take, in view of the nature of the business and the expressed preferences of the management—is the matter to which attention is first given. It is that which is established at the outset. With the skeleton agreed upon, the facts of the business—that is, the daily transactions—are posted into it in a way to maintain a balance sheet and profit and loss statement as going parts of the bookkeeping system. The balance sheet is constantly made up. The profit and loss statement goes along with the business.

By the Balance Sheet System of Accounts there is no review and making out of statements at the end of the fiscal period, nor yet a compensation for the neglected work of past months. Everything is completed as the record is written. Whatever fiscal period is established for the business relates solely to the requirements of the by-laws, and is adjusted to the convenience of the stockholders with respect to annual meetings, etc., for, so far as the accounting is concerned, one month is absolutely like another, year in and year out. The balance sheet is always ready to be inspected, and the profit and loss statement is likewise always complete and up to date.

For these reasons it would seem altogether appropriate to call the system the Balance Sheet System of Accounts.

unlike those that are made at the present time. For example, the author cites a case in which salaries and freights were debited directly to capital account, instead of making their course thereto through the proper medium, namely the profit and loss account.

The author alludes to the claim that double entry bookkeeping is of Spanish origin, and presents certain arguments in support of that theory. For example, tabulative bookkeeping was impossible until after the invention of our present system of counting and figuring. This was introduced into Spain by the Moors in the tenth century, long before it was known in Italy. Further, bookkeeping by double entry was prescribed by statute in the fourteenth century in mercantile transactions, so that it must have been well known in the country by that time. And last but not least paper mills were in existence in Spain two centuries earlier than in Italy.

Pacioli most certainly was not the inventor of the double entry system. He did, however, write the first systematic treatise on double entry and in this work he embodied the existing practice of the Venetians. In further support of the contention that Spain is the birthplace of double entry bookkeeping, it is asserted that account books dating back to 1339 are in existence which were kept on double entry. These were found at a point in the south of France, and it is argued that it is quite improbable that the system should be known on one side of the Pyrrinees and not on the other. Nevertheless, all research has failed to bring out anything absolutely certain. Finally it is shown that Spanish treatises on bookkeeping, so far as known, all date subsequently to the great "Summa de Arithmetica" of Pacioli.

A Man of Honor

A Man of Honor, or Percy Leroy: By Helen F. Potter. 250 pages; octavo; bound in cloth, gilt side and back titles. Published by F. Tennyson Neely.

It is hard to describe a volume in a sentence. It is also hard to give an indication of a story in few words. The book before us is likely to have a wider sale by reason of the introduction written by Bishop Henry C. Potter, than for any interest that the average reader will find in the story. The author is a kinswoman of the Bishop; but, notwithstanding this fact he states that he has been moved to write the introduction because the author has a story to tell, of tender and genuine interest, and as shown in it, a singularly noble type of character to describe, which she does with clear and unaffected strokes.

Reviews and Criticisms

Kheil's Researches

Valentin Mennher und Antich Rocha (1550-1565). Ein Beitrag zur Geschlete der Buchhaltung. By Carl Peter Kheil. Prag. 1898.

The literature of accounting is receiving marked attention at the hands of competent writers and investigators at the present time, the world over. It would seem from the activity that is being displayed just now in various directions, that authors in this field appreciating its neglect in the past, are endeavoring by special exertion to make up for it in the present.

Carl Peter Kheil, of Prague, has been an investigator into the early history of bookkeeping for some time past, and has recently brought out a new work, the title of which appears at the head of this notice. It contains sketches of the work of Pacioli in Italy and of Ympyn in the Netherlands; but more particularly deals with the writings of Valentin Mennher,

the second oldest Dutch author on bookkeeping, whose book was translated into Spanish by Antich Rocha in 1565. Evidently what we know at the present time as double entry bookkeeping was at the date named measurably complete; and, therefore, it does not surprise us to be informed that Mennher's book contained nothing more than improvements in details.

Up to the date named, it would seem that there had been a lack of consistency in the practice of bookkeepers employing the double entry method; for there was evidently no agreement between them as to whether a debit or a credit should precede. That is to say, there was no fixed position for debits and credits, for sometimes the debits occurred on the left and sometimes on the right. The author draws attention to the fact that the custom of placing the debit first in arranging a journal entry became current at about this date.

The mistakes of bookkeepers 300 and 350 years ago it would seem were not

---

A man born in a state of poverty never feels its keenest pangs; but he who has fallen from a life of luxury feels them with all their bitterness.—James Ellis.

In friendship, as in love, we are often happier through our ignorance than our knowledge.—Shakespeare.

Accountics

The Office Magazine.

Published Monthly.

A. O. KITTREDGE, F. I. A., C. P. A., Editor.

E. R. KITTREDGE, Associate.

Accountics is devoted to the Science of Accounting, to the Art of Bookkeeping and to the advocacy of improved Office Methods.

Subscription.—One dollar a year, payable in advance.

Postage is prepaid by the publishers in the United States, Canada and Mexico. For all other countries in the Postal Union, subscribers must add 50 cents a year.

Discontinuances.—In the absence of specific orders to discontinue at the end of the subscription term the magazine will be continued and a bill sent.

Remittances should be by Draft, P. O. Order or Express Order, payable to the order of the Accountics Association. Money and postage stamps are at the risk of the sender, unless sent by express or in registered letters. Add 10 cents each to checks on local banks to defray collection charges.

Advertising Rates will be quoted on application.

Official Journal.—This publication, by resolutions duly passed, has been made the official publication of the following organizations :—

The Institute of Accounts.
The New York Chapter of the Institute of Accounts.
The Washington Chapter of the Institute of Accounts.
The Hartford Chapter of the Institute of Accounts.

Accountics is the accredited medium of intercommunication between members of the Institute of Accounts wherever located.

ACCOUNTICS ASSOCIATION, Publishers,

Lancashire Bldg., Pine St., near Nassau, New York.

Publisher's Desk

We are indebted to Theo. Koehler, C.P.A., conductor of the recently established New York School of Accounts, St. James Building, New York, for the prospectus which he has issued, outlining the courses conducted therein, which are described as practical bookkeeping, higher accountancy, auditing and commercial law. In the prospectus very little is offered with regard to elementary education or the attainments qualifying the students for each or all of the courses offered. With respect to mathematics we are informed that everything is dispensed with "beyond the four fundamental rules." Nothing is said about grammar and rhetoric. The following excerpt explains itself:

"The inadequacy of commercial schools, or so-called 'business colleges,' to fulfill the requirements of adult students of accounts, arising from their course in bookkeeping partaking too much of a primary nature suitable for children, and the consequent protracted drills in petty details, as well as in their curriculum, including penmanship, shorthand, typewriting, arithmetic, and other allied studies upon which a student of accounts may neither need nor wish to enter, has prompted the establishment of the 'New York School of Accounts' for the purpose of giving instruction exclusively in bookkeeping and accountancy in a manner especially suited to adult students."

To save the reader the trouble of counting we will state that there are only 101 words in the sentence. Notwithstanding

its length, there are several things omitted which may be gained by reading between the lines.

Our esteemed contemporary, Printers' Ink, which, in this connection, may be introduced as the weekly mouthpiece of a newspaper directory that makes a business of rating the various periodicals of the country in the matter of circulation, etc., seems to "have it in" for The Bookkeeper, of Detroit. In its issue for October 18, Printers' Ink refers briefly to the history of The Bookkeeper, which it says has been published for some twelve years and is at present a monthly of the size of the popular magazines. After alluding to the character of the advertising which it contains, it contrasts the rating of the directory with the circulation which the magazine declares that it has. The directory holds to the modest figures of 12,500 copies monthly. The publishers of The Bookkeeper in 1897 made a statement to the directory of a circulation of 17,262 copies, but have made no report since. Its published circulation is at present 50,000 copies, which, Printers' Ink insinuates, is an unsupported claim. Evidently Brother Beach has failed to square himself with the publishers of the American Newspaper Directory. Even though he should adjust matters in this direction, it would not change the facts of the actual circulation. At least that is the common sense of the situation, and the public might be in as much doubt thereafter as they are at present, with respect to this matter.

Gaming has been resorted to by the affluent as a refuge from ennui. It is a mental dram, and may succeed for a moment; but, like all other stimuli, it produces indirect debility.—Colton.

MULTIPLICATION TABLE.

Simple, Practical, Comprehensive. The only practical device on the market to save figuring in multiplication. Time-saving, Brain saving, Assures Accuracy. A complete table of the products of multiplication, so constructed that you can find the results at a glance. Gives easily, quickly, accurately any calculation in multiplication required in business. Will last ten years. Send for circulars. Price, postpaid, $1.00.

ROBERT S. AYARS, Louisville, Ky.

The Evolution of Accountancy

The Society of Accountants and Auditors (of England) held its Autumnal Conference on the 5th of October, at Manchester. The Lord Mayor very courteously set apart the room in the Town Hall, known as the Lord Mayor's Parlor, for the use of the visitors and at the opening of the conference extended to them in person a hearty welcome. The first paper read after the usual preliminaries was by the Secretary of the Society, Mr. James Martin, on "The Evolution of Accountancy." Though Mr. Martin confined himself to the development of accountancy in Great Britain, still there is so much in common in the business methods and interests of America and England that members of the profession on this side of the water cannot fail to appreciate his lucid statement of the situation there. He said in substance:

We may date the rise of accountancy from the year 1800, Scotland taking the lead of England by some twenty-five years and keeping well in advance for over half a century. The first formal organizations were also made in Scotland, the Society of Accountants in Edinburgh being incorporated by Royal Charter in 1854, and the next year the Institute of Accountants and Actuaries of Glasgow, and in 1867 the Society of Accountants in Aberdeen.

It was not till 1870 that we find an organized body in England, when the Institute of Accountants of London appeared. As this society would not admit provincial accountants, local societies arose at Liverpool, Manchester and Sheffield. An effort to harmonize the jealousies existing between these various organizations resulted, in 1880, in the Institute of Chartered Accountants in England and Wales, but the object sought was not realized. The influence of the London branch was paramount and within five years of the granting of the charter, a meeting of accountants from all parts of the country was held and a license was obtained from the Board of Trade on December 31, 1885, for the incorporation of the Society of Accountants and Auditors. Matters in Scotland had not progressed as favorably as the happy beginning gave promise, owing to a want of elasticity in the structure of the local societies, and steps were taken for the organization of an Institute for all Scotland, which after an existence of nineteen years, became the Scottish branch of the Society of Accountants and Auditors.

Mr. Martin then gave a passing mention of other societies in Great Britain and her colonies, of which the following is a list: Corporation of Accountants (Limited) of Glasgow; the Institute of Chartered Accountants in Ireland (Incorporated in 1888); the Institute of Chartered Accountants of Ontario (Incorporated in 1883 by Act of Parliament); the Institute of Accountants of South Australia (Incorporated); the Incorporated Institute of Accountants, Victoria (Incorporated 1887); Queensland Institute of Accountants (Incorporated 1891); Australian Institute of Incorporated Accountants, (Founded 1892); Incorporated Institute of Accountants, New Zealand (Founded 1894); Sidney Institute of Public Accountants (Incorporated 1894); Tasmanian Institute of Accountants (Incorporated 1897); New Zealand Accountants and Auditors' Association (Founded 1898); Institute of Accountants in Natal (Founded 1899); Federal Institute of Accountants (Incorporated), Melbourne; Association of Accountants in Montreal.

In regard to the United States Mr. Martin said: Before leaving this part of my paper, I would like to say that I am conscious of the splendid work that is being done by American Accountancy Institutions, but as I cannot possibly do justice to them in this paper, I prefer not to attempt an injustice.

Having followed the growth of the organizations, Mr. Martin next turned to the objects which underlie their formation. He put these as the elevation of the status of accountancy as a profession, the promotion of professional interests of the respective members and the protection of the public in their dealing with professional accountants.

Attempts have been made from time to time to obtain legislation by Parliament in furtherance of these objects, but so far without avail, due in part to the attitude of the members of the Institute of Chartered Accountants in England and Wales. The policy of the Institute has been to conserve the interests of its members without regard to the status of the profession as a whole. Feeling itself protected by the charter of 1880, it considers any attempt to increase outside proficiency as detrimental to the Institute. The Society of Accountants and Auditors takes a broader view of the situation, but its efforts looking towards governmental protection of the public by Act of Parliament have not thus far been productive of results.

The following memorandum, which was endorsed upon a bill in April last, embodies the proposals of the Society in this regard:

"The object of this bill is to complete the organization of the profession of accountant throughout the United Kingdom on lines similar to the legal and medical and other professions, and for this purpose to establish a uniform standard of apprenticeship examinations and admissions throughout the United Kingdom. By the establishment of a register it is proposed to recognize only qualified accountants and to debar unqualified persons from practicing. The council sought to be set up will also exercise disciplinary powers which will secure the public against the risk of employing unqualified or untrustworthy persons in the confidential relations of an accountant. It has been intended to make the Council representative of the principal societies of accountants now existing in Great Britain and Ireland.

Mr. Martin asked the question whether the position of the professional accountant is a satisfactory one in the eyes of the public and answered it in this wise:
Clearly not! Let us examine for a mo-

ment how Her Majesty's Judges and Her Majesty's Government regard it. When in the High Court of Justice the appointment of a receiver or liquidator comes on for consideration, what course is pursued? An accountant is generally nominated for the office. Does the judge or the registrar ask whether the person nominated is "Chartered" or "Incorporated," or whatever he may be? No. He calls for an affidavit of the fitness of the applicant, which must be made by a solicitor of the court. So in spite of training, examinations and what not, unless a solicitor is prepared to swear to the accountant's qualifications, the appointment cannot be made. In other words, membership of any existing body is not accepted by the courts in England as evidence of qualification.

With regard to the Government, matters are infinitely worse. The legal profession are always ready to back us up in the courts, but no one is disposed to help us with the Government, and I have no doubt we are despised as being incapable of helping ourselves. In keeping and auditing the voluminous accounts of the Government departments are any professional accountants employed? The only case I can remember is one where the War Office was in a mess and called in outside aid. Take the case of the audit of the accounts of county councils, school boards, boards of guardians, etc., whose accounts are audited by Local Government Board auditors. Has anyone ever heard of the Local Government Board placing a professional accountant on the staff? I have not. Even in the case of official receivers in bankruptcy and companies winding-up, with a few notable exceptions the tendency is not to give these appointments to accountants who are the most qualified persons to fill them.

Some of our Chartered friends say time will alter all this; I say on the contrary the position is going from bad to worse, and this is illustrated by the fact that when the London Government Bill was before the House last session, the Opposition induced the Government to exclude us from the audit of the accounts of the new municipalities, although we are extensively employed by the great corporations both in the City of London and throughout the country in similar business.

In view of their condition, Mr. Martin

asserted that the only course to pursue is to continue endeavors on the lines that have been followed for so many years past. He said: We are attempting nothing that is impossible; a little common sense and a little self-sacrifice are the qualities most urgently required for success. American accountants, with characteristic energy, have already shown what can be done by statute in the State of New York. Victorian Accountants, as represented by our own committee, and the other societies in that colony, have agreed amongst themselves as to the procedure to be adopted in their Parliament. There is no need for me to appeal to Incorporated Accountants; the splendid position of the Society to-day is the result of unity of heart and mind both at home and abroad, and we are bound together by a bond that no foe can break. I may, however, by virtue of that friendship with which I, as your Secretary, have been privileged by so many of the Chartered Accountants of England, Scotland and Ireland, appeal once more to them to consider the position calmly and dispassionately, and to grant us their co-operation, so that whereas the commencement of the nineteenth century saw the rise of the professional accountant, the opening of the twentieth century may witness his enrollment by statute as a member of one of the great professions which have so largely contributed to the welfare of the community and the prosperity of the Empire.

The fortunate circumstances of our lives are generally found at last to be of our own producing.—Goldsmith.

There is but one good throw upon the dice, which is, to throw them away.—Chatfield.

The Tall Buildings of the Metropolis

A very considerable number of the office men of New York are the occupants of offices from the windows of which are views which many people would be willing to undertake long journeys for the privilege of seeing, even for a short space of time. The buildings themselves are also marvels to be carefully examined by the tourist and enthusiastically described to the home-people upon his return. The occupants of the buildings likewise come in for observation and comment.

In one tall building downtown, overlooking the bay, there are a dozen foreign consulates. As one scoots skyward in the elevator he may see on doors across the halls of the several floors "Consul-General of the So-and-so," and "Consulate of this" and "Consulate of that," and when he gets up to where he is going and looks out seaward this seems a very appropriate place for such offices. For from the windows of this building may be seen coming in the steamers from the various countries represented within it, as, in due course, they may be seen passing out. From one land and another the steamers are coming and going all the time. Where one can thus see the means of actual communication the other land is brought nearer; and where there are so many boats all the time going and coming one is more and more inclined to regard them simply as plying on so many ocean ferries; and it seems appropriate, indeed, that the consulates should be right here at one end of them.

Another thing likely to impress the visitor to the tall building overlooking the bay is the bay itself, with its shipping. Doubtless, many times, he has looked at the tall buildings from the waters, from the decks of ferryboats or other steam craft, and thought they were great; now let him look down upon the bay and its boats, and he will find that from the tall building point of view the water and the craft upon it have decidedly a novel interest. From the shore or from the deck of another boat he sees only the side and the elevation of a passing steamer; from here, upon the nearer ones at least, he may look down upon them, and take in their shape and dimensions; and he gets a new idea of their sharpness and their narrowness; and as he sees a steamer coming up, say, to a wharf, to make a landing, she seems, seen from here, more than ever to be endowed with some sort of life, and to be feeling her own way, cautiously, to the landing-place. Seen from this elevation, the bay, with its varied moving boats, takes on a pictorial aspect, and the scene that it presents is one of great interest.

One of the marvellous sights among the works of man is the spectacle presented by the tall buildings of this city after nightfall in the winter season, when, on account of darkness coming on before the closing hour of business, these cliff-like buildings are all lighted up. This is a sight that is peculiarly modern and wonderful. The rivers and bay, seen after nightfall from the tall building, do not present so wonderful a spectacle as the buildings themselves do, seen at that hour from the river; but from this point of view, the silently moving boats, some brilliantly, some dimly lighted, and all picked out with red lights and green, do present a striking and fascinating picture.

The possession of wealth is, as it were, prepayment, and involves an obligation of honor to the doing of correspondent work.—George Macdonald.

Never put much confidence in such as put no confidence in others.—Hare.

Examinations

The word examination to the average mortal has an uncomfortable sound. Few arrive at that degree of proficiency in any line where they regard with indifference the crucial process. Charles Kingsley, in his story of "Water Babies," as perhaps some of us are not too old to remember, has given an amusing picture of the dreadful torture inflicted upon children by those officers of the government called Examiners. There once prevailed a feeling that the threshold of the school-house crossed for the last time, examinations were left behind, but in these later days the nerve-wearing, head-splitting, heart-rending process awaits each forward step. Does a man seek a government position? Stern civil service examiners bar the way. Would he become a doctor or lawyer? The State has provided a multitude of questions that must first be answered. Is he wishing to put up the prescriptions that the doctors make? He must first show the proper authorities that he is competent. Or would he become a C.P.A.? He has to give evidence of his proficiency in accounts before those legally qualified to pass upon his abilities.

Here is the humorous report of a committee appointed to examine two applicants for admission to the Bar as it is spread upon the record in the proceedings of the District Court of Kingfisher County, O. T.:

The committee selected from the Kingfisher Bar
To learn what the attainments of applicants are,
Convened, their laborious task to pursue,
At the Probate Court room, time quarter
past two.

The committee were welcomed with ur-
bane smile
By the candidates, who were provided the
while
To supply such refreshments as sorely
were needed,
To have the great learning of aspirants
conceded.

The subjects discussed, and the questions
propounded.
Taxed the mem'ry of committee, the students confounded,
And but for refreshments then on the
spot,
'Tmight have been a close guess, if they'd
"got there" or not.

The committee probed deeply and without compunction
On the candidates' knowledge of man-
damus, injunction,
Replevin, quo warranto, and half dozen
others,
Of which 'tmay be said they knew less
than the authors.

On forms and procedure both were well
posted,
While on bills and notes, the committee
them roasted,
Till five in the evening, 'twas considered
sufficient
To warrant report: "We find them proficient."

We do not happen to have in hand the reports of any of the numerous examining boards filed in this part of the country to publish by way of comparison, but we venture to assert that few if any of them are as strikingly original as the above.

A Slight Misunderstanding

"Smithkin," said the employer, "you may take a month off."

"Oh, sir," replied the clerk as soon as he could command his voice, "it is so good of you to suggest it! I have felt the need of a rest for some time, but have hesitated to ask for it, knowing how busy we are. But it will do me no end of good, and I thank you most heartily for your consideration."

"Smithkin," said the employer, "are you crazy?"

"Why, no, sir. Didn't you say I might take a month off?"

"Certainly that is what I said. This is the first of the month, while last month's calendar remains over your desk. Take last month off and keep up-to-date. That's what I meant."

Private credit is wealth; public honor is security. The feather that adorns the royal bird supports its flight; strip him of his plumage and you pin him to the earth. —Junius.

Whatever distrust we may have of the sincerity of those who converse with us, we always believe they will tell us more truth than they do to others.—Rochefoucauld.

The Furniture Worker,

A SEMI-MONTHLY COMMERCIAL AND INDUSTRIAL JOURNAL.

For the interest of the Furniture, Bedding, Wood-working Industries, etc., and their branches. The production, handling and consumption intelligently discussed—not technically, but from the commercial standpoint of the manufacturer, exporter, retailer and user.

One of the few American Trade Papers receiving bronze Medal and Diploma for Editorial Merit at the Exhibition of the Trade Press Association in Brussels and Antwerp.

Always Interesting—Never Tiresome.

Subscription Price—24 Issues, $2.00.

THE FURNITURE WORKER PUBLISHING CO.,
126-180 Longworth St., Cincinnati, O.

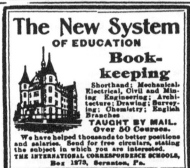

Features of the Twentieth Century

With any given date for a starting
point, a number of curious and often very
ingenious combinations can be made,
showing its relative position to other important dates. The beginning of the
twentieth century, still a little more than
a year ahead of us, has become a favorite subject for those interested in such
calculations. When the dividing line
which separates the present period of one
hundred years from the succeeding period
of one hundred years is reached, the opening of the new century will be the beginning of numerous series of times and sea-
sons, canonical and civil, and a convenient point around which to group the
results of astronomical observations. A
collection of a large amount of odd and
out-of-the-way information of this kind
has been made by Rily V. Moore, of Battle Creek, Mich. The following selection
from these peculiar statistics cannot fail
to be interesting to the reader:

The twentieth century will commence
on January 1, 1901. It will open on Tuesday and close on Sunday. It will have
the greatest number of leap years possible—twenty-four. The year 1904 will be
the first one, then every fourth year
after that, to and including the year 2000.
February will have three times five Sundays—in 1902, 1948 and 1976.

In 1901 Federal Memorial Day, Fourth
of July, and Thanksgiving Day will occur
the same day in the week. Then after
that the same thing will happen at the
following intervals: 6, 11, 11, 6, 11, 11,
years, and so on, or in 1907, 1918, 1929,
1935, and so on.

In the years 1912, 1914, 1969 and 1996
there are four holidays that will fall on
the same day in the week—the three already mentioned and Washington's Birth-
day anniversary, as also the 29th of February.

Thanksgiving Day and Christmas will
occur the same day in the week in 1906,
and then at successive intervals of 11,
6, 11, 11, 6, 11 years, and so on; also in
1928, 1956 and 1984. March 4 will fall on
Sunday in the inaugural years 1917, 1946
and 1973. The same yearly calendar that
was used in 1895 can be used again in
1901.

The following year, in order beginning
with 1901, the dates of Easter for the first
twenty-five years of the century: April
7, March 30, April 12, 3, 23, 15, March 31,
April 9, 11, March 27, April 16, 7, March
23, April 12, 4, 23, 8, March 31, April 20, 4,
March 27, April 16, 1, 20, 12. The earliest
possible date on which Easter can occur
is March 23. The last time it occurred
on this date was in 1818, but it will not
occur again until after the twentieth century. The latest Easter can occur is April
26, and it will thus occur but once in the
coming century—in 1943. The last time it
occurred was April 26, 1886. Whenever
Easter occurs on March 27 or April 3, 10,
17 or 24, Christmas also occurs on Sunday.

Though some of the objects aimed at
by the church authorities who fixed upon
the method of determining the date of
Easter was to prevent its occurring on

the same date as the Jewish Passover, nevertheless the two events will occur together four times in the twentieth century—April 12, 1903; April 1, 1923; April 17, 1927, and April 19, 1981.

The twentieth century will contain 36,-525 days, which lacks one day of being exactly 5,218 weeks. The day of the week that will not occur as often as each of the others is Monday. Fifteen out of the hundred years will begin on Wednesday and the same number on Friday. Fourteen will begin on each of the other days of the week.

Several announcements are made of changes to be inaugurated with the opening of the new century. The first of importance is that Russia will adopt the Gregorian calendar. This will be done by omitting thirteen days, the amount of the error that will have accumulated after the close of February, 1900. The Russians will then write January 1, 1901, instead of December 19, 1900.

The other important announcement is that it is not at all unlikely that the astronomical day, which now begins at noon of the civil day, will begin with the civil day, at midnight. The present method of having the astronomical day to begin twelve hours after the beginning of the civil day is apt to be confusing. On the other hand, to have the former begin at midnight will be to them somewhat inconvenient.

A New Coin

Congress has authorized the coinage of a new dollar, popularly known as the Lafayette dollar, and the first of this issue will come from the United States Mint at Philadelphia in a short time. This coin, which is made a legal tender, is of unique and artistic appearance and originated in the patriotic desire to perpetuate the memory of the assistance rendered this country by the Marquis de Lafayette during the Revolution. As only a limited number, fifty thousand, will be struck off, it may be expected that in the course of time it will become an object of interest to collectors and curiosity hunters. On the face is a double medallion of the heads of Washington and Lafayette, while this inscription appears on the reverse side: "Struck in commemoration of monument erected by school youth of United States to General Lafayette, Paris, France, 1900." This tells the purpose for which it is destined. A miniature of the equestrian statue of Lafayette which is upon the monument also appears on this side. The first piece of money to come from the mint will be presented by President McKinley, representing this Government, to the President of the French Republic.

Ignorance that knows itself is a wise and learned ignorance.—Pascal.

What is bought is cheaper than a gift. —Cervantes.

Do You Know What Your Output is Costing You?

THE **Proof-by-Balance System of Cost Accounts**, which for several years past has formed an important feature of various specifications of the **Balance-Sheet System of Accounts**, is now offered to manufacturers generally.

It is suited to every line of business and to every class of product. The principles are unvarying, but their application is adjusted to meet specified conditions. Adaptations are always intelligently made to meet requirements.

The leading features of the system include the following:—

1. The cost value of materials on hand, in gross and in as many subdivisions as may be desired, is shown at all times.
2. The cost value of work in progress, in gross and in whatever detail is required, is indicated at all times.
3. The cost value of goods completed and on hand, in gross and in as fine detail as desired, is shown at all times.
4. The correctness of the figured cost of goods is proven monthly by balancing with total charges to factory.
5. The constant employed for spreading over product the general expenses of the factory is established monthly in the light of actual facts, thus insuring perfect agreement between recorded costs and the conditions of output.
6. Inventorying is reduced to the examination of individual departments or classes of materials to verify the corresponding accounts.

The cheapest system to install and maintain, and the most efficient and satisfactory in use.

Installations are made upon the Specification Plan exclusively. Everything is in writing. No oral instruction.

No changes in your present methods until you have had a chance to become familiar with all the provisions of the new.

ACCOUNT, AUDIT & ASSURANCE CO., Limited
25 Pine Street, New York

CHICAGO, ILL.,
1308 SECURITY BUILDING

TORONTO, ONT.,
McKINNON BUILDING

AGENCIES:

DAVENPORT, IOWA,
68 McMANUS BUILDING

DETROIT, MICH.,
717 CHAMBER OF COMMERCE

MONTREAL, QUEBEC,
11-17 PLACE D'ARMES HILL

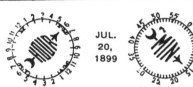

Accountics:—
T^{HE} OFFICE MAGAZINE

Volume VI Number 2	FEBRUARY, 1900	Monthly, $1 a year Single Copy, 10 cents

The Application of Advanced Accounting Methods to Modern Business Enterprises

I. The Scientific Analysis of Business Accounts.*

By A. O. KITTREDGE, F. I. A., C. P. A.

The stated title of my remarks, as presented in the notices of this meeting, is hardly satisfactory, because it might seem to convey the impression that there is possible only one scientific analysis. If it read "the" scientific analysis of business accounts, it would be better, for what I desire to emphasize to-night is scientific analysis broadly. That accounts may be scientifically analyzed I think almost every one will admit without argument, but whether the analysis presented by some one else would be the same as the analysis I might arrange is altogether another question. There are different points of view to be occupied, and very possibly there may be different objects to be served by the analysis.

Further considering the subject of title, the question well might be asked, why "analysis?" The answer to this is that analytical inquiries show where improvements are possible. Separating a thing into its component parts shows not only the relationship that the parts bear one to another, but also locates any deficiencies that the individual parts may reveal. Possibly, for our purpose this evening, the word "classification" might have served just as good a purpose. Classification, by which is meant putting things of a kind together, or arranging in groups, likewise serves to develop true relationship and to bring to view shortages and deficiencies.

However we may look at the subject, we are faced with the fact that every business has accounts, and that these accounts, to be conducted in the most satisfactory manner, require to be treat-

---

*An abstract of an address delivered before the Hartford Chapter of the Institute of Accounts. Hartford. Conn., Nov. 28, by A. O. Kittredge, F. I. A., C. P. A., President of the Account, Audit & Assurance Co., Ltd., New York.

This address was, in fact, an enlargement of the preliminary article in this series, as announced in the prospectus in the December issue, and presents the statement of principles more fully than the article as first prepared.

ed analytically and scientifically. Good results in bookkeeping are seldom secured where there is no attempt at arrangement, and where everything is left to chance. The difference between an old-time, clumsy, labor-consuming set of books and an easy-working, labor-saving set of books of the present day is to be found largely in the classification of accounts and the adjustment of the details arranged to facilitate and maintain that classification.

I sometimes think, when observing the way in which many sets of books are arranged and kept at the present day—particularly when there is recalled the fact that by far the larger majority of all the books of accounts are arranged on more or less fallacious plans, or upon no plan at all—that in the scientific progress of the day office work relatively has been left far behind. Scientific improvements have been made to a far greater extent in almost every other field than in accounting.

Again, as a conclusion following upon a careful survey of the field, I am led to believe that, as a rule, we have far too much bookkeeping and altogether too little accounting in our offices. Bookkeeping is the art, the method, the embodiment of the plan, the practice. In contradistinction, accounting is the science, the analysis, the classification, the scheme or plan in the abstract. We are prone to consider the rulings of the journal and cash book, the form of the ledger, and the designs of blanks, to the exclusion of the fundamental accounting plan upon which these very important bookkeeping adjuncts are to be employed.

It is quite possible to conceive of an accounting system, applicable to a given line of business, without any reference whatsoever to the bookkeeping dress that is to be employed in interpreting and arranging it for use in the office. To make this plain it may be asserted that a very few lines from the artist's pencil will suggest to the mind, so clearly as to be instantly recognized, a land-

scape, a building, a face, or any other familiar object about us. But an outline is not a picture. However much we may enjoy a finished picture, we are forced to admit that an outline permits of study, without the distraction caused by fine details, minute features of form and color to divert the mind and thereby defeat the object in view.

To put it otherwise, accounting may be likened to the boney framework or skeleton, while the bookkeeping accompanying it is flesh and blood. The skeleton is the strength of the system, but is concealed by the outer covering or dress.

I have already remarked that I think we have too much bookkeeping and too little accounting. We have too much in our office practice that is empirical and too little that is really systematic. Before we go further, let us consider what is meant by system in such a phrase as "an accounting system." System, in the precise meaning of the word, conveys the idea of completeness and sufficiency, and yet the word is often employed to indicate not a complete circle, but a mere arc or fragment.

I frequently encounter men—bookkeepers, accountants, business managers and others—who seem to have no adequate conception of an accounting system, nor yet of a bookkeeping system, using the word in both cases in the sense of something adequate to the purpose and complete. For example, one says, "I keep my books upon the voucher system." I ponder this assertion. Bookkeeping surely is more than the record of the payment of one's indebtedness, and yet the voucher method goes no further than to record in most excellent shape the disbursement of funds. Another man says, "I keep my accounts upon the loose leaf ledger system." Again I stop to think. Accounts are more than mere ledger records, and in a large business there exists the requirement of more than one kind of ledger in order to meet in the best way the demands of the various groups of accounts that occur. If he uses only one style of ledger some portions of his accounts are poorly served. The loose leaf ledger is certainly a most excellent office adjunct, but it has its limitations, and, after all, it is only a ledger. It may be used upon any one of several plans and in conjunction with various details, but in itself it is only an insignificant fragment of a system. So again I conclude that the man who is using this expression has no conception of an accounting system in the proper sense of the term.

Still others whom I occasionally meet say: "I use the seven-account system," and "I use the card system," and "I use the columnar system," but, after all, there is nothing in these terms that indicate a system that embraces all that is done in the office and upon which all the necessary details can be hung. Each of them is merely a fragment.

There is no "system of accounts" worthy of a moment's consideration except a complete system. We should not employ the word "system" save only as we convey thereby the idea of an adequate and comprehensive plan.

An inquiry that is pertinent at this point is: What is the object of all accounting? A very prominent author of treatises, whose books are standards both in this country and in Great Britain, using the term "bookkeeping" in the inclusive sense, meaning both the plan and the method of interpretation, has asserted that "the object of all bookkeeping is to produce a correct balance sheet." He defines a balance sheet, in substance, as being the orderly arrangement of all the assets and liabilities of a business. Right here the business man will join us and say: "That is exactly what I want of accounts. That is the reason why I have books kept in my office. My financial relationship to the world, as expressed by the orderly arrangement of all my assets and liabilities, is just what I am after."

We all know the conventional form of a balance sheet, and how first are put down the assets, and how in the second place are put down the active liabilities. Finally, in the liability column, is inserted an amount which is the difference between the assets and the active or actual liabilities, and this is called capital. business first owes the creditors of the or present worth. The theory is that the business, and after them owes the proprietors the remainder of whatever there is in the business. So our assets and our liabilities always balance.

In constructing a balance sheet, there always precedes it a profit and loss statement. We cannot do business without expenses, which are very generally called losses. Again there are real losses; for example, the result of selling goods for less than their cost. Each transaction in business results in either a loss or a gain. When our gains exceed our expenses and our losses we have remaining a profit; but when our expenses and our losses exceed our gains we have a loss. A profit and loss statement, therefore, takes into account the ex-

penses of the business, together with the real losses and the gains of the business, and shows the net result, the actual profit or the actual loss, as the case may be. Whenever this amount has been ascertained, it is carried to a proper division of the capital account. We have either added to our capital or we have lost a part of our capital, as the result of the business done in the period under review. When this part of the work has been finished, we are ready to complete our balance sheet.

If what the business man most desires to see is a balance sheet, and if the object of all bookkeeping is to produce a correct balance sheet, then it follows that to have the balance sheet always ready, continuous, perpetual, would be the ideal result to be accomplished by an accounting system in conjunction with the bookkeeping details with which it is dressed. Business is continuous; therefore the balance sheet should be continuous.

A going or perpetual balance sheet is not such an abstract theory, nor yet nearly so difficult a matter of accomplishment as many would suppose. Let me illustrate this in the simplest posible way. Suppose, first, that we have the balance sheet of a business, as of the date of January 1. Suppose, second, that the figures representing the assets and liabilities, instead of being arranged in columnar form in two groups, as is the conventional method, are written in a horizontal line, shoulder to shoulder. We would first have cash and then notes receivable, following which would be accounts receivable, real estate, manufacturing plant, materials, manufactured goods and so on to the end of the assets. Following these would be the liabilities, under such heads as notes payable, accounts payable, etc., and finally the capital account in as many subdivisions as are appropriate. The subdivisions of capital to which I refer include current profits, surplus and capital stock. Suppose, further, that each of these accounts or titles in the balance sheet is supplied with a pair of columns, Dr. and Cr., and that the amounts representing these accounts are written either in the debit or the credit column of the respective pairs, as circumstances determine. Suppose still further that the business transactions of each day in the new year are analyzed upon balance-sheet principles, and that the totals of the transactions of each day are written under these balance-sheet amounts, which have been extended across the columns on the first line.

Now, starting with a balance sheet and adding thereto the daily transactions, classified upon balance-sheet principles, will we not have a balance sheet whenever the columns are footed?

You answer, "Yes."

That is strictly true, with one exception. As already mentioned, we cannot

do business without expenses, and we seldom make a transaction without a loss or a gain. There is concealed in these figures, written in the form described, the profit or the loss of our business. When we make out the conventional balance sheet, as already stated, we first construct a profit and loss statement, and after transferring to the proper division of our capital account the net result—profit or loss, as the case may be—we have our accounts in shape for the construction of a balance sheet. If we are going to have the perpetual balance sheet, as suggested by the illustration we are considering, we must arrange, in connection therewith, for a showing of profits and losses, and for the transfer to capital account of the net results of the business as we go along. We therefore extend the horizontal arrangement of accounts far enough to include the items of a profit and loss statement.

One group of the new columns added will include the expenses of doing business, and another group will show the revenues or earning. Now, this is a somewhat clumsy illustration of a going balance sheet, but perhaps it will answer our purpose, if to no greater extent than to indicate what is necessary to be done to make the scheme actually practicable.

We have seen that analysis or classification, in addition to other objects, serves to point out deficiencies. If we take up the individual accounts contained in the ordinary ledger and apply thereto the balance sheet tape line, we shall find in some cases redundancies and excesses, and in other cases shortages and deficiencies. Arranging the groups of accounts with respect to each other, in the way necessary to produce a going or perpetual balance sheet, we shall discover that we are short certain accounts that are absolutely necessary to express the condition of the business that we are attempting to represent upon this plan.

(To be continued.)

Professional Secrecy

In the October number of ACCOUNTICS, the confidential relations existing between the accountant and his client were discussed at some length. Attention was called to the fact that there is very little in the way of legal decisions to serve as precedent and guide, when the question of professional secrecy is in controversy.

A case in point has recently come up in the City Court of Meriden, Conn. It arose in the suit of Walter R. Bristol, a traveling salesman, to recover a month's salary from C. B. Rogers & Brothers Co., silver manufacturers. Mr. George Rockwell, auditor of the International Silver Co., a rival manufacturing company, was called as an expert to prove the value of the plaintiff's services. On cross-examination he was asked to give the name of salesmen for whom he had audited an account concerning which he had testified, and also the amount of salary received. He refused to answer on the ground that he was confidential man for the International Silver Company, and that it was not proper for him to divulge the secrets of the cost of selling goods. The judge held that he must answer or go to jail for contempt of court. "I still decline to answer," said the witness. The matter was at last adjusted by agreement between the lawyers, by which his whole testimony was stricken out and the question in controversy withdrawn. This settlement of the difficulty leaves the legal status undecided, but similar questions are likely at any time to come before the courts, and at a day not far distant will receive authoritive decision.

How are the Profits of the Year to be Ascertained?

BY BERNARD DALE.

(Continued from page 122 December number.)

The Single Account System

This system is explained by Mr. Palmer in the fifth edition of his well-known "Company Precedents" as follows:

According to this system profit is to be ascertained by a balance-sheet showing the true financial position of the company. If the balance-sheet shows that the joint stock assets exceed in value of the debts and liabilities, including paid-up capital, the excess is considered profit. And if the balance-sheet shows that the assets are less in value than the amount of the debts and liabilities, including paid-up capital, the deficiency is considered loss. "The essence of this system," Mr. Palmer says, "is that the company may apply its net revenue to the payment of dividends so long as its capital is intact."

The following are some observations on this system:

1. The system works well enough in the case of an "entire venture," where the profit has not to be ascertained until the conclusion of the venture. In such a venture any excess in the value of the returns over the amount of the advances, represented in this instance by the paid-up capital, is profit, and any defect, loss.

2. The system is inapplicable to the case of a "continuous venture," where the regulations of the company provide for an annual division of profit, for here the advances of the succeeding year consist of the value of the assets of the preceding year brought forward, less the amount of the external liabilities, which value, in the event of a loss sustained in the preceding year, may be less than the paid-up share capital. Suppose a manufacturing company, which starts with a paid-up share capital of £100,000, and loses £10,000 on the first year's operations, thus reducing the capital to £90,000, but whose trading operations for the second year produce, say, returns of the value of £100,000, that is £10,000 in excess of £90,000, the reduced capital forming the

advances for the second year? Such excess of £10,000 would be "profit" for the second year. But if the Single Account System had been applied it would have shown neither profit nor loss for the second year, for, among the liabilities, there would have been included the paid-up share capital of £100,000, notwithstanding that none of this capital had been received in the second year, and £10,000 of it had, by the supposition, been lost in the first year's trading, and could not, therefore, have formed any part of the advances for the second year.

The error which the advocates of the Single Account System appear to have fallen into is in concluding that, because the profit of an "entire venture" are ascertained by means of a balance-sheet, in which the paid-up capital figures among the advances, and the unrealized assets at their form of account, without modification, must be applied to the by no means similar operation of ascertaining the "profits for a year" of a "continuous venture." There may be, of course, no reason why "profits for a year" should not be ascertained by a single account rather than by two or more, but, if the single account selected for this purpose be a balance-sheet, then it must first be made to accord with the facts and (a) among the liabilities for the year must be included the real advances for that year, and not the paid-up share capital, unless actually received in that year; (b) the assets used as "fixed" capital must be entered at cost value, less deterioration, and not at market value, as would be the case if they were items figuring in the balance-sheet of an "entire venture."

It is submitted, however, that the proper function of a balance-sheet is merely to exhibit the position at a given date, and that, save in the case of an "entire venture," it cannot with propriety be used as an instrument for determining profit.

(To be continued.)

Reviews and Criticisms

The Dictator

The Dictator. A Collection of Graded Dictation Exercises, etc. By Mina Ward. 180 pages. 5x7 inches. Bound in cloth, gilt side title, published by the Phonographic Institute. Price, $1.

This little book will be welcomed by many who are studying shorthand, whether in schools or in a private capacity, and who, very naturally, are anxious for speed, accuracy and good style. It is adapted to the use of those who are following various systems of shorthand. The lessons are graded, and inserted numerals give the number of words at different points in the articles in a way to be of the greatest advantage. The

mere fact that the stenographer can write 125 or 150 words a minute really gives no definite idea of speed. He might easily be able to write 150 a minute from an ordinary newspaper, and still find it impossible to write 100 words from a technical article in a scientific magazine. The exercises in this little book are therefore graded for the purpose of making a stenographer's speed a known quantity. In addition to the words being counted, as above indicated, the syllables have also been counted, and the average number of syllables to the word is given at the end of each article. The first article, for example, has words of one syllable. Others average 1.25, 1.45, 1.65, and so on, up to 2.19, the latter being a phrenological examination and introducing such pretty

words for practice as "acquisitiveness," "conscientious," "metaphysics," "psychology," "theosophy," etc.

Civil Service Examinations

How to Prepare for a Civil Service Examination, with Recent Questions and Answers. By Francis E. Leup. Octavo, 560 pages. Bound in cloth, side title. Published by Hinds & Noble. Price, $2.

Since the classified civil service was established and civil service examinations became the rule, there has been a general desire upon the part of every one who has the least ambition for government employment to test his accomplishments. No one wants to apply for a position and be turned down for lack of ability. There is also the need of training or preparation for taking the examination. For such purposes the book before us is a most admirable aid. One of the initial chapters defines the classified civil service, indicating the branches and the classes maintained. With the latter there is a schedule of the rates of pay. There is also a statement of the qualifications which are considered. Several pages are devoted to the form of application to be made, etc. A sub-chapter describes the examinations, telling what they are like, and also gives a list of the positions to be filled, with the page in the book, and where other particulars are presented. The book is a useful one to all who desire to test their accomplishments, whether intending to apply for a governmental position or not. It is supplemented by a very complete index.

Try It and See

It is getting time to hustle;
Don't be afraid to rustle;
Just look—you'll see prosperity coming
　　o'er the land.
Don't say, with look rejected,
"Hard times, as I expected!"
You can surely make the riffle if you
　　　　　　have
　　　　　　　　the
　　　　　　　　　　sand!

Don't look so glum and surly—
But get up bright and early—
And you'll find enough to busy you on
　　every hand.
If with care you'll do your sowing,
The Lord'll push the growing—
Later on you'll reap the harvest if you
　　　　　　have
　　　　　　　　the
　　　　　　　　　　sand!

Bear On

From St. Anthony's Monthly.

Oh, never from thy tempted heart
Let thine integrity depart!
When Disappointment fills thy cup,
Undaunted, nobly drink it up;
Truth will prevail, and Justice show
Her tardy honors, sure though slow.
Bear on! Our life is not a dream:
Though often such its mazes seem:
We were not born for lives of ease,
Ourselves alone to aid and please.
To each a daily task is given,
A labor which shall fit for Heaven;
When Duty calls let love grow warm;
Amid the sunshine and the storm,
With Faith life's trials boldly breast,
And come a conqueror to thy rest.
　　　　　　　　　　Bear on.

The Monthly Statement

Comparatively few of us at the present day stop to think how much business is facilitated by modern improvements or how much easier it is to do business under present conditions than under the conditions that existed in the days of our grandparents. A survey of what has taken place in the last one hundred years is pregnant with suggestion. To contrast the conditions that existed one hundred years since and those of to-day is all that a single paragraph could contain. Then the transaction of business in whatever line was slow and difficult. The merchant, in a majority of cases, kept his own books, or as he would have expressed it at that time, his own "accounts." He wrote all his letters with a quill, and when they were written, instead of using a blotting-pad, which was something unknown at that time, he allowed the ink to dry or else sprinkled it with sand. Envelopes had not been invented, and accordingly letters were laboriously folded in a way to enclose them and at the same time provide space for the superscription. There were no postage stamps, no letter-boxes in the street and no collections of the mail. While there were postmasters, each business man had to do for himself much that is at present done by the Post Office Department.

❧

To send a letter, which was a single sheet of paper, large or small, from New York to Boston or from New York to Philadelphia, cost eighteen-and-a-half cents, and from Boston to Washington cost twenty-five cents. These rates were at a time, it should be remembered, when the purchasing power of a cent was several times what it is at present. To carry a letter from Philadelphia, which was then the capital of the United States, to Boston, for example, and bring back an answer by return mail, consumed twelve to eighteen days, according to the season of the year and the weather.

❧

In contrast with these conditions, put first the mail service, then the telegraph, and finally the telephone, which the present generation enjoys. The business man who at the present time is not in instant touch by telegraph, or, preferably, by telephone, with a very considerable part of his trade is far behind the times.

❧

If such has been the development of business facilities in the last one hundred years, what is it to be in the one hundred years next to come? No one can imagine, no one can give a guess, as to what the future may hold. We regard the telephone at present as the perfection of communication, and yet only a little while ago any one who would have suggested such a means of communication would have been considered wild and fanciful.

In the one hundred years that have passed, while these remarkable changes and improvements have been taking place, many fortunes have been made by those who were able to project themselves, so to speak, somewhat ahead of their day, and perceive the changes before they were fairly inaugurated. That business man who has been entirely satisfied with keeping step in the ranks has found himself still in the (rear) ranks, while his neighbor, who was not content with an ordinary place, but was constantly looking ahead to anticipate the changes that were coming, has made a fortune and also a name for himself. The same, it is fair to infer, will always be true.

❧

The same rule applies to those in subordinate positions. That bookkeeper who is content to keep books as they have always been kept will always keep books in a way that secures only a small salary. On the other hand, that bookkeeper who uses his knowledge of bookkeeping merely as a means to something better, who aspires to accounting, and who by energy and enterprise makes himself worth more than a bookkeeper's salary to his employers, gets on in the world. Still other lessons might be drawn from this statement of the remarkable development of the last one hundred years, but enough has been presented to put the thoughtful reader into a mood for careful self-examination. Where are we relatively? Are we in the ranks, keeping step, or are we scouts in advance of the army, spying out the new country and learning what there is ahead which we may properly use to our own advantage?

❧ ❧

A very common definition of dirt is matter out of place. Accepting this definition as correct, what a dirty place the average office is, and what a particularly dirty thing is the desk of the average office man! Leave out of the question entirely the matter of dust, cigar ashes, etc., and consider only the matter that is out of place therein, relating to the tangible and important affairs of business. What is a desk for? The shortest and most appropriate answer to this question would be, "to use." How much of the desk is used, employing this term now in the sense of regular employment and leaving out the question of storage? We have seen elegantly finished rolltop desks, large and spacious, so thoroughly loaded with matter out of place that there was no room for use, no chance to do any work at the desk, the person who is supposed to use the desk being driven thereby to a table for a space on which to spread his paper for writing. Who is to blame for such a state of affairs? Certainly no one but the user of the desk.

❧

Storage of papers is an important problem in every office, but a desk, we submit, should not be devoted to storage, save

only of those things which are in current demand. That which is permanently disposed of should be filed away or stored in less expensive room than that afforded by a desk, thereby leaving to the desk capacity for those things to which it should be specially devoted. If you accept this proposition, dear reader, make the application in your own case, by examining the drawers and pigeon-holes of your desk. What do they contain? How much is simply matter out of place, or dirt? You have been thinking for a long time that you needed a larger desk. How much could you increase the capacity of your present desk by simply putting away in proper place those things which your desk contains and which do not rightfully belong therein?

❧

The office man, as well as men of other classes, is a creature of habit. Out of sight is out of mind. When something is to be disposed of it is gotten rid of with the smallest amount of labor. Therefore things are put away in drawers and pigeon-holes that ought never to have found resting room therein. So much is this habit of putting things out of sight in the easiest way indulged in that many business men, fitting up large offices, object to the roll-top desk. They say it is only a catch-all for things that do not need to be kept; that it is only something to be abused, and therefore they restrict their clerks to flat-top desks, thereby compelling them to put away their books and papers each night in the drawer room of the desk, instead of having a convenient roll-top to close down over them. We risk nothing in saying that seventy-five out of every hundred roll-top desks whether used by subordinates or principals, have their drawers so full of dirt, by which we mean matter out of place, or papers and other articles that do not need to be kept, that it would be impossible to put away every night the accumulation of papers with which the user of the desk has been working during the day. If there is any one among our readers who desires to start upon a crusade and to work a little reform of his own along lines of utility and economy, we suggest that he commence in his own office and that he do what he can to clear the desks therein of dirt.

Unusual demand for the January Accountics has exhausted our supply, and we are not able to meet requests for that number. To enable us in a measure to do so, we request subscribers to return to us the magazine for that month, for which we will extend subscriptions two months for each copy received.

The synonyme of usury is ruin.—Dr. Johnson.

He who believes in nobody knows that he himself is not to be trusted.—Auerbach.

One solitary philosopher may be great, virtuous and happy in the depth of poverty, but not a whole people.—Isaac Iselin.

What the Credit Men Are Doing

By A. O. Kittredge.

The new year with the National Association of Credit Men opened auspiciously, with Secretary Prendergast full of good works and at the same time with demands upon him that were more than convenient to meet. Of specific results accomplished in the early part of January, particular attention should be directed to the arrangement made with the American Surety Company, whereby that corporation agrees to furnish bonds to the members of the National Association of Credit Men at the low rate of one-quarter of 1 per cent. This most advantageous contract with a prominent bonding corporation will have the effect of enabling members of the association who are required to give bonds in court, away from home, and on short notice, to arrange for the same in an expeditious manner, and with the smallest amount of trouble. The proposition is open to all the members of the organization who desire to avail themselves of it, and does not involve any obligation upon their part to give all their business to the company. The general method of procedure will perhaps interest the reader: Each applicant is required to file with the American Surety Company a general agreement of indemnity, on acceptance of which the company indicates to its local offices in the city where the applicant resides that such a party is to be furnished with bonds immediately on application, at the rates quoted. Accordingly, after these preliminaries have been accomplished, it will only be necessary for members of the organization to call upon the local representative of the American Surety Company in their city for such services as they require. Of course, the same privileges, under proper restrictions, will be extended to the members in cities remote from their residences, as, for example, in cases where they are engaged in protecting their interests with failed debtors, etc.

* * *

At the meeting of the Board of Directors of the National Association of Credit Men held in Chicago, late in November, resolutions were adopted providing for a fund of ten thousand dollars to be raised for the prosecution of fraudulent debtors. Members of the association were urged to correspond with each other in respect to the financial standing and responsibility of customers and applicants for credit. W. H. Preston, of Sioux City, ex-President of the National Association, was authorized to visit the cities of San Francisco and Seattle in February, for the purpose of organizing local associations. After the discussion of the claims of rival cities, Milwaukee was chosen as the place of meeting of the next annual convention, which will be held June 12th, 13th and 14th.

* * *

Not the least enjoyable among the pleasant entertainments at which Secretary Prendergast was an honored guest during his Western trip was that given by the Credit Men of Sioux City. W. H. Preston, as chairman of the evening, in a graceful way introduced the National Secretary to the members of the association, all of whom listened with evident interest to his address. E. W. Caldwell followed with remarks in which he happily combined both wit and wisdom.

* * *

The interest of Baltimore business men in the work of the Baltimore Credit Men's Association was evidenced by their attendance at the third annual meeting held in December. President Field and Secretary Prendergast, of the National Association were present and made addresses, and there were presented the annual reports on the year's work by the local officers. An interesting feature of the meeting was the address by John C. Rose, United States District Attorney, on the Credit System from the standpoint of the Federal Court. An election of officers followed the address and resulted in the re-election of Samuel Rosenthal, Jr., as President, and J. Harry Tregoe as Secretary of the association. M. F. Burgess was elected Vice-President, and J. H. Stone, Treasurer. The members of the executive board for the past year were continued in office.

* * *

The Kansas City Association of Credit Men held its regular monthly meeting for December at the Coates House. The dinner which preceded the business session has become an established feature of these meetings, and is an occasion for social reunion of which the members are glad to avail themselves. The presence of National Secretary Prendergast as a guest made this one of more than ordinary interest.

* * *

The West is well to the front in activity in credit men's work, as witness the second annual banquet of the Denver Association. The eighty-six members, gathered at Brown Palace Hotel on the evening of December 12th, were ready to unite with Secretary Prendergast in a vigorous effort to organize local associations in every town of importance in the State. Inspiring addresses were given by C. D. Griffith on "Our Record in the Past," A. C. Foster, on "The Relations of the Retail to the Wholesale Credit Man;" J. T. Plummer, on "System and Hustle," and by Hon. W. B. Harrison, Referee in Bankruptcy for the district. At the annual meeting of this organization on the 26th of December the employers, as entertainers, tendered to the employes an elaborate dinner. President F. J. Arnold acted as toastmaster and Mr. J. W. Hudston, of the Denver National Bank, and Major Daniels and Mr. J. H. Middlebrook spoke in response to appropriate toasts.

* * *

The Detroit Credit Men varied the regular order of business meetings in December by a social entertainment in the Turkish Room of the Cadillac Hotel, to which the ladies were invited. Music, refreshments and some short addresses helped to make the informal gathering interesting to those who were present. All went home with a desire that such occasions should be of more frequent occurrence. At the annual meeting on the 23d of January, Philo E. Hall was re-elected President; H. B. Gillespie was elected Vice-President, and Wm. D. Gridley, Treasurer. After the annual address by the President and report by the Secretary, a general debate followed as to the means to be adopted to secure the interest and attendance of members, and the hearty co-operation of all present was promised for the coming year.

* * *

The annual meeting of the St. Louis Credit Men at the Mercantile Club Rooms, December 16th, was more largely attended than any similar gathering in that city. After two hours spent around the bountifully covered tables which the committee in charge had prepared, President Richard Hanlon introduced Frank P. Hays, President of the Missouri Bankers' Association, who spoke on trusts and their amenability to the natural laws which govern trade. Secretary Prendergast, O'Neill Ryan and Albert Arnstein were the other speakers of the evening.

* * *

The second annual dinner of the Rochester Credit Men's Association was held in the rooms of the Genesee Valley Club, Rochester, on January 12. Some 150 of Rochester's representative business men attended the dinner, and the banquet is described as a credit to the credit men and an emphatic demonstration of the success which attends that organization's efforts in the field. President John H. Gregory presided, and at the conclusion of the menu introduced the first speaker of the evening, John Field, of Philadelphia, president of the National Association of Credit Men. His subject was "The National Association and Its Work." This topic Mr. Field handled in his customary able and interesting manner, to the delight of all who heard him. The next address was by National Secretary Prendergast, the subject being "American Shipping." This was in a sense a variation from the ordinary topics introduced at the gatherings of credit men, but the subject was handled in such a way as to be of special interest to all who are concerned in it. William C. Sprague, editor of The Collector and Commercial Lawyer, of Detroit, who was present, spoke of the man behind the gun. This subject, the speaker said, permitted him to take random shots, and these he proceeded to fire in directions that had the approval of his listeners. Other addresses were made by guests, including A. J. Barnes, of Buffalo. The banquet was brought to a close at midnight with the singing of "America," in which all heartily joined.

* * *

The annual meeting of the Credit Men's Association, of Milwaukee, was held on the 11th of January. Since the death of President T. W. Brockus, in October,

Vice-President Max Landauer has been the presiding officer. The election for the present year resulted as follows: President, H. M. Battin, of the Standard Oil Co.; Vice-President, James McLeod, of Roundy, Peckham & Co.; Secretary, F. H. Benson, and Treasurer, O. C. Hansen, of the Cream City Hat Co. In addition to the regular routine work, committees were appointed preparatory to the entertainment of the National Association in June.

* * *

A good representation of the Credit Men's Association of Chicago assembled at the regular meeting in December to listen to an address by F. H. McAdow, on "The Treatment of Fraudulent Failures." Mr. McAdow gave in a vivid manner a description of a case where the credit man is confronted with a fraudulent failure, and carefully analyzed the situation. What, he asks, is the proper course to pursue? The debtor is fighting the battle on his chosen field, with the aid of the best legal advice procurable in his vicinity, surrounded by a sympathetic community, and, if brought into court, will be tried before a judge inclined to charity. Is it better to accept the settlement that is offered, or to prosecute the case? Mr. McAdow is strongly of the opinion that the latter course is the one to pursue, on the ground that one offender brought to justice will deter many from attempting to follow in his footsteps. Should, however, the compromise be entered into, and the debtor be allowed to resume business again, "the standard of public conscience is lowered, instead of being raised—and right here is a difficulty or an obstacle in the way of reform that is not always recognized. It is the lack of a decided and positive public sentiment against such things in this country." He claims that the one thing needful to remedy the present condition is co-operation, the provision of a liberal fund for the prosecution of fraudulent debtors, and an advertisement of the fact throughout the country.

* *

The annual meeting of the St. Paul Credit Men was held at the Minnesota Club, in December, and was preceded by an informal dinner. Secretary Prendergast was present and outlined the work of the National Association since its organization. Addresses by Chauncey Seabury and Mr. Kirk from the employers' standpoint were listened to with appreciative interest. The officers elected for the ensuing year are C. D. Maclaren, President; H. D. Brown, Vice-President; L. Beardslee, Treasurer, and J. H. Beek, Secretary. In a short and appropriate speech, E. A. Young, the retiring President, expressed his gratitude to the association for the co-operation and consideration which he had received, and the association in turn acknowledged his zeal and efficiency by a vote of thanks.

Education of Accountants

The New York State Society of Certified Public Accountants is engaged upon the discussion of very comprehensive plans for courses of study adapted to the requirements of accounting students, accountants' assistants, and all others who expect to devote their time to public accounting and who aspire to the degree "C. P. A." The project of inaugurating some adequate and efficient educational facilities was brought to the attention of prominent accountants, all members of the New York State Society of Certified Public Accountants, at a dinner given early in November last by Charles W. Haskins, president of the society.

It was formally brought to the notice of the society at the November meeting, in a brief address with resolutions, by H. R. M. Cook. The resolutions recited that, whereas it is the sense of the society that it is expedient and necessary to the development of the profession of public accountancy that the same should be established primarily upon an educational

basis, as is the case of other professions, and that means should be taken to render the proposition effective, therefore the president of the society was requested to confer with the trustees of Columbia University and of the University of the City of New York, or other collegiate bodies, at his discretion, with the object of effecting an arrangement for the establishment of a class and for the conduct of a course of study in the science of accounts, in finance and economy, in business practice, in commercial law, and in such other subjects as are necessary to the special education of persons intending to enter the profession. The president was also empowered, at his discretion, to invite co-operation of kindred societies and all members of the profession interested in the future success of public accountancy, to the end that adequate provision should be made for accomplishing the object in view.

At the meeting of the society, on December 11th, President Haskins submitted a report of a conference with President Low, of Columbia University, and also one with certain officials of the University of the City of New York. It was evident from his report that in the first instance co-operation in a movement already started by the Chamber of Commerce, New York, looking to the higher educa-

Home Office of Provident Mutual Building-Loan Association, Los Angeles, Cal.

tion of business men in commerce, financial and various technical subdivisions of business, would secure the desired result in the form of a four years' course, with more or less of elective studies in connection therewith. It was also evident that, in the case of the University of the City of New York, a night course could be arranged on less elaborate lines, but especially adapted to the requirements of those who are employed during the day. The report of the chairman was discussed with much interest by various members present and resulted in the appointment of a committee to outline a syllabus of study and to propose such further measures as to it might seem appropriate in the premises. This committee is at present at work upon the project, with every prospect of evolving something that will meet requirements and be generally acceptable.

Attractive Offices

A generation back, when the man of business went from his cheery, bright home downtown to his office, he left be-

hind him all evidence of comfort and pleasantness. His hours of labor were spent in a dreary, unkept room, devoid of anything that would attract a cultivated or refined person. It is difficult to understand why men with a keen appreciation of beautiful surroundings allowed the office to remain so long a barren and unsightly place. If pressed for an explanation some doubtless would have said that their fathers used it in that state and they had accepted it as it came to them; others, that it was like those about them.

In these latter days, however, there has come a radical change in the appearance of the office. The rude, unsightly desks have been banished, the unvarnished chairs have been replaced by modern ones, the walls are fresh from the hands of the decorator, the dust-laden shelves and disorderly cabinets have vanished as if by magic, and the elegance of the appointments show that those who planned have the inclination and the means to make the place in which they pass a large part of their time beautiful and attractive.

The feeling that there is anything incongruous between business and graceful, or even elegant, surroundings has passed away, and the artist and the artisan have united to make the office and the office building a source of pleasure to all cultivated persons who have occasion either daily or at rarer intervals to be there.

Nor has the advance been entirely along the line of the aesthetic, for utility has had consideration and modern inventions have facilitated clerical work by numerous contrivances. Offices of this character are found all over the country from the Atlantic to the Pacific.

The accompanying cut of the home office of the Provident Mutual Building-Loan Association, of Los Angeles, California, is an illustration of this type we have last referred to above. The telephone and the electric light are not wanting, and, to add to the cheerfulness and brightness of the scene, some appreciative hand has placed a bunch of roses upon the counter. In the rear there is a hint of rooms where the officers of the company may hold counsel, and where conversation may be had with customers and others, free from interruption and distraction. We have but to fill the foreground with a busy throng to make it a living picture of Western energy and activity.

Accountics

The Office Magazine.

Published Monthly.

A. O. KITTREDGE, F. I. A., C. P. A., Editor.

E. R. KITTREDGE, Associate.

Accountics is devoted to the Science of Accounting, to the Art of Bookkeeping and to the advocacy of Improved Office Methods.

Subscription.—One dollar a year, payable in advance.

Postage is prepaid by the publishers in the United States, Canada and Mexico. For all other countries in the Postal Union, subscribers must add 50 cents a year.

Discontinuances.—In the absence of specific orders to discontinue at the end of the subscription term the magazine will be continued and a bill sent.

Remittances should be by Draft, P. O. Order or Express Order, payable to the order of the Accountics Association. Money and postage stamps are at the risk of the sender, unless sent by express or in registered letters. Add 10 cents each to checks on local banks to defray collection charges.

Advertising Rates will be quoted on application.

Official Journal.—This publication, by resolutions duly passed, has been made the official publication of the following organizations :—

THE INSTITUTE OF ACCOUNTS.

THE NEW YORK CHAPTER of the Institute of Accounts.

THE WASHINGTON CHAPTER of the Institute of Accounts.

THE HARTFORD CHAPTER of the Institute of Accounts.

ACCOUNTICS is the accredited medium of intercommunication between members of the Institute of Accounts wherever located.

ACCOUNTICS ASSOCIATION, Publishers,

Lancashire Bldg., Pine St., near Nassau,

New York.

Publisher's Desk

The daily increasing clerical work necessary to transact the business of the country has given an impetus to inventions for aiding computations in a way to insure accuracy and obtain rapidity. A multiplication table compiled by Robert S. Ayars, of Louisville, Ky., has been designed with a view to giving the products of multiplication at a glance. The results shown on the tables form the basis of all calculations, and it is but a simple matter in the use of decimals and fractions to obtain the product from any combination of figures. These tables are printed on three sheets of heavy cardboard (11x14 inches) fastened together so that they can be opened and propped up in a convenient position for consultation. A railway clerk in figuring freight on way bills, a bookkeeper in making out accounts or a clerical man in any department demanding accuracy and speed in multiplication of figures, can, by the aid of these tables, greatly shorten his calculations while also making sure of accuracy.

Some people have money to burn, others have it to give away. It is said of advertisers that they spend money like water, but it has remained for the John Hancock Mutual Life Insurance Company, of Boston, to scatter money broadcast in connection with their advertising. We are careful in phrasing the above sentence, for, in addition to the cost of advertising, they have been presenting the recipients of the advertisements with actual money. We have referred in the past on several occasions to the series of cards that this company has been sending out for some time past. One that reached us at Christmas time was a folder, that to be opened required a per-

forated end to be detached. Within was a picture of Santa Claus, in fur-trimmed clothes, holding aloft a bundle, on which was printed the word "Token." Removing the rubber band which held the cover in place and opening it, there appeared a bright new penny. The text on the card was as follows: "We enclose a token, with wishes for a merry Christmas. The token is modest but a bright fellow withal, and joined with many others of its kind is potent for much good or ill." Then follows an argument with reference to life insurance, which every one could afford to endorse.

"What It Means to Be a Librarian," is the title of an article by Herbert Putnam in a recent issue of the Ladies' Home Journal. Anything from this source pertaining to the conduct of libraries is an authority, and will doubtless be stimulating to better work in this rapidly widening field of employment. Mr. Putnam's long experience at the head of the Boston Public Library has made his name familiar to the reading public throughout the country, and his recent appointment to the position of librarian of the Congressional Library at Washington is a matter of national interest.

Although Accountics has had but a short time in which to win the favor of the public, its genuine usefulness and adaptation to the needs of business men is evidenced by the fact that the same mail in addition to the usual quota of domestic letters brings us inquiries from New Zealand, China, England and Germany. Neither do the newer parts of our own country fail to show appreciation, and our new protege, Cuba, likewise falls into line in this, as she will in other American interests. Wherever business is done Accountics is in demand.

We are favored by the Pope Manufacturing Co., of Hartford, the makers of the celebrated Columbia bicycle, with a sample of the Columbia calendar for 1900. It is of the same general description as the calendars or desk tablets which this company has put out for a number of years past.

MULTIPLICATION TABLE.

Simple, Practical, Comprehensive. The only practical device on the market to save figuring in multiplication. *Time saving, Brain-saving, Assures Accuracy. A compiled table of the products of multiplication, so constructed that you can find the results at a glance.* Gives easily, quickly, accurately any calculation in multiplication required in business. Will last ten years. Send for circulars. Price, postpaid, $1.00.

ROBERT S. AYARS, Louisville, Ky.

Do You Ever Have Occasion to Use A Legal Directory?

Forty-two law firms, who jointly forward over two hundred and fifty thousand items of business to their legal correspondents annually, and who are necessarily posted as to the best attorneys to use at a distance, communicate to a central office constantly their experience with their various correspondents, and from this information is compiled monthly the directory which they use. That such a list is superior to one compiled in the ordinary way and published annually or semi-annually, goes without saying. Each issue contains, in addition to the legal list, a complete Bank Directory, the collection laws of the various States, tabulated, besides a good deal of general information of value to lawyers and credit men.

This directory (*complete* each month—*no supplements*) can be obtained for Five Dollars per annum by addressing

The Mercantile Adjuster,

P. O. BOX 609   NEW YORK.

150 NASSAU STREET.

HELPFUL BOOKS
For Young and Old.

JUST OUT.

GILGAL,

Stones That Pave The Way To Success.
A New Book of Proverbs by MRS. CALVIN KRYDER REIFSNIDER. Charles Scribner's Sons' Holiday "Book Buyer" says:
"Not since the publication of the proverbs of King Solomon has such an exhaustive compendium of maxims been issued as appear under the title 'Gilgal; Stones That Pave The Way to Success,' the work of Mrs. Calvin Kryder Reifsnider. Many of these nuggets of wisdom are compressed in a single brief line."
A neat little Pocket Volume, Designed for Presentation, at Popular Prices. Flexible Cloth, 25c.; Cloth, 50c.; Leather, gilt top, $1.00.

Mrs. Reifsnider's Other Books.

TRUE MEMORY,
The Philosopher's Stone, Its Loss Through Adam, Its Recovery through Christ.
A New Presentation Concerning the Creation of the World, the Fall of Man, the Life and Mission of Christ, the Present Condition of the Earth and the future of the Race.
"The Greatest Book of the Century Just Closing."—The Arena.
Handsomely Illustrated. Elegantly Bound. Just out. Price $1.00.

BETWEEN TWO WORLDS,
Third Edition in Five Months, 300 pages. Strikingly Illustrated, handsomely bound in Cloth and silver, $1.00. It is a plain, helpful presentation of the relation and connection between this World of Matter and that of Spirit. It illustrates clearly what the Spirit is, where and how it lives, works, etc.

HOW SHE EARNED IT,
Or, $25,000 in Eleven Years. Fourth Edition. Illustrated. Cloth, $1.00. Acknowledged to be the best guide ever published for those honestly striving to get on in the world.

UNFORGIVEN.
A Romance. Fourth Edition. Handsomely Illustrated. Cloth, $1.00.

For Sale by all Booksellers. Sent Postpaid on Receipt of Price. Address

The Anna C. Reifsnider Book Co.,
ST. LOUIS, MO.

The Globe Rotary Copier

The Globe-Wernicke Co., Cincinnati, Chicago, New York and Boston, have recently put upon the market a perfected and up-to-date form of rotary copier that is giving most excellent satisfaction wherever employed. The speed with which letters and other documents can be copied is alone a great recommendation for the use of this device, while the superior character and evenness of the

Fig. 1.—Globe Rotary Copier.

copying also support it in public favor. In appearance, as an office adjunct, the machine is greatly to be preferred to the old-time copy-press. It is cleanly and always ready for use. Even though the copy clerk is not at hand, a copy can be had instantly of any sheet of manuscript or typewriting by simply entering its edge between the rolls and giving two or three turns to the crank. There is no

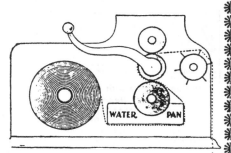

Fig. 2.—Cross Section Globe Rotary Copier.

brush or dampened pad, or wet cloth to be handled—in fact, there is nothing whatever required except to lay the letter in place and give the handle a turn.

Fig. 1 shows the copier mounted on a cabinet of quartered oak, with paneled ends and sides, and handsomely finished. One half of the closet is devoted to the reel on which the impressions are dried,

---

and the other contains shelves for general storage.

Fig. 2 is a cross section showing the rubber rollers, water pan and roll of copying paper. The dotted lines indicate the course of the paper as it is unwound by the action of the crank, and the process of copying which occurs while the paper is passing between the rubber rollers. On each side of the metal casing which holds the copying apparatus are wire baskets, one for holding letters, etc..

to be copied, and the other for their reception as they come from the press.

Can wealth give happiness? Look round and see, what gay distress! what splendid misery!—Young.

Convenient Calendar Stand

What business man is there who does not appreciate the convenience of a calendar pad upon his desk, against dates in which he may make memorandums? The conventional diary, more or less affected by professional men in certain lines, does not seem to take the popular fancy to anything like the extent that a padded calendar, with leaves to turn over out of the way, always leaving in sight that which is wanted at the moment. Devices of this kind have been popularized by various advertisers, but those articles which have been sent out by way of advertisement have never been altogether satisfactory for use. They are inade-

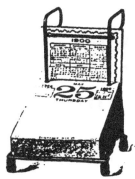

Calendar Stand.

quate in construction, and, while pleasing to the eye, are, in fact, somewhat inconvenient. The Standard Company, Limited, of 76 West Jackson Boulevard, Chicago, have evidently appreciated the wants of business men in this regard, and also have perceived the shortcomings of other devices of the kind, for they have put upon the market a well-finished, adequate device, sufficiently heavy to remain in position while being used, mounted on rubber feet to avoid scratching the desk, all as shown in the accompanying illustration. The sample that we have before us bids fair, by its utility, to hold its place on our desk for the year against all comers.

Accountants' Associations

New York Chapter of the Institute of Accounts

The January meeting of the New York Chapter of the Institute of Accounts, held at the Waldorf-Astoria, Thursday, January 25th, was largely attended both by resident members and visitors. In response to special invitations a considerable number of public accountants representing different societies in New York were present. The address of the evening was delivered by Charles W. Haskins, C. P. A., M. I. A., president of the New York State Society of Certified Public Accountants and chairman of the Board of Examiners of the Regents of the University of the State of New York, for the C. P. A. degree.

Mr. Haskins spoke on "Accounting—Its Past and Present," and from his scholarly and scientific handling of his subject, it was evident he had given it careful and thoughtful consideration. He divided his address into three general heads, first tracing the historical references to accounting and bookkeeping back to the earliest records, thereby going further into the past than any other investigator whose work has been made public, and second, giving a historical survey of public accounting and auditing in the same general manner. In this part of his address the speaker brought to light many hitherto unnoticed facts. The third or final division of the subject was more of the nature of a glance into the future than a statement of present conditions. In it Mr. Haskins referred particularly to what is now about to be put into operation in an educational way for the preparation of training of future generations of accountants. The address was listened to with much interest and at its conclusion was warmly commended in discussion, which was participated in by the various members and visitors.

Hartford Chapter of the Institute of Accounts

The regular meeting of the Hartford Chapter of the Institute of Accounts was held on the evening of January 23d. Charles Dutton, F. I. A., secretary of the National Institute of Accounts, was present by invitation and delivered the address of the evening. Mr. Dutton spoke entirely without notes, and, perhaps for that reason, his remarks were of especial interest to his auditors. The subject upon which he spoke was one of the phases of our economic life, and from information received from some of those who were present there were offered thoughts and suggestions which will be of benefit to all his hearers.

Illinois Institute of Accountants

A very encouraging and interesting report of the December meeting of the Illinois Institute of Accountants has come to us. The feature of the meeting was an address by Frank E. Webner, now auditor of the Chicago Railway Equipment Company, in the course of which he made

a careful explanation of the Balance Sheet System of Accounts. For a more complete elucidation of his subject, he read the article on "Evolution in Accounting and Cost Keeping," by A. O. Kittredge, published in the February and March (1899) numbers of ACCOUNTICS.

Associated Accountants of New Orleans

A goodly number of members and invited guests were present at the regular monthly meeting of this organization, held in December. The president, A. L. Soule, introduced as speaker of the evening W. W. Weiss, cashier of the Teutonia Bank. Mr. Weiss's address, which treated of bank bookkeeping, was listened to with much interest. He illustrated his subject by charts, and in conjunction with these, produced his improvement upon the skeleton ledger for inspection.

Chartered Accountants' Students' Association

An educational movement, of great importance to the accountants of Canada, was inaugurated early in December, at a special meeting called for the purpose. The object in view was the formation of a society to further the interests of students in preparation for the examinations conducted by the Institute of Chartered Accountants of Ontario. The need of something of this kind has long been felt both by accountants and by the business public, and the project was taken up with considerable enthusiasm. The result was that a constitution was drafted and a committee was appointed to arrange for a series of meetings to be held during the coming winter. The new organization will be known as the Chartered Accountants' Students' Association. The officers elected were as follows: Hon. President, Geo. Edwards, F. C. A.; Hon. Vice-President, Harry Vigeon, F. C. A.; President, Spencer H. Over; Vice-President, T. H. Kilgore; Secretary, Arthur H. Edwards. Fornightly meetings are proposed and promises have already been obtained from a number of prominent accountants to address the meetings.

Bookkeepers' Beneficial Association of Philadelphia

At the regular monthly meeting of this organization for December John R. Cassell, lecturer on Commercial Law in the Peirce College, delivered an address on "The Credit System," giving special attention to what constitutes a proper basis for granting credits. The meeting was well attended and interest was sustained throughout.

Usury is the land-shark and devil-fish of commerce.—J. L. Basford.

The Spaniards have a saying that there is no man whom Fortune does not visit at least once in his life.—Ik Marvel.

Interest and Discount X

By Charles W. Rohse.

Installment Companies

In installment companies it is almost the universal practice to allow simple interest on payments made between dividend dates, and the dividend periods are usually semi-annual. At each semi-annual period the previous values are compounded.

Tables have been recently published carrying out this idea and the combination of simple and compound interest both in the same table, i. e., simple interest on the first six payments, then a compound, then simple interest until the next dividend period, or the twelfth month, and then a compound. The heading of one of these tables reads as follows:

"Monthly values of $1 placed at simple interest at the end of each month, with interest compounded semi-annually at annual rates in the heading." (The speaker here exhibited a table covering thirteen months.)

The Co-Operative Savings Society of this city (Hartford, Conn.), of which I am treasurer, recently sold a piece of real estate for $4,700, agreeing to take 120 monthly payments of $52.18, payable at the end of each month. No cash was paid, but security was given not only on the property sold but on other clear property appraised at about $3,000. The principle to which I desire to call your attention, is the method of dividing the payment of $52.18 into principal and interest.

Now, the interest on $4,700 for one month at the rate of 6 per cent. per annum is $23.50, which, deducted from $52.18, leaves a balance of $28.68 to be applied each month in reduction of principal, in addition to which the borrower is entitled to interest at the rate of 6 per cent. per annum, or ½ per cent. per month; simple interest for the first six months, then a compound, and so on.

Having a table of $1 each month, computed on the basis above stated, it is a comparatively easy matter to multiply said table by $28.68, and thus ascertain the amount of sinking fund at the end of each month. However, before reaching the 120th month, the figures would, in order to be accurate, have to run into at least four places of decimals, besides three significant figures, and the multiplication by $28.68 would make the result by direct multiplication eleven figures. This would become very tedious, and unless computed in duplicate, very apt to errors. Therefore I resorted to the following method, and to illustrate the same I will copy the first thirteen steps of the table, and by deducting the payment of $1, $2, $3, etc., will obtain the difference, or interest, which I will designate as the first difference; then deducting ciphers from the second period, for the reason that no interest is allowed on the first payment, it having been paid at the end of the month, I will obtain the second difference, and in the same manner I will obtain the third difference.

I have now reduced the difference not to exceed two significant figures. The next step is to take the amount of $28.68 and make a table showing the multiplication of same from .0049 to .01 by addition. (The speaker here exhibited a table showing the result of multiplying $28.68 by numbers from 49 to 100 inclusive.)

Now for the practical application of the differences multiplied by the results obtained of once $28.68, twice $28.68, three times $28.68, etc. Opposite the second month I have a difference of five, correctly expressed decimally, is .005, or one-half of 1 per cent. per annum. Now one-half of 1 per cent. of $28.68 is .1434. There-fore, the interest from the end of the first month to the end of the second month is .1434. The second difference is .005, which produces the same amount of interest. Adding these two amounts together as illustrated in table, I have .2868. Proceeding in this manner I have the third month's interest as 43 cents, the next month as 57 cents, etc.

Now these items, from the first month to the time the thirteenth payment is made, aggregate $11.31. By these continuous additions, table can be computed to maturity by addition, which has been substituted in place of multiplication, and at the yearly intervals proofs may be made by taking the amounts as shown by the printed table and multiplying by $28.68. Now the amount shown by the printed table opposite the thirteenth month is $13.3939, and multiplying this by $28.68 produces $384.14, which gives a variation in the calculation at that point of 1 cent.

The Globe Adjustable Perforator

Every user of blanks and forms that are filed in post-binders and other similar devices, requiring the sheets to be evenly and accurately punched or perforated, will be interested in a device recently put upon the market by the Globe-Wernicke Co., of Cincinnati, Chicago, New York and Boston, which is illustrated in the accompanying engravings. As indicated by its name, its special usefulness turns upon the fact that it is adjustable, thus adapting it to use for a very large range of requirements.

Fig. 1 shows the perforator mounted on

Fig. 1.—Globe Adjustable Perforator.

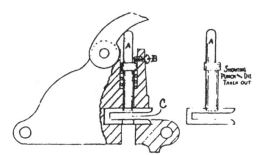

Fig. 2.—Cross Section Globe Adjustable Perforator.

a neat frame. Fig. 2 is a cross section, giving a view of the interior of the punch and showing the punch and die separately. This punch will easily and accurately perforate 35 or 40 sheets of paper at once, and can be adjusted so that the holes may be punched anywhere from 1¾ to 7 inches apart. By the aid of the gauges on the frame of the perforator the machine can be accurately set in the position desired. Additional punch heads may be added if it is necessary to make more than two holes in a sheet at one operation. The lever by which the machine is manipulated is so arranged that an expenditure of very little strength is sufficient to cut through the paper. Beneath the perforator is a hollow metal base for the reception of the cuttings. The machine is finished in appearance and occupies but a small space.

Our Sentiments Exactly

Somebody's desk crammed and crowded to its fullest capacity, with paper bulging from the pigeon-holes and jammed into the drawers till they refuse to hold more, a desk that is a daily reproach and a constant despair to its possessor, a desk whose ownership none would like to con-

fess, but which is an uncomfortable reminder, has been the inspiration of the following lines:

Wanted, an india rubber desk;
  One to expand and contract at will;
One to expand, though, most of the time—
  A desk I could never hope to fill.
Mine is one of the usual size,
  Big enough for methodical men,
But, good Lord, not a size by half
  To hold the things that come in my ken!

Day after day do I lay aside
  On my desk the things I'll take up next;
Week after week I forget these things,
  Which pile up higher, and I am vexed.
At best, once a month, I make a sweep
  Of the gathered stuff to show my zeal;
And, swearing a virtuous reform,
  Shuffle the cards for another deal.

Men may second Fortune, but they cannot thwart her.—Macchiavelli.

Let not one look of Fortune cast you down; she were not Fortune if she did not frown.—Earl of Orrery.

Avoid both courts and camps, where dilatory Fortune plays the jilt with the brave, noble, honest, gallant man, to throw herself away on fools.—Otway.

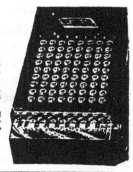

Learning to be a Manager
BY WALTON DAY.

Among a given lot of men up for examination, there will be found various kinds and degrees of talent. One will be skillful with his hands, as, for example, in mechanical employment or in penmanship; another will be quick at figures; another will be expert as a salesman; still another will succeed in trading. One will have high qualifications as a bookkeeper or accountant, and still others will be faithful to any trust of a subordinate character reposed in them. The one kind of talent, however, that will be hard to obtain, and for which, accordingly, a high market price will be paid, is that of planning and direction, or what is commonly designated as executive ability. It is safe to say that there will be found one hundred persons able to do things under directions to one who is able to plan what to do and set himself or others at the doing of it.

To be able to wind oneself up and set oneself going is a talent in itself, and in the market conception of the case is worth much more than any other phase of individual talent. To be able not only to keep oneself advantageously employed, but to direct the labor of others, is still more valuable. Who is there among men in general more helpless than the individual out of employment, skillful to a degree in certain lines and yet for the time utterly unable to find anything useful to do. The tendency of the times is in the direction of division of labor and specialization. In offices, as in factories, men are trained to certain duties and are held to those duties, to the exclusion of everything else. When finally one of this class is thrown out of his regular line and is forced to depend upon his own resources, he is in a sense more helpless than a child. What then can be done to overcome this tendency and to render men in general better able to take care of themselves and to become self-reliant and equal to the common emergencies of life?

The fault in many cases is fundamentally that of temperament or habit. The boy looks forward to a certain line of employment as being that which will give him a livelihood, and with the feeling that when he has become skilful in his chosen avocation, he will have done all that is necessary to do. Right here some friend ought to correct his planning. Every employment sooner or later fails those who are dependent upon it. Conditions change, panics occur, the demand varies. A friendly tip to the young man, therefore, would be, "Learn your trade by all means, but remember that you cannot depend upon it under all conditions. While holding yourself to it as the principal object, do not shut your eyes to other things alongside of it, for example, to adaptations and to variations, an acquaintance with which may be of considerable importance to you, first or last."

But the advice should go further: "Do not for a moment suppose that you have done all that is required of you when you have done one thing, however thor-

oughly. Do not feel that when you have learned one trade that you have earned the right thereafter to shut your eyes to all responsibilities, save only its requirements, and devote your leisure time to frivolities. Instead, keep on learning, keep on trying, and always have an alternative upon which you can depend in emergencies." It is all summed up in the advice, "think and study." While doing one thing, learn to do something else by utilizing the time that would otherwise be wasted, for, as a fact, there is more recreation and more real enjoyment in study and in planning how to do than in all the frivolities and so-called pleasures of life.

In thus learning how to do more than one thing, the young man will learn in part how to put himself to work. In thus giving attention to something else besides the routine of his daily labor the young man will learn how to adapt himself to varying conditions, and this is one of the first lessons in management or executive work. With an idea in mind of what he would himself do, facing unusual and unexpected conditions, he is, in part at least, prepared to tell others what to do under like conditions, and so, step by step, he gets to the position of a director of work, instead of a doer of work. We can by no means exhaust the thought that is in mind in the brief space that can be devoted to such a subject. A volume would be necessary to do it full justice. At least one thought that is contained in these remarks, properly understood, will be of advantage to many of the younger readers of this magazine, and that is this: To learn to be a manager, both of self and others, should be the worthy ambition of all.

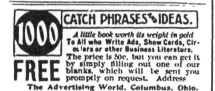

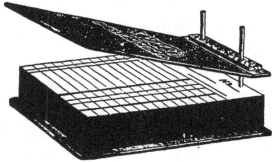

The Globe Card Index System

We have not time to prepare a list of all the uses to which the Card Index method may be applied. Suffice it to say that the system is universally applicable. It does all that can be done by book indexes, and very much more.

Our time and thought are largely devoted to the production of cards and card facilities.

We have recently prepared a catalogue of Card Index outfits, and have incorporated in it brief instructions in the use of the Card Index method. The illustrations are realistic, being fac similes in colors.

Among the special applications described are the following:

Merchandise Stock Records	Getting Orders from Inquiries
Merchandise Cost Records	Cost Records (Manufacturing)
Recording Quotations Made	Recording Quotations Received
Following up Slow Accounts	Indexing Catalogues
Keeping Credit Information	Looking after Freight Claims
Lists of Customers	Recording Advertising Contracts
Lists to Circularize	Publishers Subscription Lists
Fire Insurance Record	Life Insurance Record
Ledger Accounts	Depositors Signatures for Banks

and various others.

Individual Record and Guide Cards, together with Trays, Files, Drawers, Cabinets, etc., are also illustrated in great variety.

The goods are priced in full detail. The prices quoted are for deliveries at your railway station. We pay the freight.

The book is sent free on request. It is known as CATALOG No. 31, which please mention in writing.

THE GLOBE-WERNICKE CO.

CINCINNATI NEW YORK CHICAGO BOSTON

Accountics:—
THE OFFICE MAGAZINE

Volume VI
Number 3

MARCH, 1900

Monthly, $1 a year
Single Copy, 10 cents

Accountancy: Its Past and Its Present*

By CHARLES W. HASKINS.

If some pulpit orator will give us a good Sunday sermon on the moral aspect of business accountancy, on the value of our profession to the well-being of society, his tongue will be "the pen of a ready writer." His theme will associate itself with exalted thought, and will don the graces of language of prophet, apostle and evangelist. Divinity has long used our technical terms in the painting of its propositions; as when Udall, in 1548, speaks of the judgment as "a general daie of accoumpte and audite to be made at the throne of God"; or when the author of The Seven Sins, in 1606, says: "Those heapes of Siluer will be a passing bell calling thee to a fearefull Audit." Theologians of to-day may with great mutual advantage elevate accountancy itself to a doctrinal platform, and teach and insistently remind us that its obligations are at one with the eternal principles of righteousness and truth. My own task, in what I shall endeavor to lay before you to-night, is a comparatively unpretentious one. I restrict myself to the practical aspect of accountancy; and, within this sphere, I have brought together certain items of information relating to various phases of its history; items that admit of no rhetoric or flights of imagination, and that will be "interesting" (as we call it), mainly, if at all, from the fact that a good proportion of them are thus presented for the first time.

In trying to get at the beginning of this important subject, I have been reminded of a certain eminent Frenchman, who writes very learnedly on the history of bookkeeping. He says we really must overlook his want of erudition, for he isn't quite able to say just when or exactly how the Phoenicians, or the Tyrians, or the Carthaginians, or those early traders who came by caravan to buy the balms of Gilead, did begin to record their items of outlay and income. He thinks, on the whole, they did as a college-boy who puts down helter-skelter his weekly allowances, the marbles he loses, and the lickings he catches (1).

The beginnings of accountancy, after all, are easily enumerated. There are no beginnings. Its origin is lost in the mists

of antiquity. It is supposed, however, to be as old as the knowledge of mathematics; abstract and concrete numbers are but another name, it has been said, for theoretical and practical accounting.

The stupendous engineering feats of the ancients, as their building of the Pyramids, the Roman Roads of Britain, the Chinese Wall, the Jewish Temple, and the great works of Athenian and other architecture, assuredly presuppose some adequate system of accountancy without which all would have been a monumental tower of Babel-like confusion.

The Bible affords us many traces of a knowledge of business accountancy—in the parables of the talents, of the ten pounds, of the steward who conspired with his lord's debtors to falsify their vouchers; in Paul's telling Philemon to draw on him for the debts of Onesimus; in the very organization of that mighty fabric of accountancy, the Hebrew Theocracy.

The life and upright character of Joseph; his administration of the affairs of Pharaoh; his celebrated "corn deal" in preparation for a seven-year's famine; his wise provision for his father's household; his tactful method of bringing his brethren to account; betray an aptitude in the giving and receiving of political, economic, commercial, financial and household accountancy that ought to constitute him naturally the patron saint of the guild of accountants.

The classical writers, Greek and Latin, philosophers and poets and historians, from Herodotus and Aristophanes to Cæsar and Cicero and Tacitus, and the jurists down to the time of the Justinian Code, make frequent mention of various phases of accountancy. They have words and phrases for accounts of expenses and of debit and credit (2); for the making up of accounts (3); rendering accounts (4); giving in false accounts (5); passing a person's account (6); balances of accounts (7); account books (8); entries in account books (9); interest books (10); bookkeeping (11); bookkeepers (12); accountants (13); a chief public accountant or accountant-general (14); the auditing of accounts (15); audit rooms (16); auditors (17); salary or fees for the auditing of accounts (18).

A very few examples may suffice. Plautus says: "The account of debits and credits between us balances exactly." Cicero—"The account comes right to

a farthing." Cæsar—"Of all this money a joint account is kept."

"To audit," writes Ulpian, a Roman jurist of the second century, "is to compare receipts and payments." And Cicero after such an audit, says that "there is a big difference whether money is in your box or is only among the credits of another man's account book."

Pliny, the elder, said that in his day an intermediate deity called Fortune was universally regarded as accountant of the ins and outs of human existence. "To her," he says, "are referred all our losses and all our gains; and in casting up the accounts of mortals, she alone it is that balances the two pages of our sheet" (19).

The early kings of England had a peculiar double-entry that brought accountancy and bookkeeping into very close touch. A book called the primary account was kept by one officer, and another book, the secondary account, was kept by another functionary. These were separate and independent accounts, and neither was a copy of the other. But they were exactly alike; and line for line and page for page, they must agree; and the probatum, or sign of audit at the bottom of each page, could not be affixed until they did agree. No erasure was allowed; correction must be explained; and the probatum was separately added to every such explanation. The administrative genius of Henry II., about 1154, added a third, called the tertiary account, as a check upon the other two; "because," said he, "it is written, a three-fold cord is not easily broken" (20).

This scheme of accountancy had its origin in the Exchequer; but two concurrent accounts of the Royal Wardrobe for 1299, the second of which has recently come to light, show that it was also followed in the King's Household. As in the Exchequer, so in the Wardrobe, line almost answered to line, leaf and page quite answered to leaf and page, and the audit was carried out in like manner. Director Milman, of the Society of Antiquaries, says in describing these two accounts of the Wardrobe, "They correspond, as required by the rule derived from the Exchequer, leaf to leaf, page to page, almost line to line. The probatum, the mark of audit, has been affixed to the sum of every page, and to the sum of every leaf on its second page; and in some cases, where the sum has been apparently corrected by a second audit, a second mark is affixed to the finally stated sum. The rolls are separately kept accounts for the year, brought on the

* An address by Charles W. Haskins, C. P. A., President of the New York State Society Certified Public Accountants, delivered before the New York Chapter of the Institute of Accounts, Thursday evening, January 25, 1900.

expiration of the year into agreement in the manner described" (21).

The destruction of the Houses of Parliament, sixty-five years ago, called attention to another ancient method of security. You remember Robinson Crusoe's calendar of a notch a day cut in a stick of wood, and how he lost his reckoning when he was sick and unconscious. In some parts of England the village baker has a little stick for each customer, and cuts a nick in it for every loaf he lets him have on tick. Country bakers in France add the element of accountancy by splitting the little stick and giving the customer half; then, for every loaf taken, the split halves are fitted together and the notch is cut across both. The split-stick method, as a protection against fraud, was long in use in the English Exchequer. A depositor's name was written on the two narrow edges of a little flat stick, and notches of prescribed width, representing the amount of the deposit, were cut across the flat side. The stick was then split, and one of the halves was given to the depositor as a receipt, to be compared with its mate when presented. In 1834 it was found that there were vast piles of these old sticks, worn out, worm-eaten and absolutely worthless any longer. They were preserved at Westminster, and the order was given that they should be consumed in the stove in the House of Lords. The stove, overheated by these dry sticks, set fire to the paneling; the paneling set fire to the House of Lords; the House of Lords set fire to the House of Commons, and the two Houses were reduced to ashes (22).

The appointment of independent examiners of public and private accounts has been in vogue in Britain for untold centuries. Thirteen years ago a correspondent in Notes and Queries, an English medium of intercommunication, asked: "Can any reader give a reference to any earlier mention of an auditor than the statute 13 Edward I Cap. ii?" The editor repeated the inquiry ten years later; but as yet no reply has been received. This earliest known mention of a special examiner of accounts in Great Britain is dated 1285, and reads: "When the masters of such servants do assign auditors to take their accounts, and they be found in arrearages upon the account, all things allowed which ought to be allowed, their bodies shall be arrested, and by the testimony of the auditors of the same account, shall be sent or delivered into the next gaol of the King's in those parts" (23).

William Thynne, who died August 10, 1546, was one of two Examiners of the Accounts of the Officers of the King's Household. Furnival's account of him, published for the Chaucer Society, contains many references to rules for the examination of accounts. The following, from Duties of the Clerks of the Greencloth, is dated 1539:

"Item the said Clerkes of the Greencloth shall safely keep all their Bookes concerning their Office, after they had ingrossed them up, privately to themselves, without the view or sight of them to any other Officer unto the yeares end.

And the said Booke shall be examined with the Accomptants and particular Clerkes for the perfecting of the same. And likewise shall the Clerkes, Comptrollers and Clerkes Accomptants order all their Bookes touching their Offices.

"Item, that they shall make every halfe yeare a view of the expence of the Household, that it may be seen what the Charge amounteth to for the said halfe yeare" (24).

The Vision of Piers Plowman, written about 1340, shows that the appointment of special auditors was at that time common among the nobility. "I hold it right and reason," says a certain lord, "to take of my reeve all that mine auditor, or else my steward, counseleth me by his account and my clerk's writing. With 'Spiritus intellectus' they took the reeve-rolls, and with 'Spiritus fortitudinis,' I fetch it, wol he, nol he." And Dr. Whitaker, commenting on this passage, says: "These reeve-rolls, of which I have seen some, little later than our author's time, consisted, for one year, of several sheets stitched together, and contained very curious and minute details of all the receipts and expenses of these officers. There was more order and exactness," he continues, "in the economy of our old nobility than we are apt to imagine" (25).

On a mural slab in the chancel of the old church of St. Mary at Chesham, England, is the following inscription: "Heere lyeth part of Richard Bowle, who faithfully served divers great lordes as auditor on earth, but above all he prepared himself to give up his account to the Lord of Heaven, and now hath his quietus est, and rests from his torments and labours. He was a lover of God's ministers, a father of God's poore, a help to all God's people, and beleeves that his flesh, which with the soule was long tormented, shall with the same soule be eternally glorified. He died the 16th of December, 1626, and of his age 77" (26).

The profession of accountancy ranked with that of barrister, at least in Scotland, as early as about 1650; and in England the historian Fuller (1655) thinks it worthy of exceptional remark that, in some things, "the Dean and Chapter of Paul's were both their own accomptants and auditors" (27).

Samuel Pepys writes, in 1667, of "the King displeasing the Commons by evading their bill for examining accounts." He makes frequent mention of this bill for accountancy; and speaks of accountants as public officers. On June 3 of that year, he says he was "in the Treasury-chamber an hour or two, where he saw the country receivers and accountants come to attend. I, upon desire, was called in, and delivered in my report of my accounts." And at one of these accountants he has his characteristic little fling: "A brisk young fellow," he calls him, "with his hat cocked like a fool behind, as the present fashion among the blades is" (28).

Others, also, had their little joke in passing; and some gave the accountant a word of good advice. Tom D'Urfey, in his Pills to Purge Melancholy, sings of

"A British accountant that's frolic and free,
Who does wondrous Feats by the Rule of Three."

"Admonish accontants," writes Camden in 1605, "to be circumspect in entring."

The earliest known certificate of a professional examination of accounts is that of Snell, of London. The bursting of the famous South Sea Bubble in 1720 was followed by a Parliamentary investigation into the affairs of the South Sea Company; of which one Sawbridge, of the banking firm of Turner, Caswall & Co., was a director. A professional accountant of the name of Snell was engaged to examine the books; and his printed report is entitled, "Observations made upon examining the Books of Sawbridge and Company: By Charles Snell, Writing Master and Accountant in Foster Lane, London" (29).

In 1740, Horace Walpole, "His Majesty's Auditor-General of all his revenues of America," wrote privately to certain Governors complaining that the colonies were not voting him any tips over and above his Royal salary for auditing their accounts. Governor Clarke, of New York, bestirred himself as a true henchman in the matter; but Governor Belcher, of New England, read the letter out loud in a meeting of the Assembly. In the ensuing newspaper controversy in the Old Country it was recalled that a Mr. Blathwaite had been voted an allowance in 1709 for auditing some accounts in New England; and that up to that date such allowances had been frequently voted in New York and New England "from the time of the Revolution" of 1688 (30).

In 1794, a book showing "how to qualify any person for business without the help of a master," was published in Massachusetts by George Fisher, who styles himself an "accomptant." About the same time, three separate mathematical and commercial works, all entitled The American Accountant or Accomptant, were issued by different authors. One of these, by Chauncey Lee, to whom Columbia College afterwards gave the degree of D.D., is notable for its early use of the dollar mark, "a rude representation," says the editor of the Mathematical Magazine, "of the character now in use" (31).

Further investigation will doubtless increase this accumulation of historical notes; but the references I have given, covering every period except the dark ages and prehistoric times, and gathered from whatever sources were available—the Bible, the classics, and miscellaneous chroniclers—will serve as no mean testimony to the antiquity, the respectability, and the importance of the profession of accountancy. If now we look about us, at home and abroad, we see that new conditions in the progress of civilization are bringing the art and science of the accountant into relations of the gravest import, and into a new importance and prominence in the universe of affairs that may well cause every one of us to ask himself, "Shall I be of those who are equal to the occasion?"

(To be continued.)

The Application of Advanced Accounting Methods to Modern Business Enterprises

BY A. O. KITTREDGE, F. I. A., C. P. A.

(Continued from page 18, February number.)

Consider for a moment the overworked merchandise account. I say "overworked," because I think that before I am through you will agree with me that the merchandise account is called upon to perform more functions than any other one account in the entire list. The merchandise account is opened at the beginning of the fiscal period by being debited with the stock of goods on hand —that is, the inventory. As business proceeds it is debited with the new goods that are bought. Of course these debit charges in both cases are at cost prices. As goods are sold to customers, the merchandise account is credited with the sales. Of course the prices in these cases are selling prices. We then have two sets of values in one account—cost prices on the debit side and selling prices on the credit side. If we went no further, the account would break down by a strict application of double entry principles and demand a change. But the worst remains to be told.

On occasion we return to the seller some goods that we have bought. In order to debit him with the goods so returned, we must credit the merchandise account with the same, and this results in putting cost prices on the credit side of the account. Again, some of our customers bring back goods which we have sold them. Now, in order to credit them with the selling price, we must post the same amount to the debit of merchandise. This results in putting selling prices on the debit side. And so we go on, sometimes mixing the transactions still further, as in the case of manufacturing enterprises of moderate dimensions, by putting into the merchandise account more or less of that which is entirely foreign to merchandise and which relates solely to the making of goods. Occasionally there is put into the merchandise account that which is of the nature of expenses. In any event the rule in general is to get the account so badly mixed that when we get to the end of a business period we abandon the account entirely. We turn our backs upon the work that we have done and the record we have kept because we perceive that it is not what we require, and, with paper and pencil in hand, we proceed, upon single entry methods, to put down what we have in stock in order to determine whether a loss or a gain has attended our operations. We are obliged to resort to inventorying to complete a statement of our merchandise transactions.

No bookkeeper, no accountant can tell what the balance shown by the conventional merchandise account represents. It is a mixed quantity, and, in most cases, badly mixed.

It is evident, therefore, that if we are to have a going balance sheet, we have got to change the merchandise account. The change necessary is that two accounts shall be substituted for one. One of these accounts would take all the transactions at cost; that is the goods in and the goods out, and would be the merchandise account proper, and by classification, an asset account. The other account would record the sales, and by classification would be a revenue account. The balance in the first account would be the amount of goods on hand at all times, while the balance in the other account would show the gross profit (or loss).

And this brings me to a remark which I have frequently had occasion to make in the past, and that is that the major part of the work of closing the books at the end of a fiscal year, including inventorying, is simply making up for the shortcomings in keeping the accounts during the year. If the accounts had been correctly kept, or, I should say, adquately kept, there would be the need only of verification at that date—not an expensive search after original facts.

If an account—and we will call it merchandise, not in the conventional sense, but, as previously defined—is debited with the goods taken in, including the inventory at the beginning of the period, all at cost prices, and is credited at cost prices with the goods going out, then the balance in that account at any time should represent the goods on hand, likewise at cost prices. This balance would be subject to proof at any date by an inventory, the same as the cash account is subject to proof by counting the cash. The cashier does not count his cash for the purpose of ascertaining the sum he should write into the cash book in balancing, but, instead, to verify the balance which the cash book calls for. Again, if the credit to this merchandise account for the goods parted with were offset by a corresponding debit to a selling account, trading account, revenue account, call it what you please, and if the latter account were credited with the amounts obtained for the goods parted with, the balance in that account, as already intimated, would show the profit (or loss) on the transactions. Again, if gross profits thus ascertained were carried to the credit of the loss and gain account, and if the expenses of doing business for the period were likewise carried to the debit of the loss and gain account, the balance in that account would show the net results of the transactions. With changes and adjustments in the accounts along these lines we get very close to the possibility of a going balance sheet and a perpetual profit and loss statement.

Before dismissing the merchandise account, as it is ordinarily conducted, let us give momentary consideration to the inadequacy of the method of managing this important division of business records commonly taught by the schools and set forth in the text-books. Merchandise on hand, as, for example, in a great department store or in a large mercantile establishment in any division of trade, is certainly an asset, intrinsically valuable and quite available, as business men look upon such things. By the ordinary double entry plan, however, the actual value of this asset is shown by the books only at the extremes of the fiscal period. The books are opened with a statement of the amount of goods on hand, and they are closed with a statement of the amount of goods on hand, but between these dates the actual amount of the asset is not stated. The buying and selling of the establishment may be at such a rate as to produce a complete turnover every few weeks, and it may fluctuate greatly in amount from time to time, and yet a statement of the asset appears only at the beginning and ending of the fiscal period.

It is well known that the preferred time for taking stock, as the phrase goes, is when the stock is lowest. Therefore, this asset, so far as it can be inferentially derived from the figures in the accounts, is understated for the larger portion of the year. A merchant may have so much stock on hand fully paid for and in marketable condition as to be able to negotiate in bank a large credit, and yet this asset, sufficiently available in the banker's eye to warrant the discount of the merchant's note, does not appear upon his books. Certainly, from this point of view, ordinary double entry methods require revision and correction.

(To be continued.)

To be ignorant of one's ignorance is the malady of ignorance.—Alcott.

It is not poverty so much as pretence that harasses a ruined man.—Washington Irving.

In goodness, rich men should transcend the poor, as clouds the earth; raised by the comfort of the sun to water dry and barren grounds.—Tourneur.

There is some help for all the defects of fortune; for if a man cannot attain to the length of his wishes, he may have his remedy by cutting them shorter.—Cowley.

The Monthly Statement

Those who give most careful thought to the conduct of the public schools and who most carefully examine the character of the product produced by the public schools are most ready to admit that one of the evils of the present day is over-education, or, rather, the attempt to crowd into the limited period which a young person can spend in school, far more than can be decently covered in that period. There is also the inclination to put time upon those things which are ornamental rather than useful, to the exclusion of time upon that which is purely practical. We have no quarrel with the public schools in themselves, but we do take exception to much that is done in the name of popular education, and particularly to that which is in the nature of crowding the pupil.

It is a matter of satisfaction, therefore, to learn through certain statistics relating to the public schools which have recently been made public, that there is a tendency upon the part of the public itself to correct this evil. Where selection of studies is permitted, there is being manifested a marked preference for those studies which are directly practical in character, like the natural sciences, or those which by long use have proved their worth in the sense of real education and training. Thus language and literature are coming into a prominence at present which has been lacking for a long time past. Of course, the changes referred to cannot be found in the primary schools, nor yet in the ordinary grades in the common schools anywhere, but they do manifest themselves in high schools and academies. In addition to the change in the character of the studies, there is also to be noted a change in the percentage of students in attendance upon these schools. It appears that the the number of students has nearly doubled in the last nine years, and in the same time the change in the direction of the concentration of the pupil's attention upon comparatively few studies has occured. A few figures are of interest in this connection. The percentage of in-

crease in Latin, for example, during the years mentioned, shows the enormous gain of 174 per cent., while history shows a gain of 152 per cent., geometry 147 per cent., algebra 141 per cent., German and French 131 per cent. and 107 per cent. respectively, physics 79 per cent. and chemistry 65 per cent. Without the actual figures being presented, the statement is made that English and rhetoric are gaining in the same general proportion. Latin, which is sometimes described as the parent language, exercises an important influence in a pupil's education, and the figures which apply to it, as already remarked, are surprisingly large.

The effect of all this must be to the advantage of business interests, as well as in other directions. The educated man in business has been so little known in the past that his presence, when it was first made manifest a few years ago, was naturally surprising, but gradually we have come to look for him in all directions. The education for business and the education for a profession are in a sense of like importance, and may proceed side by side. Some of our best educated business men were in fact educated for a profession, as for example, the law, and afterwards went into business. Business is in that condition that education becomes of special importance, and that man who enters upon business without a good preliminary training is at a great disadvantage in comparison with those who are specially trained for it. Business men, therefore, are to be congratulated that their sons are at last being educated along practical lines rather than dosed with an immense amount of miscellaneous information, to digest or assimilate which is a practical impossibility. The strength of character and the remarkable attainments of certain men of generat ons just passing off the stage was due in part to the fact that their education was restricted to comparatively few studies. It is a good thing for the rising generation that the habit of few studies is once more coming into vogue.

senting them with answers thereto, all arranged in a form to be of the greatest advantage to students everywhere.

The object of the work, the author says in the preface, is primarily to supply candidates with a text-book which will assist them in preparing for their examinations. While it has been produced in the form of questions and answers, yet it must not be taken as showing specimens of the answers required by the examiners, but rather as a guide and help for future students.

The work is prefaced by a table of contents and carefully prepared alphabetical index. Under the head of Bookkeeping the questions employed in the intermediate examination and in the final examination for the years of '97 and '98 are presented. The same is true under the heads of Shareholders, Partners' Accounts, Partnership and Executorship Accounts, Joint Stock Companies, Auditing, Insolvency, Negotiable Instruments, Mercantile Law and Mercantile Arithmetic. So far as legal matters are concerned the rules and forms are of course limited to Dominion practice. With this single exception the book is quite as valuable in the States as in the Dominion, and it deserves a very wide sale.

Joint Stock Company Bookkeeping.

Joint Stock Company Bookkeeping. General technical information respecting incorporated companies: By J. W. Johnson, F. C. A. Ninth edition, revised and enlarged. 108 pages, large octavo; bound in cloth, gilt side title. Price, $1.75.

We have had the pleasure of reviewing various successive editions of Mr. Johnson's really valuable work relating to joint stock company bookkeeping, and in all instances we have had occasion to commend it not only for the excellent features which it possessed in the original edition, but also for additions made in the later editions. The author is a very wide-awake man, actively engaged in the field of business instruction, and a practical accountant as well, and he never allows an item of accounting practice to escape him that can be made of any value in a new edition of any of his works. Accordingly his books are always kept up to date. The volume before us is no exception to the rule, and the small additions that have been made to it since the last edition was issued tend to make it more satisfactory than ever to those who read it.

All the legal references in the volume are to Canadian law, and to that extent the book is less helpful on this side of the line than it would be if the laws of the several States in the Union had been codified and tabu'ated as a part of the introductory matter. The accounting however, is very much the same, whether the practice is under the laws of the Dominion or under the auspices of Uncle Sam. The former editions of the book have had very large sale, both in Canada and the United States, and this one merits a continuance of favor.

Reviews and Criticisms

Canadian Accountant's Manual.

Manual for Accountants. Canada. Vol I. Being the questions set by the Institute of Chartered Accountants (of Ontario) and the answers thereto, forming a text-book for accountants, bookkeepers and business men. 256 pages octavo, bound in cloth. Price, $3.

We think we are guilty of no exaggeration when we say that no organization in the Western Hemisphere has done more to raise the standard of accountancy by educating and training young men for the profession than the Institute of Char-

tered Accountants of Ontario. For many years past this organization has held periodical examinations as a means of testing the knowledge and experience of those students who have aspired to its diplomas and honors. Incidental to these examinations has been an experience upon the part of those who have been instrumental in conducting them that is of the greatest value to the profession and to business men everywhere, so far as it has been made available. Mr. Eddis has taken an important part in this work for a long time past, and has finally embodied in a volume a selection from the questions which have been employed, pre-

What the Credit Men Are Doing

By A. O. Kittredge.

The Reciprocal Reporting Committee submitted its report to the local associations of credit men about the middle of February. At the outset the report states that the labor of the committee, up to the present time, has been almost entirely in the line of securing information from different local organizations as to the system employed by them with respect to reciprocal reporting. The report then sets forth the routine in force at New Orleans, Baltimore, Cincinnati, Minneapolis, Sioux City, and other points. The plan in vogue in Minneapolis and Sioux City is specially endorsed by the committee and is recommended to other associations for adoption.

Secretary Prendergast announces a decided increase in membership in various local associations, including particularly the following: Rochester, Boston, Philadelphia, St. Louis, Cincinnati, New York and Buffalo. Rochester seems to lead the van, having secured sixty new members since the 10th of January.

The Legislative Committee of the New York Credit Men's Association has prepared a bill with regard to signed statements that the present legislature will be asked to pass. The article now on the statute book of the State has been found inoperative, and its inefficiency has become so widely known that counsel almost universally refuse to take the cases of creditor clients that, to the ordinary mind, seem to be teeming with fraud on the part of the debtor. It has been found almost impossible to frame a law that would hold good against selling out a stock of goods in bulk where the goods have not been paid for, and where intent of fraud is palpable to the victimized creditor. The constitutional right of every man to sell his stock out piecemeal or in bulk is unquestioned, and the only remedy, therefore, for creditors is the poor one of seeking redress by civil procedure. Every one who has resorted to this plan knows to his cost that this is difficult and an almost hopeless task, if the debtor really desires to evade payment. The only remedy, therefore, would seem to be in the National Bankruptcy Act, where, if a debtor will not and cannot pay his just debts, he is to be adjudged a bankrupt and take the consequences. The committee has in contemplation an amendment to the Bankruptcy Bill, which, it is believed, will meet the difficulty and which it will also urge for adoption.

The Credit Men's Association of New Orleans, according to a long article in La States, has undertaken a reform in credit conditions in that city. Under the present practice settlements for goods bought by retailers can hardly be made inside of forty or fifty days, a system greatly at variance with the usage of wholesale houses in other cities. This long credit induces overbuying and, consequently, has an injurious effect upon trade. The credit men are confident that united action among wholesale dealers to bring about a system of short contracts will result in mutual benefit to buyer and seller, and be conducive of a healthier financial condition.

The Sioux City Bureau of Credits, at their annual meeting, elected the following officers: President, C. B. French, Jr.; Vice-President, C. P. Kilborne; Secretary, L. T. Ford, and Treasurer, R. M. Baker. After some discussion, the unanimous vote of those assembled was given to a motion declaring against the repeal of the National Bankruptcy Law. A paper read by P. A. Sawyer on "Dishonest Failures," also contained hearty commendations of the law and the fairness of its workings.

The excellent attendance at the January meeting of the Credit Men's Association of Chicago, held at the Grand Pacific Hotel, was evidence of the interest of its members in its objects. I. E. Edgar, of the Continental National Bank, delivered an address on "Facts versus Impressions," in which he demonstrated the tendency of banks and other business institutions to extend credit when there was not sufficient data for a knowledge of the situation of the debtor. Instead of relying upon general impressions and incomplete statements, he urged that systematic and thorough personal inquiry be made into the standing of persons asking credit. As a means of obtaining better results from the credit association, he suggested that the members be divided into groups, representing allied trades, and that each group should hold occasional meetings under the direction of a chairman, for the discussion of methods and matters peculiar to the specific branch.

It will be recalled that at the annual meeting of the Board of Directors of the National Association of Credit Men, arrangements were made by which W. H. Preston, of Sioux City, Iowa, ex-President of the National Association, should visit various cities in the West, and particularly those upon the Pacific Coast, for the purpose of organizing local associations. Mr. Preston left on his missionary excursion early in February. Efforts were directed particularly to organizations in Salt Lake City, San Francisco, Seattle and Los Angeles. Preliminary work had been done in all these cities by placing before the merchants information with respect to the work of the association. Accordingly, when Mr. Preston reached them, they were in an excellent position to appreciate what he had to offer and to co-operate with him.

On Monday, February 5, Mr. Preston conferred with representative merchants of Salt Lake City, there being present members of nineteen of the most prominent business houses of the city. The result was a decision that an effort should be made to secure the assent of all the prominent concerns in Salt Lake City to form an association, and at the same time to invite the co-operation in such a movement of the merchants of Ogden and Provo, Utah. Since Mr. Preston left Salt Lake City advices have been received that the plan is being acted upon and that everything points to a successful issue.

On February 10, the merchants of Seattle tendered Mr. Preston a banquet, as the representative of the National Association of Credit Men. At this banquet, which was attended by representatives of some thirty houses, all of them the principals of their concerns, a resolution was adopted that a local credit association should be formed. A committee was appointed to draft a constitution and by-laws. The Portland Credit Men's Association took a lively interest in Mr. Preston's mission to the coast, and besides tendering him a complimentary banquet, sent a representative, in the person of E. M. Wheeler, of the Goodyear Company, to Seattle, to help him in the good work at that point.

At San Francisco, Mr. Preston presented the object of his visit to the Board of Trade and to the Merchants' Credit Association of California, as well also as to some of the more prominent business houses. Both the organizations named issued notices to their members inviting them to a meeting, to be held on Friday, February 16, for the purpose of affording Mr. Preston an opportunity to lay before the meeting the question of organizing a local association of credit men. This meeting was attended by the representatives of seventy-five of the leading concerns of San Francisco, and resulted in the appointment of a committee of five, to organize a credit association to be allied with the National Association of Credit Men, and to frame a constitution and by-laws, to be submitted at a meeting called for the purpose.

At Los Angeles, Mr. Preston met with the same active interest and co-operation which had marked the various stages of his journey. Under the auspices of the Associated Jobbers of that city the representative merchants assembled and decided unanimously to organize a credit men's association, and the President was authorized to appoint a committee of five to complete the organization.

The annual meeting of the Buffalo Credit Men's Association, held at the Ellicott Club, was more largely attended than any other previous one. John S. Gray, President of the German-American Bank of Detroit, and John F. Gregory, President of the Rochester Credit Men's Association, were the chief speakers. The election of officers resulted as follows: President, Frank Sibley, of Sibley & Holmwood; Vice-President, George W.

Farnham; Treasurer, J. J. Dolphin, of F. C. Howlett & Co. The Secretary has not yet been appointed by the Executive Committee.

—

I. D. Waggener, Secretary of the Kansas City Association of Credit Men, reports a pleasant and profitable meeting of that organization on the 16th of February. The establishment of a Credit Exchange Bureau for the exchange of information among the members was discussed, but no action was taken.

—

During a recent visit to Cincinnati, Secretary Prendergast was invited by the Chamber of Commerce to address the business men during 'Change hours. In able and well-chosen words, he called attention to the purposes for which Credit Men's Associations were being formed. His most timely remarks had good effect in awakening an interest among his hearers.

—

Through the efforts of the members of the Sioux City Bureau of Credits, a bill prohibiting the sales of stocks of goods in bulk, without due notice and protection to creditors, has been introduced in the Iowa Legislature, and is now before that body for consideration. A similar measure has been introduced in the Ohio Legislature, at the instance of the Legislative Committee of the Cincinnati Credit Men's Association. A bill also bearing on these lines is in the hands of the Baltimore Association for introduction in the Maryland Legislature.

—

The Rochester Credit Men's Association has issued circulars containing a complete membership list, and also the names of officers and committees. The president of the organization for the current year is John H. Gregory, of the Central Bank, and the secretary is A. E. Nelson, with Wright, Peters & Co. The chairman of the Executive Committee is John H. Lenahan, with H. C. Cohn & Co. Daniel B. Murphy, of Burke, Fitz Simons, Hone & Co., is chairman of the legislative committee. The organization is in a highly prosperous condition.

—

The rapid expansion which has lately characterized the general business of the country has had the inevitable effect of inducing an over-confidence and looseness in financial matters. At the beginning of a new year when each concern is, in theory at least, making a fresh start, the following words of warning from a prominent credit man come with especial fitness: "Just at the present time I might suggest to the credit men the importance of keeping close haul on all accounts concerning which there is the least doubt. The present year has been something of a long-drawn-out holiday for men handling credits. Business has been good in all lines, orders have been heavy and collections have been excellent. In fact, so much good feeling prevails in every department in business houses that the credit man, along with the rest of the force, is likely to be led off his guard by the general enthusiasm and good feeling."

Questions and Answers

Concerning the

BALANCE-SHEET SYSTEM OF ACCOUNTS

Conducted by the

Account Audit and Assurance Co., Ltd.

25 Pine Street, New York

The Balance-Sheet System of Accounts in Manufacturing and the Proof-by-Balance System of Accounts.

From W. J. B., Dayton, Ohio:

Will you give me an idea of the working of the Balance-Sheet System of Accounts applied to a factory, and will you also explain the Proof-by-Balance System of Cost Accounts? Wherein does the latter differ in results from other cost account methods?

Answer.—The Proof-by-Balance System of Cost Accounts is merely the factory part of the Balance-Sheet System of Accounts. As a cost account system it differs from any that we have ever found in use, in that it is not a mere determination of constants to be employed in calculations, nor yet an estimate of the cost of occasional lots. Instead, it is a record of every lot of goods produced, showing the actual cost of the lot, in materials, labor and factory expenses, and proving by the sum of the costs of all the lots balancing with the sum of the charges to the factory.

As a result of our methods, we have, among other exhibits, the cost of the material remaining on hand unconsumed, the cost of the work in process at all dates, and, as already stated, the cost of the finished product. These several showings are essential to a going balance sheet of the business which is the end at which we aim. The Balance-Sheet System, therefore, applied to a factory, gives a balance sheet statement of the business at all dates, without the necessity of an inventory. Accompanying it is a profit and loss statement, likewise complete at all dates.

The fiscal period, in the sense of indicating a date at which the books are to be closed, is abolished. The books are always closed, and they are likewise always open. One month is exactly like another. The business goes on, like Tennyson's brook, without intermission, and the records of the business show results without the necessity of shutting down or otherwise making special investigations to determine what has been accomplished.

Distinguishing Features and Scale of Expense

From A. P. A., Chicago:

How is the Balance Sheet System of Accounts distinguished from any other good and adequate accounting plan? Is it not attended with extra clerical expense? Are not the methods of the Proof-by-Balance System of Cost Accounts essentially expensive?

Answer.—In answering these questions, the Balance Sheet System of Accounts is to be considered as being inclusive. The Proof-by-Balance system of Cost Accounts is only the application of the principles fundamental to the Balance-Sheet System to factory operations.

Answering the last question first, we say emphatically "No!" The contrary is the actual fact. The administration of the Proof-by-Balance System is cheaper than that of any other adequate plan of keeping cost records. There is less clerical work required because there is less bookkeeping machinery to be operated.

Answering now the first question, we would say that the principal mark of distinction of the Balance-Sheet System of Accounts is the point of view from which the necessary accounting work of any business is regarded. The common rule is to regard accounts as annual or semi-annual in character—that is, that their showings are to be completed and verified at the end of a year or six months, as the case may be. When the end of the fixed period is reached, an inventory is taken, the books are "balanced" and the results of the business for the term duly declared.

With the Balance Sheet System nothing is put off to the end of a period. Everything is kept strictly up-to-date. Inventorying is dispensed with by having material accounts and product accounts arranged to show by their balances the amounts on hand, the same as the cash account shows by its balance the amount of cash on hand. The result is—not a balance sheet, and its accompanying profit and loss statement at the end of comparatively long periods—but instead, a perpetual balance sheet and a perpetual profit and loss statement. The actual results of the business are shown every day.

Now as to the second question: At first blush it would seem that there is involved a very large amount of extra labor in such up-to-date showings. The facts of the case are that we accomplish all these results without any increase of clerical labor, and in many cases with an actual reduction of clerical labor. What is usually done in the way of closing the books at the end of the fiscal period is, in reality, to make up for the deficiencies in the plan upon which the books were kept during the period. The plan, therefore, needs correction. By the Balance Sheet System of Accounts everything is done once for all, promptly and at the time. There is never any back work to make up and never any deficiencies to supply. The savings in this regard alone go far to reduce the total cost of administration. The Balance Sheet System is a cheap system to operate.

———

Confidence is a plant of slow growth in an aged bosom.—Lord Chatham.

Accountics

The Office Magazine.

Published Monthly.

A. O. KITTREDGE, F. I. A., C. P. A., Editor.

E. R. KITTREDGE, Associate.

Accountics is devoted to the Science of Accounting, to the Art of Bookkeeping and to the advocacy of Improved Office Methods.

Subscription.—One dollar a year, payable in advance.

Postage is prepaid by the publishers in the United States, Canada and Mexico. For all other countries in the Postal Union, subscribers must add 50 cents a year.

Discontinuances.—In the absence of specific orders to discontinue at the end of the subscription term the magazine will be continued and a bill sent.

Remittances should be by Draft, P. O. Order or Express Order, payable to the order of the ACCOUNTICS ASSOCIATION. Money and postage stamps are at the risk of the sender, unless sent by express or in registered letters. Add 10 cents each to checks on local banks to defray collection charges.

Advertising Rates will be quoted on application.

Official Journal.—This publication, by resolutions duly passed, has been made the official publication of the following organizations:—

THE INSTITUTE OF ACCOUNTS.

THE NEW YORK CHAPTER of the Institute of Accounts.

THE WASHINGTON CHAPTER of the Institute of Accounts.

THE HARTFORD CHAPTER of the Institute of Accounts.

ACCOUNTICS is the accredited medium of intercommunication between members of the Institute of Accounts wherever located.

ACCOUNTICS ASSOCIATION, Publishers,

Lancashire Building, Pine Street, near Nassau, New York.

Publisher's Desk

The good work that the Saturday Evening Post, of Philadelphia, is doing is aptly illustrated by almost any one of a considerable series of practical articles, which of late have characterized its pages. Perhaps the article by Thomas B. Reed, on "Monopolies," recently presented, is as good an illustration as any. The industrial combination is here and Mr. Reed does not seem to be afraid of it, nor does he characterize it, as some do, by such terms as "octopus" or "bugaboo." "My notion," says he, "is that while Providence and the higher laws, which really govern the universe, are in men's talk much inferior to the revised statutes before they are enacted, they are always found to be quite superior to them after they are enacted. In fact, nature abhors monopoly as much as it does a vacuum." This is good horse sense, as every man in active business will admit.

"The Best Business Ink" is the trademark of an ink which William H. Woglom, 239 Greenwich street, New York City, is introducing for use in office work. It is a free-flowing, blue-black fluid, which soon changes to an intense black. The ink does not gum, and its fluidity renders it particularly suitable for use in fountain pens, a quality which will recommend it to the favor of those who have hitherto found it necessary to keep on hand an ink specially made for that purpose.

Our attention has recently been called to an effort which is being made to establish an association of accountants and bookkeepers under the title of National Association of Accountants and Bookkeepers. As yet, the organization is in an experimental stage, but those who have its interest in charge intend holding a convention at Detroit in July, when a constitution will be formulated. Till the aims and purposes of the projected association are given to the public, we are unable to form an opinion as to the objects which it will subserve and its probable usefulness to the profession.

"Mr. Dooley," the new light in our literary firmament, comes forward in the Ladies' Home Journal with advice particularly applicable to this season of the year. He recommends those doctoring a man with "col' on the chist," to "get Casey's mixture f'r man an' baist, put him in bed, slap a musthard plasther on him that'll keep his mind employed, an' lave thim fight it out. May t' best man win. If the patient's alive in th' mornin' he'll not have stren'th to cough."

Notes

Wall Street brokers have confidence in the business outlook, if the price paid for a seat in the Stock Exchange is a criterion. The highest price ever recorded, $41,000, was given a few days since, exceeding by $1,000 any other purchase.

Building and loan associations are in a prosperous condition in Iowa. The Auditor of the State reports seventy-nine domestic-local, twenty-seven domestic and one foreign company doing business there, and a gain of $700,464 over previous year in receipts.

Every ledger requires an index. Of indexes there are various kinds, sizes and descriptions, but that which is closest to the ledger itself is generally preferred over that which has to be taken up as an independent proposition. Working along these lines, S. B. Kirtley, of Jefferson City, Mo., has devised what is known as the Self-Indexing Ledger, in which the opening of the account also indexes the account. He claims that the device not only prevents errors in bookkeeping, but corrects those which are made, in one-third of the time required by the ordinary plans.

Business men both in New York and outside of it will appreciate the advantages of the enlarged edition of the "Directory of Directors," which the Audit Company, of this city, has recently issued. The first, and by far the greater part of the book, consists of a list of persons holding the position of director or trustee who have New York addresses. The names of the companies with which they are connected follow in each case. In the appendix, the order is reversed, the name of the corporation being first given, and after it a list of officers and directors. While containing valuable information, the business man who consults the book may have occasion to note important omissions, for even casual examination reveals the fact that many relatively prominent corporations are entirely omitted. This fact detracts from its usefulness and is a source of regret that the work is not more exhaustive in its character. So much having been accomplished toward meeting an evident business demand, it is to be hoped that in a future year the publishers will extend the scope of the directory till it covers the entire field described in its title page and preface.

Poverty, through want, teaches evil.—Euripides.

Wealth is nothing in itself; it is not useful but when it departs from us.—Dr. Johnson.

Surely modesty never hurt any cause; and the confidence of man seems to me to be much like the wrath of man.—Tillotson.

Credit is a matter so subtle in its essence, that, as it may be obtained almost without reason, so, without reason, may it be made to melt away.—Anthony Trollope.

Datings

In an address delivered at the meeting of the New York Credit Men's Association, December 2, 1899, Hugo Kanzler, credit man for Muser Brothers, of this city, discussed the dating-ahead custom, which still prevails in various branches of the wholesale trade. After tracing the introduction of this pernicious custom, which has crept into busines during the last fifteen or twenty years, Mr. Kanzler said:

"I believe the question of dating can be well put into three classes. We have a certain class of merchants who ask dating for the purpose of anticipating, knowing full well that money may be had from time to time at a less rate of interest than 6 per cent. per annum. They are good enough in anticipating our bills to charge us that legal rate of interest, while our money is worth probably 2 or 2 1-2 per cent. Another class actually requires the time. Then comes the third class: dating or no dating, they will "stick" us if they get the chance. A most serious question for the credit men, and one hard to decide, is what is a reasonable dating, and what is the customer, under certain circumstances, entitled to?

"I do not believe it would be wise at this time to make such a radical change as to entirely remove the dating from the commercial methods of business, as it

has now become chronic. However, if we stand together and invite the Merchants' Association to assist us, we shall be able to reduce the period. Years ago dating was essential. Its origin was probably largely due to the request made by customers on the Pacific Slope, to be put on the same plane as Eastern merchants —that the loss of time in shipment should not be charged to them. Subsequently merchants generally were good enough to ask for a like benefit. In the present prosperous times we cannot conceive why we should still adhere to that principle and allow the retailers to have the benefit of our capital. The time has come when we feel justified in charging the merchant with a part of the burden of conducting his own business instead of throwing the entire burden upon the manufacturer or importer.

"If we cannot succeed in reducing the dating by other means we could do so by reducing the rate of interest allowed for anticipations. The merchant will not anticipate his bills, will not deprive you of the capital that you are entitled to in conducting your own affairs, if you reduce the rate of interest to, say, 4 per cent.

"If you insist upon thus reducing the rate, or of you cut down the dating, I am satisfied that in course of time there will be no question of dating such as is given now in the woollen, millinery and other lines. In course of time it will be reduced by from thirty to sixty days at least, and the customer will then be obliged to take some of the burden which devolves upon him."

The Post Fountain Pen

The accompanying illustration represents a new form of fountain pen which is being put upon the market by R. Caygill, trade manager, 124 West 14th street, New York. Among the advantages to which attention is directed are the following: No filler is required for this pen. Its construction is such that it never soils the fingers, and clogging or becoming filthy is impossible.

In appearance this fountain pen does

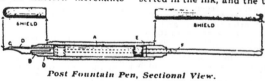

Post Fountain Pen.

not differ essentially from many others. There is the shield for both ends, each of which is removable in the ordinary manner. The central portion of the barrel of the pen carries the ink and it is filled by pneumatic pressure or by what is the equivalent of a pump. The pen is inserted in the ink, and the upper shield be-

Post Fountain Pen, Sectional View.

ing removed, a plunger, with which the barrel is provided, is drawn out by means of a rod, thus by suction filling the barrel. The operation is analogous to that of supplying ink in an ordinary pen, at least to the extent of dipping it into the ink well or reservoir, but with this important difference, that the pen once filled does not require refilling for a considerable period of time. There are various features about it that recommend it for use. In writing for circulars mention this notice in ACCOUNTICS.

Accountants' Associations

New York Chapter of the Institute of Accounts

The February meeting of the Institute, held on the 20th of that month, at the Waldorf-Astoria, was largely attended, both by members and invited guests. Among the latter were Camilus G. Kidder and George W. Sill, Attorneys, of New York; J. E. Reynolds, New York City, and Sands Olcott, of Newark. The address of the evening was given by Charles Dutton, F. I. A., Secretary of the National Institute of Accounts. His subject, "The Duality of Business," was handled in a masterly manner, and the broad and philosophic treatment was felt by his hearers to bring out new and important views. Remarks in hearty commendation followed the address. Among those speaking were Henry Harney, Samuel D. Patterson, Camilus G. Kidder, George W. Sill and Eduard Glardon.

The Illinois Institute of Accountants

The Illinois Institute of Accountants is devoting a good deal of time to the consideration of legal questions of peculiar interest to accountants. At a recent meeting Norman H. Camp, a Chicago lawyer, gave a very careful and well-arranged statement of the steps initiatory to incorporation and of the law relative to corporations under the laws of Illinois.

An address delivered before the Institute at the February meeting, by Dan Morgan Smith, Jr., of the Chicago bar, treated of the United States Bankruptcy Law. After a brief discussion of the bankruptcy acts of 1800, 1840 and 1867, Mr. Smith analyzed the law of 1898, now in force, and drew the attention of his auditors to features of the bill especially to be commended in the protection it affords to the honest debtor temporarily embarrassed, against the demands of ungenerous and unjust creditors, and the equality which it compels in the distribution of assets among creditors, placing "the firm who has extended credit upon the mercantile report upon the same footing as the personal friend." He gave a succinct statement of the procedure in the case of voluntary and involuntary bankruptcy and said in conclusion:

"The bankruptcy law, passed in 1898, has been taken advantage of by thousands, and has relieved in a great measure, the burden from the unfortunates who went down in the several crises of the last few years. It has cleared the financial atmosphere as a thunder-cloud clears the hot breath of summer, but it will soon be a thing of the past, as it is an extraordinary remedy, to be called upon only in times of great need; as a relief, it is considered only a temporary one, and will, no doubt, be repealed by the present Congress. The Fifty-fifth Congress deserves great credit for having passed a Bankruptcy Act so honest in purpose and complete in detail, that its motto may well be, 'Fairness to all; favors to none.'"

Massachusetts Society of Public Accountants

The auditors and public accountants of Massachusetts have organized the "Massachusetts Society of Public Accountants," which held its first regular meeting and dinner at Young's Hotel Thursday evening, March 6.

At this meeting a constitution and by-laws were adopted and the following-named charter members were elected: Amos D. Albee, Nicholas T. Apollonio, George S. Chase, Harvey S. Chase, Herbert F. French, William Franklin Hall, William F. Herrick, Charles F. Kellogg, C. C. Kurtz, George W. Manson, W. C. Newell, Augustus Nickerson, Edward L. Parker, Henry A. Piper, Thomas S. Spurr, George T. Stoddard, Frederick C. Tufts and A. R. Turner.

These officers were elected: President, Amos A. Albee; Vice-President, William Franklin Hall; Secretary, Charles F. Kellog; Auditor, Augustus Nickerson; three members of the Executive Committee were: George S. Chase, Frederick C. Tufts and William H. Herrick.

Six meetings, with dinners, will be held each winter, and professional subjects will be discussed.

The purpose of the society is the elevation of the profession of public accountancy and the promotion of the interests of its members.

It is the intention to embrace within its membership only those public accountants who are citizens of the United States, or have declared their intentions of becoming such citizens, who shall have continuously maintained an office and

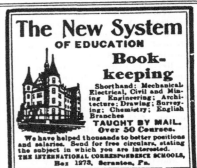

practiced as public accountants for at least five years, of which not less than one year immediately preceding the application shall have been in the State of Massachusetts, and who may be elected as provided in the by-laws.

Public Accountants Act in the Legislative Assembly of Victoria

The activity of the several Institutes of Accountants in Australia has resulted in the introduction of a bill into the Legislative Assembly of Victoria under the title of "Public Accountants Act," with a view to providing for the registration of persons practicing as accountants and auditors, so as to distinguish qualified from unqualified persons. By the enactment of the bill, a Board, which will be a body corporate, will be created, with power to issue certificates of registration to those entitled to them under the act, and to prescribe examinations to be passed by persons desirous of obtaining certificates. The board will have power to vary the subjects and conditions of such examinations whenever it may think fit. It is also its duty to appoint a Board of Examiners, and may, if occasion demands, make regulations for the appointment of special examiners.

Accountants' Students' Societies

Wider opportunities for those interested in the study of accounting and auditing are being demanded both by those already prominent in the profession and those who seek to enter it. Again and again the matter has been brought before the different Institutes, and so general is the feeling that the higher institutions of learning should provide suitable courses of study for those desirous of pursuing these subjects, along broad and scientific lines, that, one by one, university and college faculties are taking the matter under consideration.

It is well to watch what is being done in other countries, that we may profit by any advance they may make. The Accountants' Students' Society of London has instituted a method of instruction which may be followed with advantage in various communities. This is a Mock Meeting of Creditors. At one of the Society's sessions, held lately, several prominent accountants and solicitors attended, taking part in the exercises. After the meeting of the creditors was organized with the students as the body of the creditors, one of these gentlemen, representing the accountant who had examined the books of the debtor, read a statement setting forth the situation. Following this were proceedings of a nature likely to arise in the conduct of a gathering of actual creditors.

Object lessons of this kind familiarize students with the work for which they are preparing, and lectures and the instruction of the class-room may profitably be diversified in this manner. Certain forms and methods are customary and necessary in all meetings of creditors, and the accountant is daily becoming a more important feature of such

meetings. It should be part of his training to know the trend of the inquiries that will be made and to prepare himself to meet them. His value as an accountant will be largely commensurate with his ability to clearly put before the creditors a statement of the situation, and their action will often depend upon the manner in which he accomplishes this task.

The Barlow Time Book and Pay Roll

In various lines of business where a number of workmen are employed, it has been found convenient to combine in different columns on the right-hand page, as shown in "balance column."

The proper manner of using the book is to make out the check on the bank for the amount of the pay-roll, noting on the back of the check the different amounts and denominations wanted, as shown in "balance column." When the pay envelopes are filled there will, of course, be nothing left, thus proving the accuracy of the computations. One form of this time-table is made up to cover a year, with weekly payments, another is arranged so that it will last two years with fortnightly payments.

The book is neat in appearance, being

Coming to Terms

"You want a place as office boy?"

"Yes, sir."

"Where are you from?"

"Boston."

"Ah! How much pay per week do you want?"

"I want a hundred dollars, sir."

"A hundred dollars?"

"Yes, sir. That's what I want, but I expect to get about three dollars."

How to Avoid Errors

In bookkeeping and to save one-half your time in posting ledger accounts. While bookkeeping in a bank, I was greatly an-

TIME BOOK AND PAY ROLL.   For Week Ending .... 189....

NAME	M	T	W	T	F	S	Total Time	Rate per Day	Amount Advanced	Total Amt. Due	$10	$5	$2	$1	50 cents	25 cents	10 cents	5 cents	1 and 2 cents	BALANCE COL.	
J. L. Handy	1	1	1	1	0	0	4 1/2	3 00		12 00	10.		2.							$10.00	60 00
H. Peters	1	1	1/2	1	1	1	5 1/2	2 50		13 75	10.		2.	1.	.50	.25				5.00	25 00
R. B. Bacon	1	1	1	1	1	1	6	2 50		15 00	10.	5.								2.00	34 00
H. L. Jennings	1	1	1	1	1	1	6	2 00		12 00	10.		2.							1.00	7 00
B. Smith	1	1	0	0	1	1	4	2 00		8 00		5.	2.	1.						.50	4 00
A. J. Hastings	1	1	1/2	1	1		5 1/2	1 90		10 45	10					.25	.20			.25	1 00
A. Johnson	1	1	1/2	1/2	1		5	1.90		9 50		5.	4.		.50					.10	• 50
L. G. Barton	1	1	1	1	1	1	6	1.75		10 50	10				.50					.05	20
Emma Barton	1	1	1	1	1	1	6	1.10		6 60		5.		1.	.50		.10			.02 / .01	09
Ella Barker	1	1	1	1	1	1	6	1.00		6 00		5.		1.						TOTAL.	132 09
Jennie June	1	1	0	1	1	1/2	4 1/2	.90		4 05				4.				.05			
Jennie Arban	1	1	1/2	1	1	1	5 1/2	85		4 68				4.	.50		.10	.05	.03		
Nattie Green	1	1	1/2	1	1	1	5 1/2	85	50	4 18				4.			.10	.05	.03		
Mabel Hastings	1	1	1	1	1	1/2	5 1/2	80		4 40				4.		.25	.10	.05			
Grace Hastings	1	0	1	1	1	1	5	75		3 75			2.	1.	.50	.25					
Alice Carter	1	1	1	1	1	1/2	5 1/2	75	50	3 63			2.	1.	.50		.10		.03		
Jennie Lucas	1	1	1	1	1	1	6	60		3 60			2.	1.	.50		.10				
										132 09	60.	25.	34	7.	4 00	1. 00	80	20	09		

The Barlow Time Table and Pay Roll.

some form or other a time-book and pay-roll. Barlow Brothers, of Grand Rapids, Mich., have put on the market a book of this character, which, besides taking care of the time in the usual manner, also affords a ready way to divide up the complete roll into the several amounts needed to pay each person. It has the further advantage of proving itself and correcting all mistakes.

The accompanying cut shows a page of this time-book and pay-roll filled out. The sum total of footing of the column of "total amount due" on the left-hand page must equal the sum total of the

bound with red Russia back and fronts and linen sides, and is well put together.

———

Worldly wealth is the devil's bait.—Robert Burton.

———

Whatever fortune has raised to a height, she has raised only that it may fall.—Seneca.

———

We ourselves make our fortunes, good or bad; and when God lets loose a tyrant upon us, or a sickness, if we fear to die, or know not to be patient, the calamity sits heavy upon us.—Jeremy Taylor.

noyed by posting the wrong accounts and incorrect amount. I finally adopted a plan that made my work almost free from errors. Will send any one both plans on receipt of one dollar, agreeing to return dollar if claims are not proved to your satisfaction. Address, S. B. Kirtley, 202 Monroe St., Jefferson City, Mo.

Smith's Adjustable Index Tags

Anyone who has to consult many times a day heavy and unwieldly books in which there is no index, will appreciate this little invention which Charles G. Smith, of Exeter, Neb., is putting on the market. It is an adjustable index tag, made of a spring-steel clip, enclosed in leather, on which is printed or written whatever may be necessary to serve as a guide to subjects contained in the leaf to which it is attached. The clip is easily

Fig. 1. Three-quarter inch Adjustable Tag.

put in place by starting at the upper corner of the leaf and slipping it down the margin to the point desired, and it can be removed as readily by a quick movement or jerk of the hand.

Figure 1 shows a tag three-quarters of an inch in size, adapted to use on ledgers, journals, dictionaries, commercial reports,

Fig. 2. One-inch Adjustable Tag.

cards or the like, where States, numbers, letters of the alphabet, months, etc., can be advantageously employed in indexing. Fig. 2 shows the one-inch size, and is in demand by county and municipal offices, gas, water and electric companies, and other large corporations. In Fig. 3 the tags are shown as they appear when attached to a leaf.

The erasable tag is still another variety, made by the addition to the regular

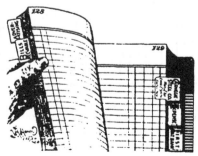

Fig. 3. Tag attached to Leaf.

leather cover of a facing on each side of Scotch linen ledger paper, on which inscriptions may be written with ink or pencil. These, the manufacturers assert, will stand from one to three erasures of ink and from twenty to fifty of pencil, and by the application of gummed stickers the facings may be renewed from

time to time, so that the tag will last indefinitely. Neat and unbroken corners and margins recommend themselves to any accountant or bookkeeper. They are secured by the use of this device. The saving in wear and tear of books is also an advantage as well as the gain in time and increased facility in manipulation.

Poverty is no sin, but it is a branch of roguery.—Calderon.

Sweeping the Floor.

BY W. E. PARTRIDGE

Sweeping a floor is such a simple matter, of course that it is always given into the hand of the youngest boy in the establishment, or to the latest comer. He is told where to find the broom and where to begin. No one ever thinks of giving any further directions for the very good reason that not a man in the place knows anything about sweeping beyond the fact that sometimes the floor is sprinkled and sometimes it is not.

To sweep is to raise a dust. The broom driver gets the dirt from off the floor and leaves twenty-five per cent. of it in the air to settle in every available place. No one protests because that is the way all boys sweep. The head of the firm knows how it is himself. When he was a boy he wore the broom out in a one-sided manner, raised a dust that took an hour to settle, and then started in with a featherduster and raised the dust a second time. This last raising was continued until the desks filled up and the bookkeepers and clerks received the remains of it on their shoes, coats, hands and faces. Yes, the boy is working in the time-honored way. If the head of the firm finds his desk dusty he makes remarks in French or Greek, calls for a duster and makes things fly a little, that is the end of it.

The janitor, the man on the sidewalk, the porter in the cellar, all sweep alike, all in the old orthodox way, and all in the wrong way. But there is the right way, and one by which no dust is raised. A store may be so swept that no dusting will be found necessary, if only the man who engineers the broom knows how. Here is the combination—First have something with which to make the floor damp. A sprinkler that will leave it wet is of no use if good work is to be done. Damp sawdust is a first-class article for the purpose. If the floor is not too warm, snow can be used in the northern states in the winter time. If the sprinkler must be employed, use the kind with the finest holes.

The next thing after dampening the floor is to handle the broom. Here is the golden rule: Never throw the dirt beyond the broom, let it stop where the broom stops. No matter how fast the broom moves, the dirt must not slide forward when the broom is taken up for a new stroke. The boy always sends the dirt flying. That is because he does not know how. By keeping the dirt under the broom and not letting it slide along beyond, there is no chance for the dust to rise. The broom holds it down on the floor, just the place for it. Give it impetus at the end of the stroke and away it will fly.

This is not an easy way of sweeping. The boy will not take kindly to it unless he is told how the first time he has to sweep, but he may find it an advantage in the end. He will not have any dusting to do unless it be to remove the dust that has come in from the outside.

There is another advantage to this plan. Sweeping can be done at any time of the day when the floor is not occupied. A corner or a room may be swept and not cause any annoyance; at least, no one will be choked with dust.

Dusting is an art that cannot be taught with a dust-brush, and therefore a word on the subject may be pardoned. Dusting properly should be the removal of dust from desk, books, papers, counter, goods, etc. With the commonly accepted methods, it is simply throwing it up in the air to settle in the same place again. In summer weather by opening doors and windows and getting up a current of air, it is hoped that a portion of it will blow out. A small part of it may do so, but in the winter it all comes down upon the surface from which it was started.

The proper way to dust? Get some very soft cloths, a yard square; then use these to wipe up the dust as though it was water. In a word, take the dust up into the cloth, then take the cloth outside and shake it where the dust will not trouble any one. Combine the quiet use of the broom with the rational method of removing the dust and the office, or the store will be transformed. The comfort of cleanliness will be a cause for daily gratitude.

Now, a word about carpets. They cannot be managed in this way. With them, all broom sweeping is a nuisance pure and simple. If you must have a carpet, make a compromise. Have the whole floor varnished or oiled. Around the edges of the office, for a space of say eighteen inches, have the floor stained somewhat darker than the ground of the carpet. The corners then can easily be kept clean by the method indicated. Better still, use rugs or have the carpet made up in the form of rugs. This has a double advantage because the rugs can be taken up any day and shaken, that is if the porter or the boy or the janitor can be induced to do such a thing.

In addition to this, there is the advantage that rugs will fit in almost anywhere and can be taken from one place to another as wear may make desirable. If this could be hammered into the brains

where it would do the most good, the comfort of those who spend a large percentage of their lives in offices and stores would be marvellously increased.

CORRESPONDENCE

Voucher Checks

From A. C. N., Toronto.

Referring to the article on "Form of of Accountics, I desire to ask if any one can throw any light upon the question of how the bank teller views a combined check and voucher. How does he manage to adapt its use to that of the ordinary check and yet leave it in form for convenient examination?

NOTE—The question raised by this correspondent is an interesting one and we should be glad to have the bank men among our readers reply to it. In this connection we may mention that we happen to know of a publisher who, on the first occasion of receiving a combined check and voucher of the general character of that recently illustrated in these columns, proceeded to cut it in two, letting one-half go to the bank and holding the other half for a purpose which perhaps was not distinctly defined in his

own mind for the moment. What was uppermost in mind at the time was getting the check to proper destination. Having cut it in two, he, of course, defeated the object of those who preferred that form and size, and accordingly were put to the trouble of getting a duplicate.

Credits and Collections

G. B. Pulfer, of the Detroit Credit Men's Association, in writing on "Credits and Collections," in an article which we are obliged to epitomise for lack of space, emphasizes the necessity of care and diligence in making collections as bills mature.

"From close observation," he says, "I am convinced beyond dispute that at least eighty per cent. of our business houses and manufacturers are too careless in their methods as regards collection of bills at maturity, and that sixty per cent. of their losses can be traced to contributory negligence on their part."

He condemns the practice of accepting orders and shipping goods to a customer when he is behind in his payments, unless a mutually satisfactory understanding has been arrived at regarding an extension of time, and gives the following advice in conclusion: "Be steadfast in your purpose, but always considerate and polite. Never write a threatening letter under any circumstances, but if it is necessary to eventually place the account in an attorney's hands, do so without warning to the customer."

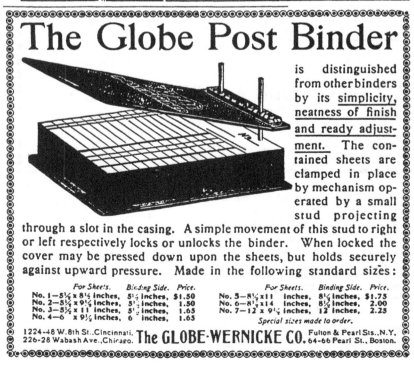

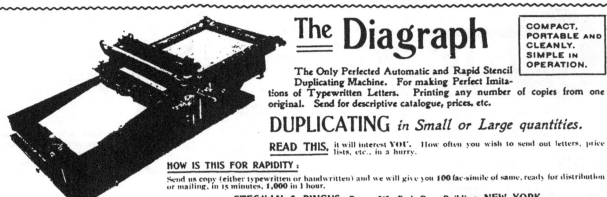

Accountics:—
THE OFFICE MAGAZINE

37

| Volume VI Number 4 | APRIL, 1900 | Monthly, $1 a year Single Copy, 10 cents |

The Duality of Business*

BY CHARLES DUTTON, F I. A.

An inspired writer in the first century of the Christian era wrote a letter to some people in Corinth in which were these words: "They measuring themselves by themselves, and comparing themselves among themselves are not wise." I am not unmindful that I am addressing the members of the Institute of Accounts, and those who by their presence here indicate their interest in accounting, that vital element of business, nevertheless, I will ask you to-night not to measure yourselves by yourselves, but standing away from your individual profession or association, to consider, not your relation to each other, but your relation to that which is the foundation and reason for all accounting.

In considering the conditions of the business world, both in times past and at present, I am convinced that the operations of fixed principles have often been overlooked and sometimes entirely forgotten. Economic specialists have multiplied impractical theories of what business should be, instead of defining and interpreting the unerring operation of irreversible law, and explanations have often been so shrouded in mystery that they needed explaining. In contradistinction to this, I shall, as best as I can, follow a more scientific method, and trace the development of those fundamental principles, which have made business not only possible, but an absolute necessity.

There are many words in the English language which we use daily and use properly, and in their use have no difficulty in conveying to others a correct understanding of the thought we would express, yet if called upon to define we are unable to do so. Such a word is "business." Almost every one has a notion concerning it, which is sufficiently correct for common use, but those who have to do with the management of affairs in our commercial world have need of something more than a mere notion. They should, in fact, have a clearly defined idea of what constitutes the warp and woof of our commercial fabric. Business was not brought to its present state

*Abstract of an address by Charles Dutton, F. I. A., Supervising Auditor of the Account. Audit and Assurance Company, Limited, delivered before the New York Chapter of the Institute of Accounts, Tuesday evening, February 20, 1900.

by legislative enactment, and certainly not by accident nor chance. It has grown out of the wants and demands of the human race by a gradual advance through the successive changes which have developed both civilization and society. It is as essential to the well-being of society as life itself.

Go back with me, away back, into the years when man was in a state of isolation, when he satisfied his wants by his own efforts, raised his own food, made his own clothing. There was no society; there was not—there could not have been —any form of business, however crude. Under these conditions man could not rise very much above the brutes. Many difficulties and obstacles had to be overcome before his desires and wants could be satisfied. Any attempt to meet more than the simplest of them would have been a miserable failure.

As man rose in the scale of civilization, his wants, his needs, his demand for comfort increased, and it was beyond his power unaided to satisfy them. When he devoted himself to overcoming one class of obstacles and to the production of one article, his wants were more than satisfied. He was in a position to extend the benefit of his labor to others. Here arose the necessity of society and when man was in a position to supply some of his neighbors' wants and have in turn some of his own wants supplied by his neighbors, the era of exchange, of business, began. It is not necessary to dwell upon the details of the development of exchanging or to enumerate the mediums by which it was accomplished. All are familiar with the steps and stages from the crude forms of early times to the complex monetary system of to-day. I will, however, call attention to one important feature of business development. The determination of what constitutes value has been of slow growth. During the ages when society was distracted by war, when the crowning desire of the people was conquest, when the great mass of humanity was looked upon and treated as slaves, it was difficult to consider an exchange except of material things.

Aristotle has been called the Father of Political Economy, which is the science of exchange, and therefore the science of business, for business is exchanging of values and nothing more, yet Aristotle

could not conceive of personal service or labor as value. The Greeks did not understand that there was any value in rights or claims. The Roman lawyers were the first to contend that labor and rights were property, which they define as being "what is exclusively one's own and can be exchanged and become another's." Thus in the evolution of business, intangible things have become exchangeable, and therefore are values. Hence, it was that man came to realize in the growth of society and the development of civilization that through his association with others, more could be produced, more could be exchanged, and more desires could be satisfied. From helping himself he was led to help others help themselves, and to accumulate more than this his own needs required.

Thus the problem of business has been wrought out. The demand for mere food and shelter has grown into the far-reaching demands of modern civilization. All the way the supply has kept pace with the demand. The progress of the two will continue; the limit cannot be fixed, for in the future, as in the past the one will be the regulator of the other. Business is thus seen to spring from an active principle, one and the same, everywhere and with all people. Opposition to this principle has always caused trouble in the past and always will in the future. As in physics, mathematics, all the phenomenon of the natural world, so in business there reigns an immutable, eternal law. Nothing that happens comes by chance. As expressed by Professor Henry Drummond, "one all-embracing series of causes and effects, must have existed eternally, of which our world and its activities is a part and of which all future activity will be an outgrowth."

The law which governs business is not separate and distinct from, but rather a subdivision of, universal law. By this is not meant human law, an enactment of man with reference to human conduct, but as defined by another, "that Law of which no less can be acknowledged than that her seat is in the Infinite, and her voice the harmony of the world." It is safe to affirm that business advancement has been in just the proportion that this law has been understood and interpreted, or, as Professor Drummond says, "the key to all progress is conformity to Law." If, then, the principles which pervade business are subject to the general law, it must of necessity follow that business is a unit, that underlying the diversity of form in which it manifests itself, one condition of the dualism must be the unity of business. If we subdivide business, as economists have done, into production, accumulation, distribution and consumption, the unity is preserved; in fact, is emphasized. It makes no difference what the motives or the ultimate purposes of exchanging may be or whether tangible or intangible things are exchanged, the process is the same. "Saint and sinner must plow with the same heifer." Prof. Walker makes each of the subdivisions separate and distinct and exchange distinct from all the others. In this I must differ with him, for exchange accompanies all the processes of production, accumulation, distribution or consumption. It is hardly possible to conceive of them as independent of exchange. The value of production is its distribution, and the value of distribution is its consumption. The idea that producers are more worthy of encouragement, as being a separate class in the business world, is shallow and false. The wants of an ever-advancing civilization have compelled the farmer to substitute a mowing machine for a scythe, that he might supply the increasing demand. They have forced the manufacturer to employ improved methods of production, to take advantage of the results of inventive genius. All this increased production would be of no avail if there were not relatively an increased distribution. Imagine for a moment, the effect upon the world if distribution should suddenly cease. Consider what would be the result if the brain labor represented in distribution should enter into combination as the brawn labor has done at times and for forty-eight hours lay down the implements of its occupation and leave the desk and the counting room. In such an event business would be paralyzed. Farmers and manufacturers are not more essential to business than are bankers, shippers and accountants.

Go into one of the grocery stores of this city, one of the smallest of them, the contents of which would barely fill an ordinary box-car, and note what an intimate relation it bears to the entirety of business. The tea is produced and gathered in China, the coffee in Brazil, the flour in the far West. That small mercantile enterprise is one link in the chain of production and distribution which encircles the globe. The inconceivable number of enterprises which are the component parts of business are not independent of each other. On the contrary, they are absolutely dependent upon the foreign lands, the islands of the seas, the forests, the prairies, for their products, and it is this unity of business that has widened the possibilities of gathering, distributing and exchanging.

If the business of the world be not a unit, why is it that a financial disturbance in Lombard street should cause a tremor in Wall street? Why is it that changes in conditions of stock values in the Bourse of Paris should affect values this side of the Atlantic? Why is it that a tornado, cyclone or drought in the far West should cause consternation in the wheat pits of Chicago, New York and other cities? The fact is the business of

one place is but a part of the business of the whole world.

The business of New York is enormous in its proportions, but it is not something in and of itself? If a wall were built around this city, isolating it, in a short time, there would be no business conducted in it, and a little later, there would be no New York. In other words, business is a unit like the human body, composed of different members whose functions are unlike, but which together form a complete whole. Emerson says: "An inevitable dualism bisects nature, so that each thing is a half, and suggests another thing to make it whole —as spirit, matter—man, woman—odd, even, subjective—objective," and he adds, "the same dualism underlies the nature and condition of man." If, then, this unity of business is one half, what is the other half needed to make the whole?

It has been shown that business in its entirety is governed and controlled by the law which runs through it, working constant and complete order in it, and that, nevertheless, the component parts of business are not alike, that on the contrary, there is a positive difference between them, no two of its almost incalculable forms being exactly the same.

Again, as man is the motive power of business and upon him depends its activities, man must be considered in the analysis of dualism. If the unity of business and the operation of law made up the whole circle of the conduct of business, man would be nothing more than a human machine, cut off from the exercise of his God-given faculties, the free use of which mark him as the highest creation of our universe. Laws originate nothing and they do not sustain anything. They are responsible for uniformity in sustaining what has been originated. But man is responsible for, and must originate and conduct the operations, processes or transactions of business, not only in harmony with the general law of unity, but also in conformity to the conditions of his own environment. In this, he can and must express both his own individuality and that of the industry with which he is connected. This is the duality: the unity of business and the individuality in business.

The absolute, determined principles of business are alike to every one, everywhere, but the circumstances materially differ with each case. A principle of business is exchange, giving something for something: the circumstances in each transaction compel the determination of value to be affixed to the articles exchanged, the choice of individuals with whom the exchange shall be made, the conditions and terms, the method of production and distribution.

You have seen a piece of woven fabric upon which a beautiful pattern of intricate detail has been wrought. Hold it up a little distance from you and only the design appears. Bring it closer and you will see that it is made by the crossing of innumerable threads, but you cannot see where one begins and another ends. Go to the mill and stand by the loom and you will see that the threads which consti-

tute the warp run the entire length of the fabric, while those of the woof are intertwined in the warp and are changed in color and direction from time to time under the manipulation of the weaver. And so in business, the lines of law correspond to the warp, and have all through the years run the entire length of our economic fabric. Into those lines of economic warp have been wrought the woof of individuality, bringing out a series of harmonious and wonderful results through the centuries, weaving independence through the lines of dependence, art through the lines of science, individuality through the lines of unity. Into this warp of Natural Law has been woven the woof of invention, enterprise, genius, experience, until there has been wrought the marvellous, economic fabric of to-day, combining the industries of the whole civilized world. The weaving has gone on just the same whatever the design to be wrought. The process was the same, whether the pattern was made up of small scattered figures or a complicated grouping of many figures.

Professor Ely, in his " Political Economy," makes this statement: "A study of corporations reveals another aspect of the industrial revolution." There is one letter too many in the last word. It should be not 'revolution,' but 'evolution.' A corporation is but a union of individuals, and an industrial combination or trust, so-called, is but a union of corporations, evolved by reason of the growth and demands of mankind. The underlying principles are the same. Size makes no difference in the legitimate operations. The Law acts the same at all times.

The processes of years ago
Were crude, were clumsy and slow:
But in the changes, year by year,
We see the crudeness disappear,
The old plans altered or relaid,
Old methods dropped and new ones
        made:
A natural development
That has no limit or extent:
But the forces have not been changed,
Only adapted, rearranged,
Or appropriated by man
For use upon a broader plan.

New Words in the Language of Business

Imagine a business man of a hundred years ago transported to the present time, and attempting to read down the "want" columns of a modern newspaper. The motorman, the conductor, the district manager, the telegraph operator, the telephone girl, the elevator boy, the electrician, the lineman, the typewriter, the stenographer, the engineer—would convey no idea to his mind of the requirements and duties of the situations wanted. Fancy his inability to comprehend the shipping news, the commercial items, with the hosts of new words which modern transportation has introduced, such as the steamboat, the railroad, the express train, the freight train, the grain elevator. This gentleman of the olden time, who might have been a power in his financial world, could go to school to his nine-year-old great-grandchild with advantage, for an understanding of the most simple terms of commerce and trade.

Accountancy: Its Past and Its Present

By Charles W. Haskins.

(Continued from page 34, March number.)

It might be supposed that any movement to establish the profession of accountancy upon a solid basis of reliability and security would be found to have originated in some part of continental Europe, where the art of bookkeeping has attained its highest development. Accountancy, however, in the higher sense and as a distinct profession, is not as yet so well known upon the continent as in Great Britain and the United States.

Italy, which gave to the money centre of the commercial metropolis of the world its Lombards or "Long Beards," has her licensed professors of accountancy; and a number of Exhibitions of Accounts have been held in the principal Italian cities—Turin, Milan, Bologna, Palermo, and notably, in 1892, at Genoa, where two special sections were devoted to exhibits of educational and professional literature. "To the Italians," writes Gibbins in his "History of Commerce in Europe," we owe the progress of mercantile science in nearly every department—in banking, currency, marine insurance, and so forth. Several textbooks on commercial subjects were published in Florence before 1400 A. D. Bookkeeping by double entry was also a Florentine invention, seemingly first in use about the fifteenth century." To this let me add that logismography, a system of keeping accounts invented by the director of the department of government accounts in Italy, and now taught in all her technical schools, is believed by many to be superior to any other in exactness and celerity of registration, and in its almost automatic detection of error.

Accountancy in France is not yet wholly disconnected from other and often very miscellaneous employments; though Paris has a Chamber of Accountants, the conditions of membership in which are, that the accountant must be a native or naturalized Frenchman, of twenty-one years of age, not an immoral person, and must pay three francs upon entrance and a franc a month thereafter.

In Germany, the work of the accountant falls, as a rule, upon the notary. It may be said, however, that in Germany, France, Italy, Austria, Belgium, and some other continental countries, the foundation of a recognized profession is being laid by the introduction of the study of accounting as a prominent part of the system of national education. In the work of higher commercial education in continental Europe, and in the study of accounting connected therewith, Germany is in the lead. Her commercial secondary schools have developed with the aid of provincial and State support, till at last a university has opened its doors for higher commercial education. On February 22, 1898, the University of Leipzig received an addition to its various courses in the shape of a higher commercial course. The cities of Madgeburg and Cologne are making earnest efforts to establish independent commercial universities. In Italy the State subsidizes the higher commercial school at Venice, reserving the privilege of having its consuls and consular agents prepared at that school. In Belgium the Government chooses its consuls from the graduates of the higher commercial school at Antwerp.

A report to the American Bankers' Association, commenting on the comparative indifference to commercial education in England, says: "Instead of taking hold of the subject at the right end and organizing a great institution in London which might serve as a model for such schools elsewhere, the English began their work in this field, as in many similar instances, by establishing examinations, and granting commercial certificates to all such pupils as could pass them. As there were no schools where the candidates could prepare for these examinations, they had to wait until existing classical or scientific schools could see their way to the profitable introduction of the commercial side. When a school here and there finally decided to open a commercial department it was found that in all England there were no properly qualified teachers for this work. The outcome of the examinations has been, therefore, most unsatisfactory" (32).

The recognition of accountancy as a distinct profession, demanding character, fitness, education, training and lifelong devotion to an ideal of duty, originated in the wants and—shall I say?—the disasters of the modern business world. It is not true that the accountant lives on the failure of others; but it is true, and too often true, that not until after a spell of sickness does one see that prevention would have been better than cure. "The Chartered Accountant," said a recent writer in the New York Sun, "is the one valuable acquisition of many years of financial storm and disaster."

The Institute of Chartered Accountants in England and Wales was incorporated by royal charter May 11, 1880; its objects being, the elevation of the profession of public accountants as a whole, and the promotion of their efficiency and usefulness, by compelling the observance of strict rules of conduct as a condition of membership, and by setting up a high standard of professional and general education and knowledge. At that time there were already three incorporated societies of accountants in Scotland; and since then the "English idea," so called, of incorporation under governmental protection, has spread and taken root throughout the English-speaking world, until there are now many such recognized societies of accountants in the United Kingdom of Great Britain and Ireland, in her dependencies, and in the States of the American Union.

This new departure, this steady advance of an ancient and honorable profession to the very van of material progress, has brought into the language a number of words as yet hardly known to our dictionaries; so that for any adequate definition of "accountics," "accounting" or "accountancy," the inquirer must go to men of affairs.

The following definition, from the standpoint of the business man, was given by Mr. James G. Cannon at the first annual dinner of the New York State Society of Certified Public Accountants in 1897: "Those who are familiar with the course of events must recognize the fact that the work of the world is resolving itself into special departments. This is true of every branch of industry, not excepting bookkeeping. Time was when, under this heading, everything pertaining to entries in books was included; but we have come to recognize the difference between the mechanism and the art—between the skill of properly recording and balancing and the science of technical examination and development. 'Bookkeeping' is still the name of the one, but 'accountancy' is the title of the other."

President Guthrie, of the Birmingham Chartered Accountants' Students' Society, said, a few weeks ago: "The mere technical ability to record mercantile and financial transactions in proper books, and to render statements of account in suitable and tasteful form, may be said to describe the limits of the journeyman bookkeeper. But an accountant, to practice in an industrial, financial and metropolitan centre, is called upon not only to record transactions and give expression to their aggregation, the incidence of their debits, and the destinations of their credits, in suitable figures and forms; he is called upon to initiate, to organize, to negotiate, to advocate, to arbitrate, and to administer affairs, businesses, and estates of every description and kind, and between all sorts and conditions of men and women. In the daily practice of his profession an accountant never knows what department of manufacture, concern, or affairs he may be called upon to deal with on the morrow."

(To be continued.)

Impossible Conditions

"The kind of a drummer we want is a convincing talker who has a large circle of friends."

"You'll not find him."

"Why not?"

"Convincing talkers never have a large circle of friends."

Has a Record for Quickness

Mr. Wholesale—Your former employer tells me you were the quickest bookkeeper in the place.

Applicant (dubiously)—He does?

Mr. Wholesale—Yes. He says you could chuck the books in the safe, lock up, and get ready to go home in just one minute and ten seconds.

When wealthy, show thy wisdom not to be to wealth a servant, but make wealth serve thee.—Sir J. Denham.

The Monthly Statement

Appreciation of the benefits from the official recognition and establishment of the profession of accounting is increasing. Again from beyond the Mississippi an appeal is made for State legislation regulating the status of the accountant. In a letter recently published in the St. Louis Globe-Democrat, the writer calls attention to the governmental action in England, Canada, and some of our own States, notably New York and Pennsylvania, in granting charters and establishing boards of examiners, and contrasts with it the indifference of a large number of States to this important and growing profession.

We are glad to see the attention of the public called to the necessity of statutory laws giving protection and security in the field of work covered by the professional accountant. It is only by discussion that education in the demands of the situation can be accomplished, and action on the part of the legislature compelled. The public must be taught the two fold advantage arising from a system of periodic expert supervision of accounts. On the one hand, to the man on whom the burden of a great trust is imposed, the public accountant will commend himself as a relief from the responsibility assumed in guaranteeing the accuracy of numerous agents and subordinates, and on the other hand, to the people, entrusting large funds to the keeping of a single individual, the public accountant will prove a safeguard and an insurance of honest dealing.

Again, not only as check upon dishonesty, but as a means of guarding against loose and unscientific methods in the management of the financial affairs of public institutions or corporations of a quasi-public character, the official accountant will come as the authoritative adviser. These considerations are gradually receiving recognition from practical men, and the demand for honest and enlightened methods in the conduct of the business of the government is being made in every part of the country.

The advisability of having a bookkeeping and auditing department for the city separate from the comptroller's or paymaster's department is being agitated in Chicago. This is but another instance of the growing feeling that the systems of accounting in use in municipal bodies are faulty, and that a more business-like and scientific manner of conducting the financial affairs of such corporations will be conducive of healthier political conditions. The business man has been too reluctant to spend his time in helping in the management of municipal affairs, but if he wishes to see a better state of things inaugurated and local government taken out of the hands of the professional politician, it will be necessary for him to insist upon strict and business-like methods in the various city departments.

Accurate and honest bookkeeping would bring to light dark and devious ways of dealing with public moneys, and the heavy taxpayer could see how the fund in the city treasury was distributed. For those classes who love darkness better than light, the disclosures of such an auditing and bookkeeping department would be so disastrous that they would be compelled to find some other profitable means of support than their fraudulent drafts upon the public funds. We hope that the movement begun in Chicago will be pushed till a thoroughly equipped bookkeeping and auditing department is established, which may prove an object lesson to less progressive cities.

What the Credit Men Are Doing

BY A. O. KITTREDGE.

A circular setting forth a plan for the organization and government of the Investigation and Prosecution Bureau of the National Association has been sent to credit men throughout the country by Secretary Prendergast. As a preliminary measure, the creation of a Trust Fund of ten thousand dollars is proposed, to be in charge of a board of trustees, and the active co-operation of the members of the association is invited in its formation. The purpose of the Bureau is the investigation and prosecution of cases on their legal basis and merits only, and it cannot be utilized as a means of enforcing collections. Secretary Prendergast reports that within the very short time since the plan has been published a large number of subscriptions have been received, and matters in connection with the organization of the Bureau are proceeding in a highly satisfactory manner.

The Milwaukee Association of Credit Men are making active preparations for the entertainment of the Fifth Annual Convention of the National Association in June. The following is a list of the committees with their respective chairmen:

Executive committee, H. N. Oberndorfer (David Adler & Sons' Clothing Co.); entertainment committee, H. N. Oberndorfer; committee on arrangements, James McLeod (Roundy, Peckman & Co.); transportation committee, O. C. Hansen (Cream City Hat Co.); committee on press, printing and invitation, F. H. Benson, 377 Broadway; finance committee, O. C. Hansen. The association on the 1st of February, held at the Pfister Hotel, a smoker, to give the members an opportunity of meeting President Field, of the National Association. He spoke at some length on the need of united action on the part of credit men in the prosecution of cases of fraudulent bankruptcy. Addresses were also given by John Johnson, John T. Burke, Frederick Kasten, Frank L. Larkins and James McLeod, and W. P. Rogers entertained the company by some bright and witty stories.

The Sioux City Bureau of Credits held its regular meeting at Mondamin Hotel, on the 13th of March. C. R. Marks spoke on "Commercial Honesty," and in illustration of his theme drew upon his early Western experiences. "In those days," he said, "there were none of the modern facilities for collection of accounts, and settlements were sometimes six months or a year apart. It was necessary that men in business should preserve their credit in order to be allowed to do business at all. The conditions bred a sort of spontaneous commercial honesty that was quite as reliable as that induced by any thought that collections can be enforced by the strong arm of the law." John M. Pickney added his testimony of business dealings in the early days in the far West, where he sometimes had accounts, he said, running into large amounts with men he had never seen, and none of which he ever lost. W. H. Preston told of his recent Western trip, the object of which was to organize bureaus under the direction and management of the National Association.

The business men of Salt Lake City, Ogden and Provo have completed an organization since W. H. Preston's visit to the Pacific Coast. A very creditable membership of sixty is an evidence of the interest in the work of the Association. The Seattle Association will be consummated in a few days.

"Collections" was the topic for the evening at the meeting of the Detroit Credit Men's Association, on the 20th of February. There were no set addresses, but most of the members took part in the discussion, which was introduced by D. C. Delamater. As each speaker drew from his own experience to enforce his views, the meeting was particularly interesting and beneficial.

One of the most successful meetings in the history of the Denver Credit Men's Association was held on the 28th of February. The presence of W. H. Preston, of Sioux City, Iowa, and W. H. Taylor, of Kansas City, Mo., as guests, added materially to the pleasure of the evening. Frederick W. Standart presided and addresses were delivered by Charles F. Wilson, on "Insurance and Credit;" Alexander C. Foster, on "Co-operation and Goodfellowship," and W. H. Preston, on "Credit Associations, Credit Men and Credit Departments." After an impromptu address by Lester McLean, on the Bankruptcy law, it was voted unanimously to strongly oppose its repeal.

Something for Nothing

The magic of Aladdin's lamp appealed to a quality of the mind as dominant in the human race to-day as when the Tales of the Arabian Nights were told. A philosopher's stone, changing base metal to gold, a hidden treasure, a sleight-of-hand manipulation, by which the public may be tricked into yielding its hard-earned dollars, has ever been attractive to a certain class of mind. The effort to obtain something for nothing has wasted the strength, and vitiated the morals of multitudes of every nation and every age. A modern instance of this same spirit is the eagerness with which the recent activity in manufacturing has been seized upon, as affording opportunity for the formation of numberless corporations far beyond the demands of trade, and as an excuse for the unwarranted increase of stock of those already in existence. In a discussion of the situation and the means for the prevention of a recurrence of it, the "Engineering Magazine" says:

"Secrecy made it possible to organize both the opportunity and the temptation to play the industrial game with loaded dice. The itching to get something for nothing upon the market is at any time the master vice in trade. One risk of the business boom is always that it lets loose these reckless forces that hasten every disaster of the next business collapse. The new "combines," if they can manipulate clandestinely, easily fire every passion to play with stock variations—to lay traps for the unwary, to declare dividends that never have been earned, and to unload lying values upon the public. It is evident that every form of secret control—every hidden device, as to methods of management—immensely overstimulates this dicer's spirit and, therefore, adds to the most dangerous uncertainties of business. That this evil can be greatly lessened has been proved not only by English experience—it has been clearly proved by Massachusetts experience. The degree of publicity to which these corporations must now submit in Massachusetts is far greater than is commonly supposed, and has been attended by results so hopeful as to mark a sure way for further legislation. This experience, together with the experience of the interstate commission—in spite of all its failures—may well furnish a safe basis for such federal action as shall give unity of procedure in different States.

Of Course

Mack O'Rell — There is some place where they manufacture artificial eggs. What name would you give an establishment of that kind?

Luke Warme—Why, an egg plant, of course.

The Application of Advanced Accounting Methods to Modern Business Enterprises

By A. O. Kittredge, F. I. A., C. P. A.

(Continued from page 35, March number.)

I have said that we are almost ready for our going balance sheet when we get our merchandise account properly adjusted, for we are not altogether ready. Let us consider for a moment the matter of expenses. Expenses are thoroughly abused items in ordinary bookkeeping. Very frequently they are thrown indiscriminately into a single account, and again, upon an assumed basis of analysis, they are strung out in a detail that is absurd. A very common mistake that is made is to fail to distinguish between those expenses which are part of the cost of goods made, as in a manufacturing establishment, and those which pertain alone to the distribution of product, or to the sales department. Analysis here is not only desirable, but imperative This will become apparent by brief illustration. As a fact, we make no profit on the goods that we manufacture until they are sold. We may run our factory and pile up goods until doomsday, but whether or not it were advantageous to make the goods would only be determined by selling them. Again, we can put so much extravagance into our methods of disposing of the goods that we make as to destroy all chance of profit. However intelligently the factory has been managed, the commercial end of the business may be so conducted as to leave no profit at all on the sales.

The cost of goods is one thing and the cost of selling or disposing of the goods is quite another thing. Our expense accounts, therefore, will divide, in a manufacturing establishment, into factory expenses and commercial expenses. But this division is not enough in all cases. We sometimes have to meet the fact of a president or other figure head drawing a large salary and contributing neither to the production of goods nor to the selling of the goods. Where does this expense go? Administrative expenses is a title sometimes employed for items of this kind.

Factory expenses will be figured into the cost of goods. Commercial expenses will go into the selling of goods. Taking the goods at cost and contrasting it with the selling price will show gross profits. Gross profits diminished by commercial expenses will show what would ordinarily be called net profits. Against profits at this stage would be charged administrative expenses, which in this sense must be considered simply a short circuit equivalent to a preliminary division of profits to the advantage of the one receiving the slice and at the expense of dividends, or to the disadvan-

tage of the rank and file of the stockholders. We occasionally run against expenses, also, which are of the nature of conducting incidental operations, like the care of tenement property in connection with a large mill and the conduct of the store, where there is a trading annex to the manufacturing operation. But I have gone quite far enough to show that expenses must be analyzed as carefully as our merchandise account.

And this reminds me to say that in talking about merchandise we naturally refer to a mercantile operation. The term merchandise, it seems to me, finds no place in a factory. I cannot imagine a condition where the term merchandise is technically correct in a factory, save only as the factory, considered as an operation, buys some classes of goods which it sells instead of making them; that which is made by a factory is never merchandise in the strict sense of the word. It should be called product, or output, or some other term that will distinguish the results of factory operations from goods which are bought to sell again, as in a merchandising or mercantile enterprise. Never should merchandise be used to indicate the materials consumed in factory operations. To conduct the producing account of a factory under the name of merchandise, debiting the costs on the one side and crediting the sales on the other, is not only technically wrong but is quite absurd.

Going a step further into manufacturing accounts, and I may presume that every one here, in view of the fact of the large manufacturing interests in and about Hartford, is more or less familiar with manufacturing operations, we may profitably devote a few moments to the elements of cost in factory product. Here again comes in the question of analysis. Whatever we make in the factory is composed of three items—materials, labor and manufacturing expenses. The cost accounts in the factory, therefore, should be so arranged as to show the amount of material, the amount of labor and the pro rata of manufacturing expenses that enter into the several articles produced. A proper distribution of costs will result in each article produced bearing its proper share of these items, and the total cost of all the articles produced, so figured, will be equal to the total of the charges to the factory, thus establishing a proof by balance.

With these fragmentary analyses in mind, let us go a step further and consider the accounts of an average or representative business enterprise—we will say those of a small factory. All the accounts of the business will divide into two general classes, namely, those which make up the balance sheet and those which constitute the profit and loss statement. All the accounts in the balance sheet are comprised in two groups, first, assets; second, liabilities. All the accounts comprised in the profit and loss statement are likewise in two groups; first, expenses; and, second, revenues.

The assets of an average enterprise, omitting some that are obviously special, will be made up about as follows: Cash, notes receivable, accounts receivable, land and buildings, machinery and fixtures, materials, factory account or manufacturing operations, finished product and items in suspense.

We have already considered some of the new accounts necessary to a going balance sheet. In the list above there is another, namely, items in suspense. A going balance sheet anticipates such a distribution of expenses or costs as will be fair to each day, week or month, according to the time schedule upon which the profit showings are arranged, without an excess or deficiency occurring in any month. If, for example, we pay insurance the first of the year for twelve months in advance, it will not do to charge to the first month the whole of that insurance. Instead, we must throw it into suspense and pro rate out of suspense into the proper expense account as we go along. Items in suspense, therefore, are assets, being expenses paid in advance, for financial reasons, and there lodged, to be pro rated out as the months roll by.

The liabilities of the typical business under review will consist of such items as notes payable, accounts payable, reserves and capital. Here again we encounter another account special to the scheme under review. The name may not be new, but the use of it is restricted. I refer to the group called reserves. The use of this account may be variously illustrated. For example, our machinery is constantly wearing out. It is constantly breaking down, and requires repairs to keep it in order. We make the repairs only when they become necessary, but sometimes, where a very serious break down occurs, the necessary repairs are large in amount. To charge repairs into months where the breakdowns occur would result in heavy charges to some months, with no charges at all to other months, and yet the cause of the breakdown is common to all the months. In other words, the wear and tear is regular and incessant, although the times of repairs are irregular in occurrence. Here comes in the utility of a reserve account. We charge into product an allowance for repairs month by month, thereby accumulating a fund out

of which to make repairs, when the accident occurs or when the need of repairs becomes very apparent. Again, take it in the matter of taxes. Taxes are an expense of every month in the year, although they are only payable at certain dates fixed by law.* We know in advance about what our taxes are to be. We should therefore charge into the proper expense account an allowance for taxes as we go on, crediting that amount to a reserve account, which account, in turn, is to be debited with the disbursement for taxes, whenever the pay-day comes around.

The profit and loss statement, as already mentioned, embraces expenses and revenues. Expenses we have already analyzed. Those which are here to be considered are the commercial expenses, or, possibly, the commercial and administrative expenses combined, if the latter division is necessary by reason of the way in which the business is being managed. Revenue accounts embrace the sales accounts (these being debited with the cost of the goods sold and credited with the selling prices), discounts on purchases, interest earned, dividends receivable, rentals, etc.

(As his address proceeded, the speaker illustrated his remarks by diagrams on the blackboard, showing in detail all the classes of accounts here enumerated and the analysis proposed. He finally put upon the blackboard a diagram illustrating factory accounts, showing the relationship of the elements of cost, one to the other, and also indicating how finished parts may be carried in stock as well as finished product. Questions proposed by his hearers were answered, and the replies made served to further illustrate the methods of analysis proposed and the reasons for certain steps demanded.)

The Business Man's Dinner Hour

The close relation between national prosperity and commercial success has not till recently been supposed to be affected by the time and manner in which a man takes the principal meal of the day, but now the dinner hour of the merchant is becoming of grave importance from a governmental standpoint. There is a reason for all things, the scientific investigator declares, and there is an abstruse connection between the dinner hour and the financial standing of our country. No longer is it a matter of indifference to the State whether the business man dines with his children, home from school for the noon hour, or smokes

*In some states taxes are due and payable at the end of the year for which they are assessed. In such cases a reserve account is used. In other states they are payable in advance, in which case a suspense account is used.

his post-prandial cigar when the day's work is done. A generation or two back, the dinner hour was a synonymous term for the time between twelve and one o'clock, but in these latter days, the lunch has taken its place. Such is the rule in the larger cities along the seaboard, and in the great commercial centers in the interior. This condition of things is owing in part to the fact that the area required for the transaction of business has become widely extended, and the home has been transferred from the thickly settled district to the suburban town. The time necessary for traveling the intervening space has led to the crowding of work into the fewest hours possible. Hence, the hasty lunch with a view to an early closing.

What the effect of the change may be upon the amount and quality of the work performed, is a question which is being discussed. We clip the following from one of the city papers, as showing the feeling of the German Government on the subject.

"Some reckless innovator in Bremen lately undertook to change the immemorial custom of the merchants of that free city of dining at the noon hour, and to substitute in its place the English fashion of dining late in the evening. The Kaiser's ever-watchful government at once ordered an investigation, and for some reason selected the postmaster-general to conduct it. Herr von Pobbielski was, fortunately, able to reassure the government and the people of Germany at once. The innovation had fallen flat, and the Bremen merchants still dine, as did their forefathers back to the days of the Hermannschlacht, at the good old German hour of noon. An echt deutsches Mittagessen can be eaten only at midday . . . . By eating at noon, it seems, the Bremen merchant is enabled to keep late office hours. He waits for the latest mails and telegrams, and answers them at once. The Englishman, on the other hand, who dines at seven or eight o'clock, is in a hurry to leave his office at six, and is likely to let communications that come in the latter part of the afternoon remain unanswered till next day. Bremen promptness, where competition is close, therefore often wins the day. It is an instance of the late bird catching the early worm. For business reasons, therefore, Bremen will not dine at eight.

It is a delightful picture of German thrift and industry which is presented to the Kaiser, that of the industrious Bremen merchant sustained by his midday meal, burning the midnight oil as he waits for Herr von Podbielski's mails, while his greedy and fashionable British competitor gorges on a late dinner."

An Explanation

Little Willie—Say, pa, what is the meaning of "commercial activity?"

Pa—Borrowing $5 for a day and dodging the lender for a year.

We all covet wealth, but not its perils.
—Bruyere.

Accountics

The Office Magazine.

Published Monthly.

A. O. KITTREDGE, F. I. A., C. P. A., Editor.

E. R. KITTREDGE, Associate.

Accountics is devoted to the Science of Accounting, to the Art of Bookkeeping and to the advocacy of Improved Office Methods.

Subscription.—One dollar a year, payable in advance.

Postage is prepaid by the publishers in the United States, Canada and Mexico. For all other countries in the Postal Union, subscribers must add 50 cents a year.

Discontinuances.—In the absence of specific orders to discontinue at the end of the subscription term the magazine will be continued and a bill sent.

Remittances should be by Draft, P. O. Order or Express Order, payable to the order of the Accountics Association. Money and postage stamps are at the risk of the sender, unless sent by express or in registered letters. Add 10 cents each to checks on local banks to defray collection charges.

Advertising Rates will be quoted on application.

Official Journal.—This publication, by resolutions duly passed, has been made the official publication of the following organizations :—

The Institute of Accounts.

The New York Chapter of the Institute of Accounts.

The Washington Chapter of the Institute of Accounts.

The Hartford Chapter of the Institute of Accounts.

Accountics is the accredited medium of intercommunication between members of the Institute of Accounts wherever located.

ACCOUNTICS ASSOCIATION, Publishers,

Lancashire Building, Pine Street, near Nassau, New York.

Copyright 1900 by the Accountics Association. Entered at the Post Office New York as Second Class Matter.

Publishers' Desk

France is about to inaugurate a change in the enumeration of the hours of the day. Instead of the twelve-hour system to which the civilized world is generally accustomed, all clocks will be run hereafter in France on the twenty-four-hour division, the hour of twenty-four being midnight. What we call 1 p. m., will be 13 o'clock, and a 6 o'clock dinner hour will fall on 18 o'clock. The new system has been used satisfactorily by some of the continental railroads, but whether it will meet with popular acceptance by the French people is yet to be seen.

The United States Government has some peculiar obligations on account of its international relations, of which the public is not generally informed. Asiatic countries do not usually provide prisons which are deemed suitable for the detention of American convicts, and in such instances our Government is compelled to bear the expense of furnishing these prisons, which is the cause of no small outlay. In the interests of commerce an International Bureau of Weights and Measures, and a similar bureau for the publication of customs tariff are located at Brussels. To the first our Government pays annually $2,270, and to the second about half that sum. For the advancement of science it contributes $1,500 each year to the International Geodetic Association, the object of which is the determination of the size of the earth by accurate measurements. The International Bureau for the Repression of the African Slave Trade, also with headquarters at Brussels, receives $100 from our Treasury. Along the coast of Morocco there is a necessity for light-houses, and that state has not reached the stage of civilization where it feels its obligations to furnish protection to mariners against the dangers on its own shores, hence the great commercial nations unite to provide this means of safety for their sailors. This country gives as its share of that expense, $325 each year.

Stickfast & Co., is the appropriate nom-de-plume of the manufacturers of Perfumed Albastin Paste. This paste is prepared for use in office work, for mounting photographs, and, in fact, for any purpose where mucilage has been hitherto employed. It is a white jelly-like substance, with a pleasant odor, and is put up in neat glass jars. William H. Woglom, 239 Greenwich street, New York City, is placing it on the market.

In another part of this issue, S. B. Kirtley, of Jefferson City, Mo., calls attention to a method of avoiding bookkeeping errors and at the same time saving labor in posting ledger accounts. The improvement he refers to is based upon practical experience in bank work.

A good copying ink and writing fluid is an important part of an office equipment. We call the attention of our readers to the advertisement on another page of the I. Pomeroy Co., manufacturers of copying fluids and inks of all colors, paste, sealing, etc., at 264-266 Halsey street, Newark, N. J. This company claims to furnish the best ink for ledgers, books of account and legal documents.

Bismarck had a high appreciation of the qualities necessary to make a successful business man, and showed his fitness to judge by the manner in which he brought several neglected estates left him by devise into prosperous condition. "Whoever can do this," he said, in discussing the requisite capacity for a statesman, "will in similar circumstances, given the necessary education, knowledge and position, generally be found equally capable of restoring the prosperity and dignity of nations."

Our contemporary, the "Billboard," of Cincinnati, has been making a scientific investigation of the subject of advertising. As yet only a partial report has been published, but the following table gives an idea of the manner in which it is doing the work.

Style	.001
Display	.012
Plausibility	.091
Position	.099
Circulation	.122
Iteration	.775
Total	1.000

We call attention to the fact that iteration gets more than three-fourths of the entire credit. We cannot judge of the correctness of the division until we are better informed of the data upon which it is based. Since the "Billboard," as well as other periodicals, prosper by reason of the continuous patronage of customers, it is possible that its opinion and its selection of material from which to make the computations has been influenced in this regard. It is an important question to all advertisers, and is one upon which they pass judgment every time they make a contract with a publisher.

All of the divisions named unite in making a successful advertisement, and it is probable that different matter is affected differently—no rule holding good in all cases. Each customer may have to make an estimate for himself, in view of the character of his goods, the class of buyers he wishes to attract and the time within which he wishes to meet them.

The man who worries advertises the fact that he is lacking in courage. The man of nerve and force does not exhaust his strength in useless forebodings. It is the cool head and strong heart that win in every struggle, and no venture is ever carried to a successful issue by the man who permits himself to worry over complicated situations or the disasters of trade and commerce. The level head and calm judgment belong not to the man who wastes his time and vitiates his energies in a timorous dread of impending disaster. Therefore, stop worrying.

Society is built upon trust.—South.

A great fortune is a great servitude.—Seneca.

Fortune brings in some boats that are not steered.—Shakespeare.

He is safe who admits no one to his confidence.—Rochefoucauld.

Wise men have but few confidants, and cunning ones none.—H. W. Shaw.

Standard Fountain Pen

The Sterling Fountain Pen Co., of 19 Milk street, Boston, are introducing three fountain pens of high grade. known as the "Standard," "Reliable" and "Sterling." A cut of the "Standard" is presented herewith, from which the reader can gain an excellent idea of its construction. It unscrews near the middle of the barrel. The long feed section, with which it is provided, permits a firm grasp without risk of touching the pen, a fact that will be appreciated by all users of fountain pens. In other respects the pen is carefully constructed. Special attention has been given to all those points which

Standard Fountain Pen

tend to render pens satisfactory for use. In the directions, or, rather, "Hints to Users," which the company are sending out with these goods, various points are made, which it is to the interest of users of fountains pens in general to observe. We suggest to our readers that they correspond with the Sterling Fountain Pen Co. for the purpose of obtaining these particulars, which will be of special advantage to them. In writing mention this notice in ACCOUNTICS.

Obedience to Orders

Employers may be divided into two general classes. Some men wish those working under them to assume responsibilities, be ready to meet emergencies, and think for themselves. When they are looking about for someone to fill a vacancy, they seek a man who knows what the situation demands, and can go ahead with meagre directions. They rejoice to find one who, if a dilemma unlooked for arises, will make for himself a way out of the difficulty. The advancement of such an employee is certain with them.

But there are employers of a different stamp. Orders must be obeyed in any event, is their motto. They wish to feel that once having issued instructions, they can depend upon their being followed out. The servant who takes upon himself to vary his course because situations have apparently changed, is useless in their eyes. They prefer to do the thinking, and to have the employees respond with ready service.

There is room in the business world for each kind of employer, and each kind of service. As an illustration of a case where obedience to orders was considered of prime importance, we give the following story, which we clip from an exchange:

A young man with a decidedly seedy appearance entered the superintendent's office, and placing his hand familiarly upon the superintendent's shoulder accosted him thus:

"Boss, can you gimme a job?"

"What department?"

"Either brakin' or firin'."

"Do you know the Book of Rules?"

"Some."

"Well, let me see how well you are posted. We will suppose you were firing a train that was running from Jersey City to Philadelphia; the engineer would get killed and you would take his place. you would find on his clip that the train had orders to take the side track for another train somewhere in the woods where there was no telegraph office. Now, suppose that train did not arrive there for, say, twelve hours, what would you do?"

"That would be the affair of the conductor, not mine."

"I will take your name, and if we have need of your services we will send for you. Good day."

The next applicant to enter seated himself back of the superintendent and waited for him to break the silence, which he did shortly.

"Well, sir, what can I do for you?"

"I would like to have a job, boss."

"In what department?"

"Train service."

"Are you familiar with the Book of Rules?"

"A little."

The superintendent then asked him the same question as the first.

The fellow scratched his head, then looking the superintendent square in the eye he replied: "Boss, if the orders looked good, and were positive, I would stay on that side track till hades froze over."

"Go down and report to Mr. ——, the train master, for duty."

Security is mortal's chiefest enemy.—Shakespeare.

It is only when the rich are sick that they feel the impotence of wealth.—Colton.

There is some help for all the defects of fortune; for if a man cannot attain to the length of his wishes, he may have his remedy by cutting of them shorter.—Cowley.

Accountants' Association

New York Chapter of the Institute of Accounts

The regular meeting of the New York Chapter of the Institute of Accounts was held March 29th, at the Waldorf-Astoria. The address of the evening was given by A. O. Kittredge, on "Accounting for Cotton Mills," a subject in which, owing to long experience in that line of accounting, the speaker feels a lively interest. He enlivened his address, and made it more attractive to the profession and to guests by the display of samples of the raw materials used by cotton mills, and specimens of the product at various stages of manufacture up to the completion of the finest goods. A chart and specification of the system as actually in force in certain cotton mills were introduced, and it was shown that while especially applicable to such mills, it can with appropriate variation be employed by any manufacturing concern. An important feature brought out by the speaker was the fact that it would exhibit at stated periods, either daily, weekly or monthly, the cost value of the raw material, the cost of the work in progress, and the cost of the finished product, in gross or in as fine detail as desired. Following Mr. Kittredge's address were remarks by W. B. Jaudon, E. Glardon, F. W. Child and others.

Massachusetts Society of Public Accountants

Through the courtesy of Harvey S. Chase, secretary of the Massachusetts Society of Public Accountants, we are in receipt of a copy of its constitution and by-laws. The next meeting will be held on the 19th of April, when an appropriate programme will be provided, and subjects of interest to the profession will be discussed. It is felt that the society has a useful future before it, and members of the older organizations take a hearty interest in this newcomer into the ranks of the association work.

We wish to correct an error in the notice published in the March number of ACCOUNTICS of the meeting of March 6th of this society. The office of secretary is filled by Harvey S. Chase, and Charles F. Kellogg, who was there named as secretary, is the treasurer.

Illinois Institute of Accountants

The members and guests who were present at the meeting of the Illinois Institute of Accountants, held on the 8th of March, united in expressions of appreciation of the programme furnished by those charged with that duty. J. Hoefman, of the Republic Iron and Steel Co., delivered an address on "Factory Accounting," and was listened to with the attention to which his wide experience as an accountant entitled him. W. I. Watson discussed the "Trial Balance," a subject to which he has given careful study, and in regard to which he has developed interesting features.

Hartford Chapter of the Institute of Accounts

As the result of the election at the annual meeting of the Hartford Chapter of the Institute of Accounts, the following is the list of officers for the coming year: President, Henry A. Hovey; secretary and treasurer, John A. Butler; member of the board of governors for the term of three years, Frederick Plimpton; members of the board of governors holding over, J. Henry Turner, term expiring March, 1901; Clarkson N. Fowler, term expiring 1902.

Bookkeepers' Beneficial Association of Philadelphia

The officers of the Bookkeepers' Beneficial Association of Philadelphia gave the members and friends of the association a very pleasant entertainment on the evening of April 2d, at Odd Fellows' Temple. Music on various instruments from the piano to musical glasses and spinning coins, songs, both sombre and humorous, and recitations made up the varied programme.

Financial Combinations in China

According to the author of "Village Life in China" (Rev. Arthur H. Smith), the Chinese moukehs exhibit a higher degree of co-operation than do any similar European institutions.

Other examples of the Chinese capacity for combination, pointed out by this author, are the loan societies, which abound everywhere. Every Chinaman has occasion to use money in sums which it is very difficult for him to command. The rate of interest is so high that a man, compelled to borrow a considerable amount upon which he must pay interest at from 2½ to 4 per cent. a month, will be, not improbably, swamped by the endeavor to make good his promise to his creditors. By eliminating interest altogether, distributing the payments over a long period and introducing an element of friendship into a commercial transaction, the Chinaman is able to achieve the happy result of uniting business with pleasure.

The simplest of the many plans by which mutual loans are effected is the contribution of a definite sum by each member of the society to some other one in rotation. The man who is in need of money invites certain of his friends to co-operate with him, and to invite some of their friends to do the same. When the requisite number is secured the members assemble and fix the order in which each shall have the use of the common fund. The order is generally decided by lot. Unless the amount subscribed is a very trifling one, every meeting of the members for business purposes is accompanied with a feast attended by all the partners, and paid for either by the one for whose benefit the association was organized or by the person whose turn it is to use the common funds.

At the first feast given by the organizer of the association, each of the other members, say six, attends with the sum agreed upon, let us suppose 10,000 cash, which is paid over to the head man, 60,000 cash in all, to be used by him for a certain period, say a year. The next year, the feast is given by the person who drew the second lot; the head man puts 10,000 cash into the treasury, and each of the five other members the same sum, all of which is paid over to No. 2, who, in like manner, employs it for a year. At the end of seven years, each of the seven members will have had a turn, each will have received 60,000 cash without interest, and each will have paid out 60,000 cash, for which he has likewise received no interest. Each one will have been accommodated with the temporary handling of a larger sum than he could otherwise have obtained, and, at the end, each one has lost nothing in money, but has had seven more or less excellent feasts, a matter which, from a Chinese point of view, is of considerable importance.

There are also co-operative societies which exact interest for loans. Their methods differ in detail. If, as often happens, the interest is left open to competition, the competition may take place by a kind of auction, each one announcing orally when he is willing to pay for the use of the joint capital for one term.. To the highest bidder is awarded the sum, but to no member is a second term conceded. The operation of these Chinese loan societies throws light upon many aspects of Chinese life. Of course, nobody is willing to enter into an association of this kind unless it is reasonably certain that every member will meet every assessment, for, if any individual fails to pay, everything is at a deadlock. To guard against such a default, it is customary to exact security, or bondsmen, in some instances the headman acting as bail for all the rest. When the number of members in a loan society is enlarged to more than a score, the probability that some one will fail to meet his obligations is greatly increased. It is also a grave objection to such long loans that, before the whole term of years elapses, it is almost certain that something will occur to disturb the financial equilibrium of the members. The Tai-ping rebellion and the frequent famines and floods which have occurred of late years in northern China have tended to bring the loan societies into discredit. A Chinaman of easy-going disposition told our author that he had been six times a member of a loan society, but that, while once the capital had been doubled by a fortunate speculation, on each of the other occasions he had lost nearly all put in.

Financial Difficulties

"Pa, what is financial difficulty?"

"Well, it is having so much money you don't know what to do with it; or having so little money that you can't do a thing."

The Magician of the Nineteenth Century

The magician, who has wrought marvelous changes in the economy of our daily life, who has spread a network of railroads over the land and. covered the sea with ships, who has multiplied a thousand fold the spindles that whirl in the factories, and touched with his wand the wilderness till it has been transformed into a city full of busy men and women, this modern wonder worker, the wizard of to-day, is known to us by the name of engineer. It is his occult science, the manufacturer, the ship owner, and the capitalist employ when they wish something to act as the philosopher's stone to change the forces of nature into money. These forces lying dormant benefit 1.o one; money hoarded in vaults is useless. The engineer knows the secret of bringing the former into action by means of the latter; or, in other words, he can tell how investments may be made, the cost, the feasibility of a project. He knows how to minimize expenditure of production. He makes possible a dozen ships where one sailed before. He puts the engine in place of the horse, and the telegraph for the post-boy. He creates wants for the capitalist to supply by making production so cheap that the luxury has grown to a necessity. People ride, who once walked.

Pocket-Knife Sharpener

The only possible reason for going about with a dull knife is that no whetstone is available. In this era of compact devices and miniature editions there is no excuse for a man to be found anywhere with anything less than a full equipment of tools and provisions for keeping them in order, upon his person. These general premises admitted, the need of a pocket grindstone, or at least a pocket whetstone is manifest. The device shown in the accompanying cut is described by the manufacturers, Baldwin, Tuthill & Bolton, Grand Rapids, Mich., as a knife and eraser sharpener. It does not need to be

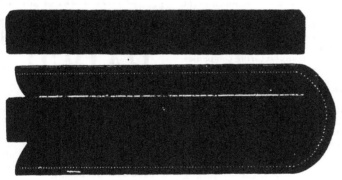

Pocket-Knife Sharpener.

They read the machine-printed page whose fathers could not spell the letters of the costly volume.

The engineer has welded capital and labor. Without his directing hand capital would lie idle and powerless, and labor spend its strength in profitless effort. United and controlled by him, money multiplies itself incredibly, and labor increases its productiveness a hundredfold. No careful man dares venture his fortune in an enterprise till he has invoked the power of his magic. The capitalist who acts alone and unassisted by him finds himself engulfed by disasters, while his rival under the guidance of the sorcerer moves steadily on to success. The financial world bases its calculations on data furnished by him, and the economy of our modern civilization would utterly fail, and the business of the world would come to a sudden stand and crumble into nothingness, were the secrets which he controls eliminated from the knowledge of mankind.

carried in the pocket unless one wants it always with him. It is of a shape to be put away in a corner of a drawer without mussing other contents or occupying much space. The sharpener is of exactly the variety required by office men for keeping their edge tools in good condition. The case is Russia leather, and altogether the device is extremely attractive as well as convenient.

Fortune, to show us her power in all things, and to abate our presumption, seeing she could not make fools wise, has made them fortunate.—Montaigne.

How are the Profits of the Year to be Ascertained?

By Bernard Dale.

(Continued from page 19, February number.)

The Double Account System

The Chief Exponent of this System is Mr. Buckley, Q. C. In the sixth edition of his "Companies' Acts," Mr. Buckley, after stating that the profits of an undertaking "are not such sum as may remain after the payment of every debt, but are the excess of revenue receipts over expenses properly chargeable to revenue account," proceeds to say:

"Capital may be lost in either one or two ways, which may be distinguished as loss on capital account, and loss on revenue account. If a shipowning company's capital be represented by ten ships with which it trades, and one is totally lost, and is uninsured, such a loss would be what is here called a loss on capital account. But if the same company begins the year with the ten ships, value, say, £100,000 and ends the year with the same ten ships, and the result of the trading, after allowing for depreciation of the ships, is a loss of £1,000, this would be what is here called a loss on revenue account.

"Where a loss on revenue account has been sustained, there is, of course, no profit until that loss has been made good, either by set off of previous undivided profits still in hand, or by profit subsequently earned. But until Lee vs. Neuchatel Asphalte Company, the question was open whether a company under the 'Companies' Acts,' which has lost part of its capital by loss on capital account, can continue to pay dividends until the lost capital has been made good.

"Lee vs. Neuchatel Asphalte Company has now shown the true principle to be that capital account and revenue account are distinct accounts, and that for the purpose of determining profits you must disregard accretions to or diminutions of capital."

Here follows the illustration of the £100 consols purchased at par and fallen to £97, to which we have referred above:

"Suppose a tramway company lays its line when materials and labor are both dear; both subsequently fall, and the same line could be laid for half the money, and as an asset (independent of deterioration from wear), would cost for construction only half what it did cost. Is the company to make this good to capital before it pays further dividend? If so, then if the cost of materials and labor had risen after the line was laid might not the company have divided as dividend this accretion to capital? Upon such a principle dividends would vary enormously, and sometimes inversely to the actual profit of the concern."

It will be noticed that in the above extracts, Mr. Buckley makes no reference to the distinction between the profits of an "entire venture" and the "annual profits" of a "continuous venture," or to the distinction between assets used as "fixed" capital, and assets used as "circulating" capital. The principal objections to this system are:

1. That it seeks to draw a distinction between capital account and revenue account, which has no existence in fact, implying, as it does, that the former account deals with capital, and the latter account does not. Mr. Buckley himself, in the extracts above quoted, states that there may be a loss of capital on revenue account, and directly it be conceded that the revenue account deals with capital, the basis of the distinction falls to the ground, and it becomes inaccurate to say "that capital account and revenue account are distinct accounts, and that for the purpose of determining profits, you must disregard accretions to or diminutions of capital."

As we have previously shown, so much of the revenue of a railway as is required for its working is as much capital as the moneys received from the shareholders and debenture holders.

2. The system is inapplicable to the case of an "entire venture" in which the profits not having to be ascertained until the conclusion of the venture, every accretion to capital must be so much profit, and every diminution so much loss.

3. The system is inapplicable to companies formed to make a profit by means of a "circulating" capital, such as banking companies, manufacturing companies, land and stock-jobbing companies. In the case of these companies the paid-up share capital is expended in the production or purchase of commodities for sale. How can accretions to the value of such commodities be disregarded in determining profits?

The views expressed by the Lord Justices, in Verner vs. General and Commercial Investment Trust, Limited, infra., are distinctly opposed to such a conclusion, both Lord Justice Lindley and Lord Justice Kay taking care to point out that, had the company in that case been formed to job or deal in its investments, his decision would have been different.

"If," asks Mr. Palmer, "accretion to capital is not to to be taken into account, how is a company which buys and sells land or stocks, shares and securities or merchandise, to make profit? Such a company buys (if it can) cheap, and sells (if it can) for more than it gave, and its profits are made up of accretion to capital. If I buy 100 tons of copper for £4,000 and sell next day for £5,000, the additional £1,000 is undoubtedly an accretion to capital; nevertheless, it is profit according to the view of every business man."

4. The statement that, "Where a loss on revenue account has been sustained, there is, of course, no profit until that loss has been made good, either by set off of previous undivided profits still in hand, or by profit subsequently earned," has, it is submitted, no foundation in principle, and is unsupported by authority. It is in direct conflict with the decision of Sir George Jessel, in Dent vs. London Tramways Company, infra., that dividends may be paid out of the profits of a year without making good loss of capital in previous years.

If the regulations of a company provide, as the regulations of ninety-nine companies out of a hundred do, that the accounts are to be balanced annually, and a profit and loss account prepared for each year, what can the intention of such a provision be, but to make the operations of one year independent of those of another. And if this be the intention, on what principle is the provision to be disregarded and the loss on the revenue account of one year debited to that of another?

It is certainly remarkable that this continuity of revenue account or carrying on the loss of one year to another, is a feature common to both the Double Account System and the Single Account System. According to the latter system, Mr. Palmer points out, "If the company has a revenue account as distinguished from its general trading account, the balance to the credit or debit, as the case may be, of the revenue account of the year, is carried into the balance sheet and stands as an item there; but the mere fact that there is a credit balance on the revenue account, is not treated as establishing the fact that the company has made any profit for the year, since that credit balance may in the balance sheet be counter-balanced by an equivalent or greater loss of capital sustained during the year or previously." It is, as above stated, precisely to prevent such a result that the regulations of a company are made to provide for the preparation of a profit and loss account for each year, and unless such a provision can be shown to be ultra vires, it, of course, gives the law to the situation.

Reference is sometimes made to the words of Sir George Jessel when confirming the reduction of capital of the Ebbw Vale Company, under the Act of 1877, "That this was a matter which was now very properly left in the discretion of the company, which might desire to reduce its capital by writing off losses. The power was extremely beneficial, inasmuch as it enabled companies to declare dividends, where, but for the power, no dividend would be possible."—Times, 20th January, 1878. This passage is quite consistent with his Lordship's definition of "profit for the year," in Dent vs. the London Tramways Company, infra., for if there be a loss of "circulating" capital during the period selected by the regulations of the company, as its trading interval, in practice generally a year, no dividends are possible for that period without taking such loss into account.

Proposition I.

In the case of an "entire venture" the profits are to be determined by means of a balance sheet, to be prepared on its conclusion, in which the assets, whether used as fixed or circulating capital during its continuance will be stated at their then value, and in which the paid-up capital will be included amongst the debts and liabilities. Any excess in value of the assets over the amount of the debts and liabilities, including paid-up capital, will be profit, and any defect loss.

This is in accord with the Single Account System, and with the practice generally adopted by the commercial world.

As the venture is at an end when the profits have to be ascertained, the distinction between "fixed" and "circulating" capital disappears.

By "entire venture" we mean a venture, the financial results of which are not to be ascertained until its conclusion.

Proposition II.

In the case of a "continuous venture,"

where there is a provision in the regulations for an annual division of profit, any increase or decrease of the selling or market value of assets used as "fixed" capital should be disregarded in arriving at the year's profits.

The reason is that the owner of "fixed" capital is not a seller, and does not, therefore, intend to make his profit out of the selling, or market, value of the asset; hence the variations of such value, during the currency of the venture, have no importance to him in determining his yearly profits.

A depreciation of market or selling value is not the same thing as a depreciation from wear and tear, and may, in fact, vary inversely to it; thus, the fleet of a shipping company may at the end of a year be so much the worse for wear and tear; but owing, say, to a sudden demand for ocean steamers might, if put up for sale, sell for a sum considerably in excess of its cost.

That diminution of the market value of "fixed" capital must be disregarded, see Verner vs. General and Commercial Investment Trust, Limited, infra. That accretion to the market value of "fixed" capital must be disregarded, see Salisbury vs. Metropolitan Railway Company, infra.

The proposition is in accord with the Double Account System advanced by Mr. Buckley, Q. C.; but it is not in accord with the Single Account System, as explained by Mr. Palmer.

In his able commentary on the Single Account System, Mr. Palmer points out, "Company Precedents," fifth edition, p. 326, that, according to that system, "if the value of the company's property goes up, and the directors are satisfied that the increase in value is to be regarded as a permanent increase, the property may appear on the balance sheet as an asset valued at the increased figure," and that "it is generally considered that there need be no revaluation of assets of a permanent character as long as there is no reason to suppose that they have become depreciated, and that what are bona fide regarded as casual and temporary fluctuations in the value of such permanent assets should be disregarded." But it may well be asked: If a company elect to make their property profitable to them by its use and not by its value on sale, why, contrary to such intention, should selling value be taken into account in arriving at their year's profit? A railway is incontestably "an asset of a permanent character" and "property"; but if all the wear and tear of the year be made good, the railway is as efficient for earning profit in the manner intended, at the end as at the beginning of the year, and why then should an increase or decrease in its selling value, even if shown to be of a permanent character, be regarded in arriving at the year's profit? As Mr. Buckley points out: "Upon such a principal dividends would vary enormously, and sometimes inversely to the actual profits of the concern.";

Proposition III.

In the case of a "continuous venture," where there is a provision in the regulations for an annual division of profit, any increase or decrease of the market or selling value of assets used as "circulating" capital must be taken into account in arriving at the year's profits.

The reason is that those who use "circulating" capital are sellers, and look, therefore, for their profits, to the difference between cost and market or selling value. Any alteration, therefore, in such value, is an element to be considered in determining the year's profits.

That accretions to the value of assets used as "circulating" capital should be taken into account in arriving at the year's profit, see in re the Midland Land Investment Company, infra.

That diminution of the value of assets used as "circulating" capital should be taken into account in arriving at the year's profits, see the judgments of Lord Justice Lindley and Lord Justice Kay in Verner vs. General and Commercial Investment Trust, Limited; and in re Oxford Benefit Building Society, L. R. 35, Ch. Div., p. 502.

The proposition is not apparently in accord with the Double Account System advocated by Mr. Buckley, Q. C., for this learned writer does not discriminate between assets used as "fixed" and assets used as "circulating" capital, but broadly lays down the same law as equally applicable to both, namely, that accretions to or diminution of capital must be disregarded. See extract quoted from his work on the Companies' Act, infra.

The proposition is in accordance with the Single Account System as explained by Mr. Palmer, subject apparently to the qualifications that the directors must be satisfied that the appreciation or depreciation, as the case may be, is "of a permanent character," and not a "casual or temporary fluctuation."

(To be continued.)

Accountics:—
T̲ʜ̲ᴇ̲ OFFICE MAGAZINE

| Volume VI
Number 5 | MAY, 1900 | Monthly, $1 a year
Single Copy, 10 cents |

The Application of Advanced Accounting Methods to Modern Business Enterprises

II. The Cotton Mill.

By A. O. Kittredge, F. I. A., C. P. A.

The old adage has it, "Out of the fullness of the heart the mouth speaketh." If I were to attempt to put into words to-night that upon which my mind has been specially dwelling the last few days, I would perhaps voice something very different from what you are expecting to hear. If, therefore, in thinking of spindles and warps and fillings, of yarns and sheetings and fustians, I, by any accident, utter such words as "book plates" and "authors' royalties," "sheet stock," "bindings" and "instalment accounts," some of you will know the reason why.

From one point of view at least, namely, that of present contact, I should speak to-night of the publishing business rather than cotton mills. However, we are obliged to take life as we find it, and therefore, putting aside those things which have occupied my attention almost without intermission for a number of days, up to the moment I started for this hall, I will do what I can to interest you in accounting for cotton mills.

My thought is not a stated address or the reading of a formal paper, but, instead, a familiar talk along the lines of practice, outlining in some respects that which every accountant must encounter, and more particularly setting forth that practice which I have found it expedient to follow in the industry named. What I shall say will be in some respects a description of an accounting system that has been put into operation in one of the large cotton corporations of this State, also into a second manufacturing enterprise likewise in this State, but somewhat less prominent in the field, and in still another mill in the South. Therefore, what I shall offer is not abstract theory, but instead, is a description of work done. From another point of view, what I shall present may be considered an exemplification of accounting principles applicable to any and every line of trade, or, rather, to any and every line

*Abstract of a lecture delivered before the New York Chapter of the Institute of Accounts, at the Waldorf-Astoria, March 29, 1900, by A. O. Kittredge, F. I. A., C. P. A., Editor of Accountics and President of the Account, Audit and Assurance Company, Limited.

of manufacture, because our subject to-night is a branch of manufacturing.

One of the reasons for laying before you the samples which are spread on the table and which will be referred to as we go along, is to illustrate, for the benefit of the younger members of the Institute particularly, a method of studying a given business, for the purpose of ascertaining its nature, in the sense of adapting an accounting system to it. It is all very well to suppose that double entry accounting is applicable everywhere; but there is double entry and double entry. Accounting, double entry though it be, must be adapted to the business in order to make it entirely satisfactory. The case is similar to that of a tailor, who must fit the coat that he makes in order to render it satisfactory to the wearer. No matter what the grade of material nor the kind of workmanship, if it binds or pinches, it will not do. So it is with the business man. If he is supplied with an accounting system which does not give him the results he wants, which is cumbersome, or is not easy to use in any respect, or which requires a word of apology or explanation whenever it is considered, he will feel toward it just as I imagine men in general feel toward ill-fitting clothes.

· · · · · · · ·

Another figure of speech may be used. The accounting system of an establishment is a machine for producing a definite product. The product is records and statements—records of the transactions of the business and the results accomplished, and statements of those results properly classified, together with showings of personal accounts. An office, when it is looked at aright, is a factory housing the machinery for turning out this product. In an ordinary factory, whether it be iron working or wood working, the product is determined very largely by the character of the machine and the skill of the operatives employed. So, too, with the product of the office. Its character is determined by the quality of the machinery that is installed and the skill of the bookkeepers and clerks in charge. In a factory, given a good machine and a

good operator, you have perfection of product. In an office, given a proper system and a skillful clerk, and you have, approximately, perfection in results.

Let us stop for a moment to inquire concerning the objects of accounting. From certain lectures delivered before the Institute in the past, we know that accounting has come down to us through long years of development. Its history has been traced back to the time when its entire machinery was nothing more than notched sticks, the simplest possible evidences of debit and credit, or the relation of man to man in business transactions. But the demands of the present day are far beyond that which is supplied by notched sticks.

It is not enough now to know that our debtors owe us so much and at such times, or that we owe our creditors so much and have agreed to pay them at such and such dates. In the ordinary business operations of to-day, whether mercantile or manufacturing, or both, what may be termed the personal accounts embrace the smaller part of accounting. What is demanded by the merchant or the manufacturer at all times is the knowledge of where he stands. Is he making money or is he losing? If he is making, where is he making and at what rate? Is he making in one department an excessive profit and standing a loss in another department? If so, the whole of the facts are required, not a general result. The business man wants full particulars at all times.

Argue the case as you will, go over all the ground from beginning to end, and you will agree with me, I think, that that which simply records our debits and our credits is one of the smallest functions of accounting. It may be one of the largest functions of bookkeeping, but still it is one of the smallest of accounting.

· · · · · · ·

Such assertions as have preceded bring us face to face with a question that has been discussed by the Institute on other occasions, and that is this, namely, the difference between accounting and bookkeeping. In order that we may have a definition before us, by which we may clearly understand that which is to follow, let us consider for a moment what accounting is and what bookkeeping is.

For our purpose it is sufficient to say that accounting is the scheme, the science, the plan, and that bookkeeping is the adaptation, the interpretation and the method. Accounting is the reason why, bookkeeping is the way it is done.

Bookkeeping is flexible. It may be adapted to almost any requirements. As a rule, business establishments are overloaded with bookkeeping.

The principles of accounting are inflexible. They cannot be changed. It is impossible to modify them. As a rule, business establishments are deficient in accounting.

It is evident that the situation requires correct and adequate accounting; otherwise the business man is likely to be lost in a maze of uncertainty. The bookkeeping, however, must be modified and adapted to the requirements of the industry, else it is unsatisfactory in the extreme.

* * * * * *

The object of the accounts of a given business is to afford the managing man such a view and knowledge of the situation as will enable him to manage his business to the best advantage. The object of a set of books is to record facts and so exhibit them in their relationship, each to the other, as to afford the business man a foundation upon which to predicate his plans for the future.

All other things being equal, that business manager is the best able to direct a given enterprise, who knows the most about the situation. On the other hand, all other things being equal, that business manager is likely to score the worst failure who knows the least about the situation. Hence the high and important function of the accountant to give the business manager a correct and exact view of the situation at all times. The requirements of the business man are best met, so far as information is concerned, when he has before him perpetually a profit and loss statement and perpetually a balance sheet—that is to say, a profit and loss statement always complete and up to date and a balance sheet likewise always complete and up to date.

A going balance sheet means a constant statement of resources or assets and a constant statement of liabilities. A going profit and loss statement means a constant showing of profits or losses, as the case may be. A constant statement of liabilities must necessarily include accrued profits. A constant statement of assets must include whatever we have on hand in the way of merchandise when it is an ordinary merchandising proposition that we are considering, or what we have got on hand in the way of finished goods, goods in process and materials out of which to make goods, if it be a manufacturing proposition that we are considering.

* * * * * *

Perhaps some of you have already thought of cost accounts, although I believe so far I have not used that term this evening. There must be records or the cost of goods produced, if we are going to know at all times what our assets are, for manufacturing at most is a conversion of or a change in assets. Of cost accounts there are almost as many ideas in vogue as there are accountants who have given attention to the subject. A definition, therefore, of what we mean by cost accounts is essential to the work in hand.

My interpretation of cost accounts is not an estimate, not an approximation, not a guess as to what the goods will cost or have cost, but the actual record of the fact that they did cost so much. Suppose, for example, we are making chairs. It is not sufficient to say that the chair will take so much of lumber, require about so much labor and so much paint or varnish, the whole amounting to, for example, $1.50. Such a memorandum is not a cost account in the proper sense of the term. It may do as an estimate for a contract, but a cost account, in my estimation, means a record of what the article has actually cost in the way of materials and labor, together with its pro rata of the general expenses of the factory. There is also included the idea that the total of the costs recorded against the individual articles shall foot an amount equal to the total of all the charges to the factory, materials, labor and incidentals inclusive.

If we are making chairs and bureaus and bedsteads, then the total number of chairs multiplied by their ascertained cost price, and the total number of bureaus multiplied by their ascertained cost price, and the total number of bedsteads multiplied by their ascertained cost price and these respective amounts added together, will equal the total charges to the factory during the period in which these goods are produced.

Right here let us consider one or two points that arise. Given a production of one hundred chairs to-day, with our factory in full swing, one cost price is produced. Given a duplicate production next month, with our factory running at half speed—that is, partly shut down—another cost price will be produced. Our cost price, it is evident, will be a constantly varying quantity, determined by the fluctuations in the management of the factory and the conditions under which it is operated. Cost price, therefore, for the purposes of this address, means the actual cost of the article at the time, not an average cost, but the actual fact as it works out.

Now, by way of indicating the advantages of this point of view with regard to cost accounts, let us inquire what the managing man says of such a showing. If he has a record before him of the costs as they come out and by it finds that his goods are becoming more and more expensive, he has something definite upon which to call his superintendent or foreman to account. The superintendent cannot dispute the manager's conclusions and say, "Your figures are not correct. You have made an undue allowance for general expenses," etc. He is faced by the fact that the same basis of pro rating is being used now as heretofore, and that, as a fact, the turnout of the factory is such that the cost is mounting up. The conclusion is inevitable. A change must be made, and the managing man has the satisfaction of directing that change to be made before very serious losses have occurred. You will think, I fear, that there is comparatively little in this talk that bears upon our subject. Nevertheless, this introduction has seemed to be necessary.

* * * * * *

What do we mean by a cotton mill? Go through the eastern part of the country, particularly the New England States, also some portions of the Southern States, and you will find in various sections industrial enterprises called cotton mills. In some cases there are a number of mills in a group. The cotton mill very generally is a rectangular building, of from three to five stories in height with a certain tower-like structure near the middle of its length, built either integral with, or slightly apart from, the building. This is the staircase tower, and through it the employes enter the different departments. The mill proper is operated either by water power or steam power.

Connected with the cotton mill, directly or remotely, is a cotton storage warehouse. Sometimes the use of this building is restricted to the raw material that is consumed by the mill, but in many cases it amounts to a public storage warehouse. Cotton is consigned to a mill by the planters in the South, by commission houses and by others, with the expectation that it will be taken over by the mill at some date for use. Various cotton mills issue warehouse receipts, which are negotiable like ordinary warehouse receipts.

In connection with many cotton mills there will be found a considerable acreage of land. Many cotton mills operate farms, so to speak. On the farm, or the acreage land, there are frequently a lot of houses built for the purpose of renting to the operatives. In many cases, particularly in the South and outside of the larger towns, there is also a store belonging to the mill. It is operated nominally for the convenience of the operatives, but, as a fact, for the profit of the owners. In many instances also the mill operates its own gas works and waterworks. It maintains a well-equipped stable for teaming, nominally restricted to the use of the mill, but as a fact frequently doing teaming for outsiders.

In connection with almost every mill there are repair shops, and in many cases allied manufacturing industries are located alongside of the mill, all operated by the same corporation. Thus there are bleacheries and dye works, and in some cases factories for the production of certain finishes on goods, and for the elaboration of certain bi-products.

* * * * * *

Finally, there is the sales department. Very frequently the sales department takes the character of a commission house in New York or some other center, to which goods are consigned as soon as produced. Independent of the commission houses, there is of late years a growing class of independent customers who buy direct of the mill instead of through the commission houses in the large cities.

(To be continued.)

What the Credit Men Are Doing

By A. O. Kittredge.

The programme for the convention of the National Association at Milwaukee, as complete as it is possible to make it at the present time, is as follows:

TUESDAY, JUNE 12.

Convention called to order by the president at 10 a. m.

Invocation by Rev. Charles Stanley Lester.

Minutes of previous convention.

Address of Welcome by Hon. David S. Rose, Mayor of Milwaukee.

Address of Welcome on behalf of Milwaukee Association—H. M. Battin.

Response to Addresses of Welcome.

President's Annual Address—President John Field.

Treasurer's Annual Report—Treasurer T. H. Green.

Appointment of Auditing Committee.

Secretary's Annual Report—Secretary Wm. A. Prendergast.

Appointment of Committees on Credentials and Resolutions.

Address—Governor Edward Scofield, of Wisconsin.

Report of Membership Committee—Frank E. Freese, Chairman.

Open Parliament on the Report of the Membership Committee.

Report of Business Literature Committee—H. E. Hutchings, Chairman.

Open Parliament on the Report of the Business Literature Committee.

Appointment of Chairmen of State Delegations.

Adjournment.

WEDNESDAY, JUNE 13.

Convention called to order by the President at 9 a. m.

Invocation by Rev. Rabbi Mayer.

General communications, announcements, etc.

Report of the Committee on Credentials.

Address, "Business Morality"—John R. Ainsley, Esq., of Brown, Durrell & Co., Boston, Mass.

Report of Committee on Improvement of Mercantile Agency Service—E. Troy, Chairman.

Open Parliament on Report of Committee, etc.

Report of Legislative Committee—George H. Hovey, Chairman.

Open Parliament on Report of Legislative Committee.

Nomination of candidates for President and Vice-President.

Informal ballot for Nominees for President and Vice-President.

Adjournment.

THURSDAY, JUNE 14.

Convention called to order by the President at 9.30 a. m.

Invocation by Rev. Judson Titsworth.

General communications, announcements, etc.

Address, "Why I Am a Member"—Dorchester Mapes, Simmons Manufacturing Co., Chicago, Ill.

Report of Committee on Credit Department Methods—Green Benton, Chairman.

Open Parliament on Report of Committee on Credit Department Methods.

Report of Investigation and Prosecution Committee—Daniel B. Murphy, Chairman.

Open Parliament on Report of Investigation and Prosecution Committee.

Election of Officers.

Selection of place for next Annual Convention.

Selection of Central Office.

Report of Committee on Resolutions.

Installation of Officers for the new year.

Adjournment.

The Milwaukee Association has arranged the following programme for the entertainment of those attending the convention:

Tuesday evening, June 12th, concert at the Deutscher Club.

Wednesday morning, June 13th, Tally-Ho Ride for the ladies attending the convention.

Wednesday, June 13th, 3 p. m. prompt, excursion on the lake, and trolley car ride to White Fish Bay, where supper will be served in the evening.

Thursday afternoon, June 14th, visit of inspection to the large factories of the city.

Thursday evening, June 14th, smoker and vaudeville entertainment.

⸺

The Buffalo Credit Men's Association held a meeting on the 26th of April, at which the following delegates to the National Convention were appointed: Wm. C. Cornwell, Geo. F. Dominick, Geo. W. Farnham, Buell G. Tallman, L. F. Gray, W. M. Edwards, W. A. Joyce; alternates, James G. Berry, John J. Dolphin, A. J. Barnes, S. C. Rogers, G. L. Lovejoy, G. D. Barr, E. C. Neal. The committee on the "Trade Excursion" made under the auspices of the Credit Men's Association and the Merchant's Exchange, of Buffalo, reported great success and full satisfaction on the part of the participants as to results. The excursion extended as far east as Binghamton and south as Oil City. After the business of the meeting was concluded, D. B. Murphy, of Rochester, N. Y., delivered an address on the "Aims and Objects of Credit Men," which by the able manner in which the subject was treated, drew forth many comments.

⸺

The New York Credit Men's Association has appointed the following delegates to the National Convention: C. S. Young, cashier of the Central National Bank; M. E. Bannin, of Converse, Stanton & Co.; Edward E. Huber, with Eberhard Faber; J. G. Cannon, vice-president of the Fourth National Bank; Charles Biggs, of the Hat Trade Credit Association; A. S. Pitt, of Marsellus & Pitt; J. R. Birch, with Merritt, Elliott & Co.; R. P. Messiter, of Minot, Hooper & Co.;

T. H. Bartindale, of Morse & Rogers; Hugo Kanzler, of Muser Bros.; Charles E. Meek, of the National Lead Co.; G. Waldo Smith, of Smith & Sills; Frank C. Travers, of Travers Bros. & Co.; W. A. H. Bogardus, of Tubular Dispatch Co.; A. H. Watson, of Watson, Porter, Giles & Co.; and O. G. Fessenden, of Hayden W. Wheeler & Co.

⸺

A large number of the members of the Sioux City Bureau of Credits, with their invited guests, met on April 10th at the Mondamin Hotel, and listened to a paper read by E. C. Peters on "Fire Insurance." Though somewhat of an innovation as to subject matter, it was both instructive and interesting, and gave rise to a lively discussion. The growth of the Bureau during the past year has been very satisfactory, the increase in the membership being about 50 per cent. All connected with the organization take an active part in its work, and a still larger increase is expected for this year. President C. B. French has just completed his list of standing committees, which, with the chairmen, are as follows: Membership, F. Bardes; Credit Department Methods, A. W. Dale; Mercantile Agency Service, George W. Scott; Business Literature, T. H. Green; Legislative, W. H. Preston.

⸺

Association work in Kansas City has not gone on as vigorously as had been anticipated. This is owing in part to the interruption caused by the resignation of the president in the fall and the election of a new one. I. D. Waggener, the secretary, says that though the meetings have not been regular the members have by no means lost interest. The annual meeting occurs in May, when officers will be elected and delegates will be appointed to the National Convention.

⸺

The Omaha Credit Men have not been active in Association work for the last few months, but on April 10th a meeting was held which was both pleasant and profitable. The members are looking forward to the National Convention in June for encouragement and fresh impetus.

Return Postal Cards.

Under the present postal arrangements a large percentage of postal cards sent out by persons seeking information or for the sale of goods is a total loss. A bill has been favorably reported by the House Committee on Post Offices and Post Roads providing for a return card and envelope, so that only those actually used need be paid for. By the terms of the bill the Postmaster-General may make contracts with private parties, allowing them to send out self-addressed cards and envelopes inclosed in prepaid outgoing letters, the postage on the return letters and cards to be paid when mailed and returned to the original office. The payment of the postage is secured by the deposit of a certain amount of cash and United States bonds with the Postmaster-General.

The Monthly Statement

Business mortality results from two causes, the fault of the concern failing, or misfortune brought about by outside circumstances. By far the larger part of disaster which overtakes members of the business world may be traced to the former cause. In fact, upon close examination, much that is accredited to the latter really had the first impetus from the fault of the sufferer. More than one-third of the failures of 1899 are claimed in the statistics as due to lack of capital, and incompetence comes in for 16.5 per cent. It is difficult, however, to draw the line between these two, for certainly a business concern which will embark in a venture without sufficient means to insure success and allow a reasonable margin for the vicissitudes of trade must be in the hands of incompetent persons. Neglect, extravagance, speculation, unwise credit, each have a share in making up the sum total. Over against these may be put specific conditions, the failure of apparently solvent debtors, special or undue competition circumstances which could not have been foreseen or overcome by care and watchfulness.

A careful study of the tables which the Bradstreet Co. issue, will prove helpful to the thoughtful business man and may warn him of breakers upon which his fortunes may be wrecked. Like causes produce like results. It is easier to learn from the misfortunes of others than gain knowledge by the thorny path of experience.

The defects of our consular system have been appreciated for a long time by those who have had opportunity to compare it with a similar service received by other nations. Though of late there has been an improvement, still there remain defects. Within the past eight or nine years several attempts have been made in Congress to carry through legislation which would eradicate these, but without success. Frequent discussion of the subject, however, by those most interested has so far aroused public attention to the needs of the situation that there is a prospect that before long some law will be enacted which will prove effective.

A bill introduced last January by Senator Lodge, entitled, "A Bill to Remodel the Consular Service of the United States," seems adapted to remedy the evils now existing. It provides that consuls shall be subject to examination, and that "No one shall be examined who is under twenty-five or over forty-five years of age, or who is not a citizen of the United States, or who is mentally, morally or physically disqualified to fulfill properly the duties of consul. The scope and method of the examination shall be determined by the board, but among the subjects shall be included either French, German or Spanish language, and questions designed to ascertain each applicant's knowledge of the commercial resources of the United States." When a consul has filled a post for twelve months creditably he cannot be dismissed except for cause. The effect of this measure will be to make the foreign service something in the nature of a profession. It will lift it out of the reach of the party politician, for a man once having demonstrated his fitness for a position cannot be deprived of his office merely to make room for a political rival.

The discussion of a reform in the consular service is drawing the attention of business men to the publications of the Bureau of Foreign Commerce as a source of information. These give the results of the investigation of consular officers over a wide range of subjects, as the market for different American products, labor situations in foreign lands, manufacturing interests, transportation, corporations, trusts, mining, tariff, cattle raising. In fact, anything which may be of benefit to the American people is noted and reported to the Government at Washington. These reports are carefully considered, and from them matter is selected which may be of use either from a business, sanitary or economic standpoint. This is published in several forms: Commercial Relations, being annual reports of the consular officers; Consular Reports, issued monthly, containing miscellaneous reports from diplomatic and consular officers; Advanced Sheets, issued daily, except Sundays and legal holidays, for the convenience of the press, commercial and manufacturing organizations, etc.; Exports Declared for the United States, issued quarterly, containing the declared values of exports from the various consular districts to the United States for the preceding three months; Special Consular Reports, containing a series of reports from consular officers on particular subjects. The advantages to be gained by a study of these official publications will readily be appreciated by those seeking a market outside of our own country, but their usefulness need not be limited to those, for valuable suggestions may be received from a study of the methods in vogue in other lands in any department of business, no matter how narrow the field in which it operates.

The bills for the establishment of a Department of Commerce and Industry, which have been introduced into the House and the Senate, are entitled to the especial attention of the business world. As the nation has developed there have been changes in the governmental departments, an increase in the number of heads and a readjustment of the work assigned to each. Within the last few years there has been a growing demand for another cabinet officer. It has been felt that the expansion of foreign commerce, the problems in connection with the manufacturing industries and the weighty questions resulting from the enormous growth of the mining interests call for representation and oversight in the Presidential Cabinet by some one not charged with other duties. The Senate bill provides for a cabinet officer and an assistant secretary, and that the department shall have general jurisdiction over foreign and internal commerce, excepting in so far as pertains to the collection of customs. Measures intended to increase foreign markets are to come within its province, also mining industries and everything pertaining to manufactures, patents, trade-marks and copyrights.

The fourth annual meeting of the American Academy of Political and Social Science was held in April at Philadelphia. These meetings call together many practical statesmen as well as students of governmental and economic subjects. The discussions this year were on corporations and public welfare. An address by Controller Bird S. Coler, of New York City, on "Financial Control, Capitalization, Methods of Accounting and Taxation," attracted much attention. In speaking of the relation of capitalization of public service corporations to municipalities, he said that it became of great moment to the municipality exercising control when the cash return of the municipality is based upon the net earnings of the corporation. "If the policy of basing the city's revenue upon the entire gross receipts of public service corporations could be universally adopted and adhered to, there would seem to be little necessity for anxiety or concern in regard to the question of capitalization, excepting where a readjustment of percentages is deemed necessary or municipal ownership of these corporations is proposed."

He called attention to the importance of having the books of accounts of all such corporations contain a true, perfect and complete record of the finances, so that reliable statements of condition can be easily extracted therefrom, and as a means to this end he proposed that there be a uniform system of accounting adopted by all such corporations, the Controller prescribing the method to be employed by each class of corporations. As a part of the plan, the books of account thus kept should be open at all reasonable times to the inspection of the Controller.

One man pursues power in order to possess wealth, and another pursues wealth in order to possess power; which last is the safer way, and generally followed.—South.

Men pursue riches under the idea that their possession will set them at ease and above the world. But the law of association often makes those who begin by loving gold as a servant finish by becoming themselves its slaves; and independence without wealth is at least as common as wealth without independence.—Colton.

Accountancy: Its Past and Its Present

BY CHARLES W. HASKINS.

(Continued from page 51, April number.)

A good bookkeeper, gentlemen, is able at any time to make out from the books he has kept a statement of the business covered by those books and of its gains and losses. So that bookkeeping in any sense—expert bookkeeping, or detective bookkeeping—is but an incident in the work of the accountant. Nor is the accountant a mere certifier to the truth or falsity of another man's bookkeeping. The profession of accountancy covers everything pertaining to the business of preparing, examining, investigating and auditing all classes of books of accounts. The accountant is called upon to plan, to arrange, to adapt books of account for any purpose, any business, any enterprise. He examines, he audits, he adjusts, he writes up, he balances any book or books for corporations, for joint stock associations, for estates, for copartnerships, for individuals. In case of their insolvency, he examines their accounts and prepares reports of their condition and statements and schedules of their assets and liabilities, and, generally, of their accounts and affairs; and he is ready to act as the assignee for the benefit of their creditors and to prepare plans and statements and schedules for the adjustment, the readjustment, the compromise, the payment of their obligations and liabilities, and for the reorganization of their business. Accountancy prepares and examines and reports upon plans and agreements and statements of all kinds of undertakings, whether financial, commercial, industrial, or manufacturing; and in the same way it has to do with the organizing, or the consolidating, or the reorganizing of business enterprises and of property interests; and the accountant is ready to act as attorney or agent for the parties in interest for the purpose of carrying the plans into effect. Accountants organize books of estates; they take charge of such books; they make proper schedules and accountings for assignees, for trustees, for executors, for administrators, whether for use in legal proceedings or in any other way. And of the accuracy of his work, whether of examinations, of audits, of balances, of investigations, the public accountant is prepared to add his authoritative signed certificate of guarantee.

The profession of accountancy looks out to-day upon a vast New World of commerce and finance; upon a boundless extent and infinite variety of debit and credit; upon a restless and resistless tide of international exchange of credit and commodities; upon a steady march and overwhelming volume of manufacture and trade and investment, at which the very kings of it all themselves stand aghast, and in all the turnings and twistings of which every man must go by rule or go under. On every book, and over every desk and bench and counter, should be written the one motto of safety, the lesson of accountancy, "Know thyself."

In this great modern monetary world the accountant finds his clientele. "Every man his own accountant" is a thing of the past, if it ever existed. Few men, without the aid of the independent accountant, could learn the condition of the joint stock company, or the firm, or the business—specially if a large one—in which he is interested or is asked to embark his fortune. The first man the accountant meets, his friend or his next-door neighbor, and from that all the way up through every branch of trade and even of government — manufacturing firms and companies, railroad and other corporations, cities, towns, counties, states, and possibly, the general Government of his country—may at any time need his independent, disinterested services as a professional expert.

As an illustration of the increasing recognition of the importance of professional accountancy, and of its employment in the very highest places of financial trust, I briefly mention the fact that in 1893 two independent professional accountants, of whom I had the honor to be one, were selected by a Joint Commission of Congress to effect a complete revision of the methods of business of the Executive Departments of the United States Government, with a view to expediting and simplifying the public business. After two years of hard labor, this important task was accomplished; the report of the experts was adopted; the new methods suggested by them, founded entirely upon the laws and principles of business, were put into immediate operation, and the success of these methods was attested by all the accounting officers of the Government after they had been in practical operation long enough to make the rendering of a judicial judgment upon them possible. This work, the most important of its kind undertaken since the foundation of the Government, resulted in a saving to the Treasury of the United States of more than $600,000 annually, as well as in greatly expediting, facilitating and safeguarding the public business. A full account of this work may be found in the reports of the Joint Commission of the Fifty-third Congress to Examine the Executive Departments (33).

Lest you may think this an altogether unheard-of proceeding, let me say that seventy years ago a Commission appointed by the British Treasury "to inquire into and state the manner in which the accounts are kept in the principal departments of income and of payments, with a view to render the system more uniform, as well as more capable of affording ready and satisfactory information on the nature and amount of expenditure," reported that in the army, navy and ordnance the correct application of funds had been fully attained by the gradual introduction of new registers, such as the increasing wants of each

office had from time to time demanded; but that the want of system, resulting from these incidental arrangements, had tended to embarrass the general statements of the accounts, and to shut out the public from a due acquaintance with the details of the expenditure. And this defect of arrangement the Commission proposed to correct by establishing throughout the departments a new general system of accounts, founded on the mercantile system of bookkeeping (34).

A few quotations—and this line of reference might be indefinitely produced—will serve to indicate the increasing appreciation of the profession of accountancy and the wide field of its operations.

Joseph Ansell, President of an English law society, said, in the latter part of 1899: "I know of no profession which is, and which ought to be, in closer touch with the members of my profession than that of the accountant. Year by year lawyers see the advantage of utilizing the services of the members of the accountants' profession. No lawyer in his senses would dream of settling draft forms of articles of partnership unless he called to his aid some accountant well-known in the profession; or of settling articles of association without the help of an accountant. And no man ought to dream of winding up the estate of a deceased client without the aid of an accountant" (35).

President Fowler, of the New York, Ontario & Western Railroad, said to a correspondent of the New York Times in 1897: "One advantage of the system is that directors of corporations which adopt it are, to some extent, relieved of responsibility, which as individuals they should not be called upon to assume. No business man who attends weekly or monthly board meetings can be expected to wade through the voluminous accounts and books of even the smallest railway company. Few of us would be able to verify the statements for ourselves, even if we had the time and inclination. The independent audit and examination by experienced and trustworthy accountants, who are directly responsible to stockholders, relieves the director of a burden which he should hesitate before assuming, as he is obliged to do under the old system" (36).

President Baldwin, of the Long Island Railroad, says: "Everywhere we turn, we find some lack of faith in the statements of public corporations, and it is only by employing such a system as is presented by the Certified Public Accountants that the truth can be ascertained. I believe that the auditor of a railroad company should be appointed by the Board of Directors of the road, and not by the President or any one official. He is then free to act independently and to the best interests of the company he is serving, and he is not hampered by the feeling that he is dependent upon this or that official for his bread and butter."

J. Lindsay Reid, in an article written some years ago for the North American Review, said: "In the case of private or 'close' corporations, a few have their books audited by expert accountants.

Now and then one encounters a president of a corporation who declares that he would not hold office for a day if the books of the concern were not audited periodically by an expert."

The Mail and Express, of New York, says of the accountant: "Much of his best work is along the line of rejuvenating the business of concerns that have for years been losing ground and gradually becoming bankrupt through the unwillingness of the managers to employ the modern methods of their competitors, or because of their ignorance of the existence of such methods. New life has been inspired in many a failing enterprise by some quick-witted accountant who has speedily recognized its need of different methods and a change of management. There is nothing so enlivening to a business as a periodical change of the point of view of the managers; and this is one of the best influences that the certified public accountant imparts."

Let us now turn our attention for a moment to the legal status of accountancy in the United States and the efforts of the profession to secure to itself a solid bulwark and vantage ground of worth and efficiency in the business world.

In 1896, the Legislature of New York, at the request of the accountants of the State and for their protection, passed an act "to regulate the profession of public accountants." This act provided for a class of public expert accountants to be known as "Certified Public Accountants," and to have the exclusive right to use the abbreviation C. P. A.; and it authorized the Regents of the University to establish examinations and to issue certificates of recognition of such Certified Public Accountants. Other States are considering, and one or two have effected, legislation based upon this law of the State of New York.

Under this law the Regents appoint a board of three examiners, who hold two examinations annually. A full C. P. A. certificate is granted only to those at least twenty-five years of age who have had three years' satisfactory experience in the practice of accounting, one of which shall have been in the office of an expert public accountant. The examinations cover the theory of accounts; practical accounting; auditing, and commercial law. They presuppose, in harmony with the law and the rules of the Regents, a high order of professional education and efficiency.

And where, it will be asked, is this education obtainable? We have theological universities; we have colleges of medicine; we have law schools. But where is there a university or college or school of accountancy?

America—"fast" as we are said to be—was not built in a day. Accountancy, as we have seen, has been a growth; a sure and steady growth. And, so far, the profession has been able satisfactorily to answer every question in its time.

The time, it would seem, has come to answer this question; a question that brings us face to face with the one great existing want of the profession— a special educational institution worthy to stand alone as the Alma mater of the coming generation of accountants—a question which, while it indicates the duty lying next in our path of progress, points back, as I believe, to an already established line of procedure to be followed in any effort to fulfill this obligation to ourselves and our successors.

It is believed that in direct line with the public accountants act of 1896 and with the Regents' examination, a school of accountancy can be established under such patronage, guidance and protection as together shall constitute a guarantee of stability and success; and that a school thus safeguarded may be so organized as at the same time to be thoroughly American in character and yet to utilize the advantages, without the disadvantages, both of the English system of articled clerkship and of the Continental system of class study.

There are colleges, not only for what have been long known as the learned professions, but for almost every calling that may have seemed in any sense to require a special education or even technical training. There are schools of mines, of agriculture, of pharmacy, of forestry, of nursing, of military and naval science, of veterinary surgery, and of a hundred other arts and sciences. And in some cases two callings will so far overlap each other that it has taken special legislation to keep them apart. Dentistry, for example, a branch of minor surgery, occupies a high position as a profession; and in our dental schools anatomy, physiology, toxicology and materia medica and therapeutics are so emphasized that it has been found necessary to make it punishable by fine or imprisonment for a dentist, as such, to practice the profession of a physician.

The educational needs of the commercial world are beginning to find recognition, especially on the continent of Europe. In the establishment of colleges for higher commercial education England is behind even the United States. As for a college of accountancy, there is not one on the face of the earth. The formation by articled clerks in Great Britain of Chartered Accountants' Students' Societies has resulted in some good lectures and debates and a certain amount of class study; and accountancy is said to be taught in two of the evening schools of the London School Board. But a London bookkeeper, writing under date January 2, 1900, says that he recently attended one of these latter and found that the tuition was ordinary elementary bookkeeping, and that the teacher's knowledge of accounts was quite theoretical.

If, then, the accountants of the United States, than whom there is not to be found among the professions a more magnanimous or public-spirited class of men, shall succeed in bringing about the foundation of a strictly professional college of accountancy, they will have led the way in one of the most important educational movements of the century—whether you call it the nineteenth or the twentieth—and will have won the gratitude, as they will doubtless have had the co-operation, of business men, of educators, of philanthropists, and of those moralists who recognize in business accountancy the "very conscience of the modern commercial world."

"We have now seen that accountants and their work have been known and recognized from time immemorial. We have caught glimpses of accountancy approaching us out of the mists of the ages. We have seen it taking shape as a kind of Levitical or thirteenth tribe distributed among the classes and callings of men of affairs. And we see it now, endeavoring, as best it may, to maintain its appointed station on the watchtowers of the business world. With increasing recognition of its indispensibility, its efficiency will increase; and, on the other hand, with an increase of efficiency, an increase of recognition will be won and accorded. As we aim at good work and high professional skill; as we exemplify a high standard of probity and honesty; as we remember, with Epicurus, that to become rich is but an alteration of our affairs and is not in itself an advantage; as we illustrate the words of Montaigne, that men should not live for themselves but for the public; so will we educate the public to understand and acknowledge this interdependent relation, and more and more cordially to welcome us to our place in the centre of the system of trade and commerce on a professional plane alongside that of the law.

FOOT NOTES.

1. Larousse; article Tenue des Livres. 2. Ratio; gramma; grammateion; logismos; accepti et expensi. 3. Ratio conficere. 4. Logizomai; apologizomai; ratio rediere. 5. Falsas ratio inferre. 6. Apoluein tina euthunas. 7. Dialogismos. 8. Codex; codex accepti et expensi; tabulae. 9. Aliquid in tabulas referre. 10. Calendarium. 11. Ars rationaria. 12. Actuarius. 13. Calculator; rationarius; actor summarum; a rationibus. 14. Logista. 15. Euthune. 16. Logisterion. 17. Euthunos; euthunter; logistes; exetastes. 18. To exetastikon. 19. Pliny, Bk. 2, ch. 7. 20. Archaeologia, Vol. 48, p. 282. 21. Report Society of Antiquaries. 22. Annual Register for 1834. 23. Stat. 13 Ed. I, cap. 2; also Notes and Queries, Jan. 15, 1887. 24. Chaucer Society Publications. 25. Piers Plowman XXII 462 (C), XIX 457 (B). 26. Notes and Queries, Dec. 22, 1894. 27. Fuller's Church History. 28. Pepys' Diary. 29. Mackay's Memoirs of Extraordinary Popular Delusions. 30. Gentleman's Magazine, 1741. 31. Report Commissioner of Education, 1888. 32. Report of Professor James. 33. Reports of the Joint Commission of the 53d Congress to Revise the Methods of Business of the Executive Departments. 34. Treasury Commission Report, 1829; also, Quarterly Review, Nov. 1829. 35. Account of Annual Dinner Birmingham C. A. S. S., 1899. 36. Times, Feb. 7, 1897.

Postage on Foreign Letters

Complaints come from foreign correspondents frequently that they receive letters on which the postage has not been properly prepaid. As a consequence they are compelled to pay double the ordinary rate. It is especially annoying to travelers, as they often order their mail sent to some boarding-house or office to await them and learn on their arrival that it has been refused by reason of the double postage which must be paid before delivery. The letter rate on foreign mail is five cents per one-half ounce, yet many letters are found to bear the two-cent stamp required for domestic postage. Care in observing this difference would insure the prompt receipt of letters which otherwise would suffer long detention or entirely fail of reaching the addressees.

Accountics

The Office Magazine.

Published Monthly.

A. O. KITTREDGE, F. I. A., C. P. A., Editor.

E. R. KITTREDGE, Associate.

Accountics is devoted to the Science of Accounting, to the Art of Bookkeeping and to the advocacy of Improved Office Methods.

Subscription.—One dollar a year, payable in advance.

Postage is prepaid by the publishers in the United States, Canada and Mexico. For all other countries in the Postal Union, subscribers must add 50 cents a year.

Discontinuances.—In the absence of specific orders to discontinue at the end of the subscription term the magazine will be continued and a bill sent.

Remittances should be by Draft, P. O. Order or Express Order, payable to the order of the Accountics Association. Money and postage stamps are at the risk of the sender, unless sent by express or in registered letters. Add 10 cents each to checks on local banks to defray collection charges.

Advertising Rates will be quoted on application.

Official Journal.—This publication, by resolutions duly passed, has been made the official publication of the following organizations :—

The Institute of Accounts.
The New York Chapter of the Institute of Accounts.
The Washington Chapter of the Institute of Accounts.
The Hartford Chapter of the Institute of Accounts.

Accountics is the accredited medium of intercommunication between members of the Institute of Accounts wherever located.

ACCOUNTICS ASSOCIATION, Publishers,

Lancashire Building, Pine Street, near Nassau, New York.

Publishers' Desk

Writing of the credulity of the business world in "The Saturday Evening Post" lately, Thomas B. Reed says: "As a race we don't like to work. Unless the sweat of the brow was the necessary precursor of eaten bread there would be very little perspiration except on horses. We would all of us rather swap jackknives than dig potatoes. Hence, when there are accumulations beyond safe and tried means of investment, the tendency is to leave off production and go to swapping. Not that we all leave off, but a good many do; and that, with the waste of misdirected effort, the making things we do not want and cannot use, soon eats up our store, and brings us back to work again. Now, although we go over the ground twice or thrice every generation, we never recognize any of the landmarks. In the midst of the speculative period we act as if it would last forever and swarm together toward the abyss."

A good typewriter ribbon is an important adjunct in obtaining neat and clear-cut work on a typewriter. The Rogers Manifold and Carbon Paper Co., of 75 Maiden lane, New York City, is introducing a ribbon which it claims is superior for several reasons. One is the woven edge, which permits the use of the full width of the ribbon without damage to type and prevents curling and bagging. Another is the quality of the material used, the ribbon being made of the best and strongest thread and inked so as to give a bright, clear, clean copy. It is put up in metallic reel boxes and can readily be wound off or on the reel. The ends are tipped with foil so that the fingers are not soiled in putting it on the machine. Those who have suffered from the annoyance of raveled, bagging ribbons, in which the type easily makes perforations and produces unequal impressions, will appreciate the advantage of an article which is not subject to these imperfections.

A system for conveying parcels post between New York and Germany has been in operation since October, 1899, and is proving very successful. Similar arrangements exist between the United States and eighteen other countries, but the volume of business with Germany is larger than all the others combined, as the Germans have quickly appreciated the advantages of this method of transportation. The weight of parcels that may be carried is limited to eleven pounds. This system being but an experiment, the arrangement between the governments is temporary, but doubtless, if the present patronage continues, it will be established on a permanent basis.

Among the books that have reached our desk is one which claims to have minimized the labor of thinking. Up to the present time there have been found no short cuts by which thought could be originated, though almost everything else has felt the benefit of modern invention; but the "Wherewithal Book" proposes to teach the merchant, the lawyer, the doctor and the minister how the mental faculties may carry on their work by a new and improved process. We imagine, however, that those who do the thinking of the world will be slow to leave the beaten tracks and will keep on grinding out their thoughts in the old laborious way.

The Rogers Manifold and Carbon Paper Co., of 75 Maiden lane, New York, claims to furnish a carbon paper which will not dry and deteriorate with age. Its freshness is preserved by the manner in which it is put up in "hermetically sealed" packages to protect it from the air and dust. Twenty-five sheets are encased in tin-foil in such a way that but a small amount is uncovered when one sheet is withdrawn. The convenience and utility of the arrangement will be appreciated by all who need to use carbon paper for manifolding on a typewriter.

When Fortune means to men most good, she looks upon them with a threatening eye.—Shakespeare.

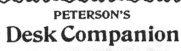

Peterson's Desk Companion

Something that will afford a relief to the crowded desk will be welcomed by every one who has to seek in the pile of papers before him the utensils that he needs. D. B. L. Peterson, of East Orange, N. J., claims to meet this want with the desk companion which he manufactures. It is a device for holding the entire writing equipment suspended under the shelf directly in front of the person using the desk. The ink wells are so arranged that they can be pushed back out of sight if it is desired to keep

Peterson's Desk Companion

the ink free from dust or to prevent evaporation. Tubes for the reception of penholders and pencils are fitted with cork to preserve the pen and pencil points from injury, and a drawer with seven compartments makes a convenient place of storage for stamps and other small articles. Useful and compact, its location above the desk leaves the entire surface unencumbered. It is neat in construction, the front being of oxidized copper, and the boxes of hard wood well put together. The accompanying cut shows the desk companion with the ink wells swung forward on the pivot ready for use.

Bankruptcy

The executive committee of the National Association of Referees in Bankruptcy issued, on March 21, 1900, its report concerning proposed amendments to the Bankruptcy Act of 1898. As a preliminary work in the investigation of the operation of the Bankruptcy Law, the committee early in the present year sent to every member of the Association a series of blanks containing questions intended to cover all the sections of the law which have been criticised. Upon the replies received generalizations have been made which are embodied in the report. As the workings of this law are of such practical interest to the business man, either as creditor or debtor, we recommend the careful consideration of the results of this investigation thus given to the public. The appendix containing a table of cases reported under the Bankruptcy Law of 1898, to March 15, 1900, will be a material aid to any one wishing to investigate the interpretation of the law by the courts.

We quote the concluding words of the committee as setting forth the end in view in conducting this work: "Alone of all the civilized, and even most uncivilized nations of the world, this nation has for the past two decades been without a bankruptcy law. In that period we have greatly grown in commercial importance, and our business, which thirty years ago was largely local or limited to great cities and the States in which they were, has now become interstate—in other words, national. With the increase of business has come an increased necessity of a national statute, regulating not merely the discharge of debtors—that is the lesser need—but more, the administration of insolvent estates. The object of the Association, as we take it, is, therefore, to formulate from time to time reports which will call attention to those sections of the law that need amendment, to the end that ultimately this country of ours may have a permanent bankruptcy statute which is scientifically constructed and fairly representative of the differing yet allied interests of the debtor and the creditor."

A Cablegram to the Philippines

Cable communication directly with the Philippines will become more and more a commercial necessity as intercourse between the United States and the islands increases. To-day a message is a costly luxury which only important governmental matters or large business interests will warrant. Now it has a long and circuitous route to travel before it reaches its destination. Leaving New York, it would go by way of Cape Breton to Heart's Content, Newfoundland, thence under the Atlantic to Ireland and from there to London. Here it would take a fresh start either across the English Channel and overland to Marseilles, or around the Spanish peninsula to Lisbon. From there it would cross to Alexandria, go through Egypt and down the Red Sea to Aden, cross the Arabian Sea to Bombay, thence through India and the Bay of Bengal to Singapore, along the coast to Hong Kong, and beneath the China Sea to Manila.

Well-gotten wealth may lose itself, but the ill-gotten loses its master also.—Cervantes.

Usury dulls and damps all industries, improvements and new inventions, wherein money would be stirring if it were not for this slug.—Bacon.

Of all pure things, purity in the acquisition of riches is the best. He who preserves purity in becoming rich is really pure, not he who is purified by

Accountants' Associations

Hartford Chapter of the Institute of Accounts

A large representation of the members of the Hartford Chapter of the Institute of Accounts had a very pleasant meeting at the Hotel Hartford on May 2. After a dinner had been served, President Henry R. Hovey introduced ex-Postmaster Furlong, who, drawing from his experience in municipal and federal life, pointed out features which he deemed radically wrong in our political system. He advocated a rural free delivery, and said: " Were much of the mail matter that is now carried through the mails placed in the class where it belongs, namely, third class, which rate of postage is a cent for two ounces, the government would then receive, after permitting legitimate newspapers and periodicals to be carried at the cent a pound rates, at least $26,000,000 additional annually. The difference between $1,750,000, the amount now received, and $26,000,000 represents the annual loss to the government from the handling of second-class matter. That amount of money would deliver mail to every home in this republic every day during the year."

P. P. Bennett, manager for Bradstreet's Mercantile Agency, spoke of the improved business methods and ways of keeping accounts. F. H. Bosson, in his talk on "Credits," called attention to the fact that the industrial community is largely indebted to the accountant, and ex-President Gershom Smith emphasized the necessity of public auditors being qualified accountants, and urged that an effort be made to obtain legislation to that end. Brief remarks were made by J. W. Green, of Pratt & Whitney Co., and Clarkson N. Fowler, concerning the laws of other states and of England, and President Hovey stated that the legislation sought would include a uniform system of accounts in town, municipal and general public affairs.

New York Chapter of the Institute of Accounts

The annual meeting of the New York Chapter of the Institute of Accounts was held at the Waldorf-Astoria on April 26th. A large number of members manifested their interest in the work of the Institute by their attendance to participate in the election of officers, which resulted as follows: F. W. Child, president; Wm. P. Plant, secretary and treasurer; Henry Harney and Samuel D. Patterson, members of the board of governors to fill vacancies caused by expiration of terms.

The various reports of the year given were in every way encouraging, and showed a larger increase of membership than had been made during either of the two preceding years. Delegates were chosen to represent the New York Chapter at the convention of the Institute to be held on the 7th of June, of which the following is a list: F. W. Child, C. E. Cheney, T. S. Whitbeck, S. D. Patterson, J. R. Loomis, H. H. Todd, A. O. Kittredge, William Dillon, W. J. Alther, W. P. Plant and Charles Dutton.

No address was made, but after the routine business was disposed of there was a general discussion of institute work and the best means of extending its influence. The feeling of enthusiasm which prevailed argued a good outlook for the future and the spontaneous expressions on all sides indicated that the New York Chapter was beginning the new year under most propitious circumstances.

Illinois Institute of Accountants

The Illinois Institute of Accountants held its regular meeting on the 12th of April, at which a programme including addresses, vocal and instrumental music was given. A paper by Y. B. Haagsma, the General Auditor of the Republic Iron and Steel Co., on "The Accountant as a Man," was a very forcible discussion of a subject which should be of interest to every member of the profession. E. B. Abbott, accountant with Fairbanks, Morse & Co., spoke on the "Evolution of the Journal," and President Abbott gave a short talk on the advantages and privileges of the Illinois Institute of Accountants.

The Illinois Institute is justifying the expectations of its friends, as is evidenced by the number of applications for membership. The good work it is doing by fostering and encouraging a professional enthusiasm and increasing a fraternal feeling among accountants is being appreciated.

Massachusetts Society of Public Accountants

The second meeting of the Massachusetts Society of Public Accountants was held at Young's Hotel, April 10th. The dinner, which is a regular feature of these meetings, was followed by a business session at which a number of applications for membership were received and matters of interest to the society were discussed. The general spirit of good-fellowship that prevailed caused the pioneers in the organization of the society to feel that they had done a good work, and that the meetings and dinners will be looked forward to with much pleasant anticipation from month to month. The arrangements for the May meeting, which it is intended to make especially attractive, include addresses on professional subjects.

Associated Accountants of New Orleans

The Associated Accountants of New Orleans will celebrate the eighth anniversary of the organization of the society by a reunion at the Capitol Hotel, West End, Lake Pontchartrain, on the 12th of May. All members of the profession will join in the hearty wish that those present have the enjoyable time of which the preparations give promise.

That Message to Garcia

BY WALTON DAY.

Some time since, when the matter was new, there was published in the columns of ACCOUNTICS "A Message to Garcia," a random article from the pen of Elbert Hubbard, editor of the "Philistine," which, in the interval, has attracted world-wide attention. More recently I have encountered a little pamphlet entitled "An Idea and Its Execution," being an answer to "A Message to Garcia." This proceeds from the pen of Shelby Downard, editor of the "Library Bulletin," and is published by the Library Company, Lima, Ohio.

"A Message to Garcia," considered as an article, was the embodiment of a fact which has been encountered by every manager of affairs, civil or military, and every director of labor, clerical or mechanical, since the very beginning. There is now and then a subordinate or employe with sufficient wit or discipline to comprehend requirements and with sufficient will and energy to execute a commission without faltering or the chance of failure. The great majority of subordinates are lacking in these qualities, but whether from natural endowment or lack of training and discipline it does not matter for the moment. The author of the "Message to Garcia" honored the man who, receiving an order or commission, proceeded at once to the efficient execution of that commission. In this respect he held up President McKinley's messenger as an example to be emulated.

So much by way of introduction. Now what says the critic? He does not detract from the honor belonging to young Rowan, but he does sneer at the New York Central road, which, through the instrumentality of General Passenger Agent Daniels, distributed nearly a million copies of the original essay for the good that they might do.

He picks out a single sentence from Hubbard's article: "It is not book-learning that young men need, nor instruction about this or that, but a stiffening of the vertebrae which will cause them to be loyal to a trust, to act promptly, to concentrate their energies, to do the thing, to carry a message to Garcia." He follows this with various dogmatic statements: "No man can concentrate his mind and energies so well as the man who has been taught to do it in our schools. No man has such stiff vertebrae as the man who knows the why of a thing. No man is so brave and fearless as an American, because he is book-learned and intelligent. No man could carry a letter to Garcia or be worthy a trust unless he be learned in the thing he undertakes."

The reader naturally wonders why our schools are so particularized in this connection. While our schools are good schools, as schools go, yet our schools, from various points of view, are conspicuous for omitting to do the very thing that is here required—namely, teaching the art of concentrating the mind and energies. Evidently the writer sees h's own literary fads or his own peculiar scholastic ideas in jeopardy, and thereupon pell mell rushes to their rescue.

However, all this occurs in the introduction and is not any part of the subject matter of the pamphlet.

Turning to that which is headed "An Idea and Its Execution," we find it to be an attack upon the employer or manager, as the case may be. He is shown to be one who demands certain things without knowing really what he wants, or stopping to explain to his subordinate that which is required. The latter necessarily fails in the execution of a commission, not by reason of his own fault, but because of the fault of the one who gave him the commission.

The picture is not overdrawn. I can indorse every word that is said, but, after all, it proves only that while there are some broad, intelligent and competent directors of subordinates, there are also many who fail in leadership. From this I infer that President McKinley stands out in the picture drawn, as one who is able to select his subordinate and properly instruct him, quite as conspicuously as Rowan in the other capacity.

Our author says: "Do not quarrel with your tools." He asserts, by way of quotation from an oft-repeated proverb, "It is a poor workman who quarrels with

his tools." Every one will admit this. But it is a far better workman who selects good tools at the outset.

The reply to "A Message to Garcia" will go thundering down the ages, not by reason of anything in it that is of importance or that by any chance can attract public attention, but simply because the author has had the presumption to put forth his ill-arranged fragments of thought under such an ambitious title. He has added nothing to knowledge or experience by his effort. He has failed to convey a lesson, but he has succeeded in making a whine heard where otherwise there would have existed only restful silence.

Of all paths a man could strike into, there is, at any given moment, a best path for every man—a thing which, here and now, it were of all things wisest for him to do; which, could he but be led or driven to do, he were then doing like a man, as we phrase it. His success, in such a case, were complete, his felicity a maximum.—Carlyle.

The Perfection Adding Machine

This ingenious device by which adding may be performed by machinery is put on the market by the Clark Manufacturing Co., 614 Race street, Cincinnati. It is made of nickel plate, and is so light and small that it can easily be carried in the pocket. The accompanying cut shows the exact size. Its manipulation is simple. Both wheels are to be set so that a cipher will appear in the open space at the top of the wheel. This is done by placing a pencil point in one of the holes and turning the wheel to the left. To add a column of figures place the pencil point in the hole of the right wheel, opposite each figure to be added,

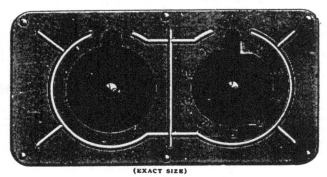

(EXACT SIZE)
The Perfection Adding Machine

and turn to the right till the figure reaches the shoulder at the top. The left wheel will record the tens and hundreds. Throw up the amount to be carried, if any, in the right wheel, throwing "0" to the top in the left one. If the machine is used as directed there can be no failure in obtaining the correct result.

Usury is the land-shark and devil-fish of commerce.—J. L. Basford.

I am amazed how men can call her (Fortune) blind, when, by the company she keeps, she seems so very discriminating.—Goldsmith.

How are the Profits of the Year to be Ascertained?

By Bernard Dale.

(Continued from page 62, April number.)

Proposition IV.

In the case of a "continuous venture," where there is a provision in the regulations for an annual division of profit, all depreciation during the current year of assets used as "fixed" capital, from wear and tear, or from waste, where the asset is of a wasting character, must be taken into account in arriving at the profits of that year.

An apparent exception to this rule occurs in the case of a venture limited solely to the working of a particular asset of a terminable nature, and not intended to be continued after that asset has been exhausted.

It is only in the case of material "fixed" capital, such as a railway, that what is known as wear and tear takes place. In the case of immaterial "fixed" capital, such as consols, held as a permanent investment, there can, strictly speaking, be no wear and tear.

The reason why wear and tear of assets used as "fixed" capital in the service of the current year should be made good before arriving at the profits of that year is, that such wear and tear represents a consumption of capital by the current year, or, as it is sometimes put, an advance from capital of the current year. This advance, with all other advances of capital, must be made good by the year receiving it before the profits for that year can be arrived at.

As to depreciation from wear and tear of a tramway see Davison vs. Gillies, infra.

In Rishton vs. Grissel, L. R., 5 Eq., p. 326, it was held that the profit and loss account in each year was rightly charged with sums representing depreciation arising from the running out of a lease.

Here, it should be pointed out, the business was entirely independent of the particular lease, and was intended to continue after that lease had run out. In order, therefore, to give effect to this intention, it was necessary, out of the annual receipts, to set aside a sum for a renewal, or, depreciation fund, so that the company might be in as good a position to go on with its business after the termination of the lease as before.

As to the exception to the rule, see Lee vs. Neuchatel Asphalte Company, infra. In that case the business of the company was solely to work a particular asset of a wasting nature, and, when that asset was exhausted, the business of the company was to come to an end, the articles expressly exonerating the company from the necessity of keeping a reserve fund. There was, therefore, no need to form a fund to enable the company to do that which, by its regulations, it had declared it had no intention of doing, namely, to carry on business after the particular asset had been exhausted.

Proposition V.

If a loss of capital arises from the loss of an asset, used as fixed capital otherwise than from wear and tear or waste in the service of the current year, such loss in the absence of any provision to the contrary in the regulations, need not be taken into account in arriving at the profits for the year.

The reason is that "profits for the year consist of the excess of the returns over the advances for the year, and when the particular year has made good the wear and tear and waste by it, of an asset used as "fixed" capital, it has restored to capital all the advances it has received from it. Hence, there is no reason why the particular year should be charged with the loss of such an asset itself, should such a loss occur during that year by accident, say, by fire or tempest.

In the case of the loss of an asset used as "circulating" capital in the ordinary course of trade, such loss must be borne by the current year, for, here, the current year has received, as part of the advances to it, not merely the right to use, but the asset itself, and, consequently, must be charged with it. Nevertheless, if the loss be of an extraordinary character, there appears to be no reason why the practice adopted by ordinary partnerships should not be followed and the loss spread over a number of years, provided it be done openly and with the sanction of the shareholders; for after all, as Sir George Jessel said in Griffith vs. Paget, 6 Ch. Div., p. 515, "These companies are commercial partnerships, and are, in the absence of express provisions, statutory or otherwise, subject to the same considerations."

In Verner vs. the General Commercial and Investment Trust, infra, an actual loss, as well as a depreciation of the value of some of the company's investments, was admitted, but the Court, having satisfied itself that the investments were made to be held permanently, and not as articles to be jobbed in, decided that such loss might be disregarded in arriving at the year's profits, at the same time intimating that if the loss had been of "circulating" capital their decision would have been different.

Proposition VI.

In the case of a venture where there is a provision in the regulations for the annual division of profit, loss of capital in a previous year need not be made good out of the receipts of the succeeding year before declaring a dividend for that year.

The reason is that "profits for a year" are the excess of the returns over the advances of the year, and that these advances in the case of a succeeding year are the value of the assets of the preceding year brought forward, less the amount of the external liabilities, which value, in the event of loss sustained in the previous year, may fall short of the value of the paid-up share capital; e. g., if a company starts with a paid-up cap-

ital of £100,000 and loses £10,000 in the first year's trading, the advances of the second year would be £90,000, and when the second year had replaced these advances, any surplus would be "profit" for the second year.

See definitions of "profit for the year," given by Sir George Jessel in Dent vs. the London Tramways Company, infra.

The proposition is opposed to the Single Account System as explained by Mr. Palmer, and to the Double Account System advocated by Mr. Buckley, Q. C., it being a cardinal feature of both these systems that the trading account, or, as Mr. Buckley terms it, the "revenue account," should be continuous, and no dividends paid until all losses on that account in previous years have been made good.

The proposition is of great importance to those companies, who, although they style themselves trust companies, are in reality nothing more than finance or stock-jobbing associations. In the case of such companies the assets being "circulating" capital, the decisions in Lee vs. Neuchatel Asphalte Company, and Verner vs. the General and Commercial Trust, Limited, do not apply, and any diminution of value of the securities held, or loss of capital, must be taken into account in arriving at the profit of the year in which such diminution or loss occurred. But—and this has too frequently been overlooked—the loss of capital need not be taken into account in arriving at the profits of subsequent years. To give an illustration: Say that on the 31st of December, 1891, one of these companies found that in consequence of the Baring crisis its investments had fallen during the year in value from £500,000 to £400,- 000, whilst the net income received on the investments during the year amounted to only £25,000. There would have been a loss for that year of £75,000, and no dividend would have been possible for that year. The capital, now reduced to £425,000, would enter at that value, as the advance for the succeeding year, and any surplus of value in the returns of the succeeding year over the £425,000, would be "profit" for that year. As these returns would include the £25,000 net income received, say, from the investments during the succeeding year, there would, on the assumption of no further fall or rise in the value of the investment during that year, be a fund of at least £25,- 000 available for dividend for the succeeding year. Indeed, if the company had issued preference shares, entitling the holders to dividends dependent upon the profits of the particular year only, there would have been no option for the company but to pay the preference dividend, and its directors might incur serious responsibilities by withholding it.

The Nimble Sixpence

The names of the different pieces of currency in use in pre-Revolutionary times still have a place in our every day language, though the coins themselves would be strange and unrecognizable to the mass of the community. Especially in the eastern portions of the United

States and those sections of the west settled by New Englanders, do phrases linger which tell of a day when the penny and the shilling, the pound and the guinea were the lawful money. The sixpence among these people is still used as indicative of a small though indefinite amount. On English soil, however, it has a fresh and ever present existence. We have no coin that is in such constant service, and so active an element in small commercial transactions.

The following remarks by a correspondent of one of the daily papers writing from London sets forth the part it plays in the daily life there in a vivid manner.

Should England ever decide upon a new coat-of-arms, let it be the lion and the unicorn rampant, holding aloft a big round penny. The present motto will answer: "God and my Right"—money, my God, and all I can get, my right. This spirit is not especially to be condemned, perhaps. With 40,000,000 people crowded into an area no larger than one of our American States, and with 20,000 persons owning all the land, the struggle for existence is terrible. Nevertheless the schemes to extract the penny are so various and unique, and they are sprung upon you so unexpectedly, as to be actually funny. In consequence you always must go about loaded down with these big, heavy copper coins, larger than our old one-cent piece which we relegated to the dark ages long ago. Several times a day you will get eleven of these in change for a shilling, and you really would have to carry a basket if they did not slip away as fast as they come. The Government could just as well put its stamp of value upon a smaller coin, but the British public would resent giving up its dear, old penny. You pay a penny for a seat in any of the parks and gardens; a penny for the use of the toilet room at all the railroad stations and restaurants; a penny for a drink of water. In fact, you will save wear and tear of patience and purse by all the time carrying a penny between your thumb and forefinger.

Americans cannot get used to the fact that this important coin is two cents instead of one. Tuppence to them seems two cents, but it really is four; thrippence is not three but six; tenpence seems a mere trifle until they reflect that it is twenty cents. The sixpence is ubiquitous; it is omnipresent; no word falls so readily from English lips. Where we say a nickel they say sixpence, which is nearly two-and-a-half times as much. I asked a shopkeeper one day why that everlasting sixpence was tacked on to everything. "Well," he said, "it sounds better; two shillings or seven shillings sounds so bald. It is much easier to say two-and-six, seven-and-six." So for the sake of euphony we pay the extra twelve cents. At the hotels they tell us the price is ten-an-six, twelve-and-six; we never can escape from the everlasting sixpence. Twenty shillings are a pound, but ten shilling are not half a pound, but half a sovereign. Then there is that exasperating coin, the half crown, two-and-six, but so little larger than the two-shilling piece that we must lay them together to see the difference. A favorite price to put upon articles is a guinea. When we ask what is a guinea we are told that there is no such coin, but it means a pound and one shilling—a pleasing variation from the extra sixpence. Twelve pence make a shilling, two shillings a florin, four shillings a double florin, five shillings a crown, two crowns a half sovereign; three columns always to add up, and, besides, there are the ha'pennies and the farthings, two of which make a ha'penny. I made this purchase yesterday—a yard and a quarter of ribbon at one shilling, thrippence ha'penny a yard. What was the bill? At the banks one must take silver or gold for all sums under five pounds ($25).

The English admit freely that their financial system is very bad, but they say, "Our money is at par all over the world, why make a change?" The silver thrippence is the same size as our diminutive three-cent piece, whose coinage was discontinued years ago. They say it is coined here for the benefit of those whose conscience will not let them put coppers into the contribution plate on Sunday, but whose generosity does not extend to a sixpence. In some churches the exact amount of the contribution, and the kind of coin, is placed on a bulletin in the vestibule. In one town, not long ago, I read, at the close of the morning service, "140 thrippence pieces."

If wealth come, beware of him, the smooth, false friend! There is treachery in his proffered hand; his tongue is eloquent to tempt; lust of many harms is lurking in his eye; he hath a hollow heart; use him cautiously.—Tupper.

Accountics:—
T... OFFICE MAGAZINE

Volume VI
Number 6

JUNE, 1900

Monthly, $1 a year
Single Copy, 10 cents'

The Application of Advanced Accounting Methods to Modern Business Enterprises

II. The Cotton Mill.

By A. O. Kittredge, F. I. A.. C. P. A.

(Concluded from page 66, May number.)

In view of this survey the accounting of a cotton mill is a problem somewhat complex in character. We have to consider not only a single phase like merchandising, but another important phase like manufacturing. Our manufacturing proposition multiplies until perhaps we have a half dozen sub-propositions to consider. If there are several mills in a group, like Mill No. 1, Mill No. 2, etc., or upper mill and lower mill, as they are frequently called, we are called upon to distinguish between the mills and to show what a given one is earning as opposed to all the others.

* * * * *

In order to make our costs correct, we must know not only what the total cost is, that is, the cost of the final product, but also what the cost is at every step or stage of manufacture.

(At this point the speaker described in considerable detail the samples of cotton manufacture displayed upon the table. They included about everything, from raw cotton to the finished product. In the course of his explanation he referred to the processes through which the cotton goes before reaching a finished stage. He pointed out that it was necessary, in the sense of correct cost accounts and for the purpose of showing the cost at all stages, to know first the cost of the raw cotton delivered to the picker; next the cost of the product when it had reached the stage called rovings; next the cost of the product in the condition of yarn, and again the cost of the product in the condition of brown or unbleached cloth. Following this he referred to the cost of bleaching, of dyeing and of imparting various finishes to the cloth. The point particularly emphasized was that the cost of each product, like roving, yarn, cloth, etc., is the material, or foundation cost, of the next stage or process.)

*Abstract of a lecture delivered before the New York Chapter of the Institute of Accounts, at the Waldorf-Astoria, March 29, 1900, by A. O. Kittredge, F. I. A., C. P. A., Editor of Accountics and President of the Account, Audit and Assuance Company, Limited.

Rovings are the raw materials for the yarn department. Rovings are frequently transferred from mill to mill, and accordingly, their cost must be known for that purpose also. In the yarn department we reach another stage. Some of the yarns produced are a commercial product. Some of the other yarns produced are either warp or fillings for the cloth that follows. The yarns produced to sell may be marketable in the shape left by the yarn department, or they may require dyeing. The yarns made for warps and fillings, in the case of a corporation operating several mills, may be transferred from mill to mill, or to any one of several weaving departments.

When we have got through with the looms and the produced cloths, then come in other processes. Some cloth is sold unbleached. Other cloths must be bleached. The bleachery is not only run for the product of our own mill, but for the accommodation of other mills. Various goods are consigned to it for bleaching. Therefore, the bleachery must be considered on an independent basis in order to show what our advantages are in manufacture.

(The speaker here dwelt at some length upon the question of profit in manufacturing. He contended that no profit could be made until goods have been sold, and that therefore the cost accounts of a factory, in whatever line, should be managed in such a way as to prove by balance. The profit should come in as a result of the commercial enterprise of the concern.)

Whatever profit there is comes when the goods are sold. How much have the goods cost? So much. How much do we get for them? So much. The difference between selling price and cost price is gross profits, assuming, of course, that we are doing business at a profit. Gross profits diminished by selling expenses or the cost of distribution, give net profits.

* * * * *

Let us consider for a moment manufacturing expenses and commercial expenses. I am sorry to say it, but in all my experience I have never encountered a manufacturing enterprise and gone through its books, either in the sense of examination or in preparation for an accounting system, where I have found throughout what seemed to me to be a proper discrimination between manufacturing expenses and selling or commercial expenses. However carefully the effort has been made to discriminate between these two, there has been a slip somewhere that has put into commercial expenses that which belongs to making, or into manufacturing expenses that which belongs to selling.

Why do we run a factory? There can be no better reason for putting money into a factory and equipping it with machinery than to make goods cheaper or better than they can be bought. If we can buy goods as cheap as we can make them and of as good quality, then we had better be spared the risk and responsibility of a factory. Here is another reason for cost accounts. We must know what our goods cost in order to contrast them with what we could buy them for.

* * * * *

This brings us back to a leading question. Where are profits made? If we have allowed the factory to show a profit, it means that the cost of our goods has been thereby so much inflated. In order to avoid deceiving ourselves, therefore, we must hold our factory product to actual cost.

* * * * *

Another point to which I would direct your attention in this connection is the relationship in manufacturing enterprises of the so-called commercial accounts and the factory accounts. I frequently find, by coming into contact with manufacturers, accountants, auditors and bookkeepers of factories, that there is in mind a complete divorce as between the office and the factory. The factory is allowed to keep its own set of books. That is, a set of books so run as to be independent and apart from the general books of the corporation. The account books of the corporation contain such accounts as Factory Property, Cash, Accounts Receivable, Accounts Payable, Notes Receivable and Notes Payable, and in many cases Manufacturing Account, together with Loss and Gain, Capital, etc. When we get to the factory, the books there are supposed to show costs, but in many cases they are restricted to so little as the pay roll and some few leading accounts with special materials.

As a broad proposition, it seems to me

there can be no division between the commercial accounts of a corporation and the factory accounts.

* * * * *

What is manufacturing? As before stated, it is only the conversion of assets. In the case under consideration, we start with raw cotton. We have as a product, cloth. What is the difference between the two? We have added labor to the cotton, and we have paid out money for the general expenses of the factory. By general expenses I mean such things as superintendence, insurance, taxes, repairs of plant, etc. What we do in manufacturing, therefore, very evidently is to change assets from one condition into another.

If, then, manufacturing is a conversion of assets or a change in the character of the assets, how much more important is it that our assets, whether commercial or manufacturing, whether in the form of materials or in any other shape, should be shown in our balance sheet! Our balance sheet must show the manufacturing accounts, not only the investment in fixed assets, like real estate, buildings, machinery, etc., but also the investment in raw cotton, in manufactured goods, and, more important than all, in that intermediate state, namely, goods in progress, representing that which occurs between raw materials on the one hand and merchantable product on the other.

* * * * *

No one will gainsay this proposition, that all the accounts that there can be in any enterprise whatsoever are embraced in two classes, namely, those that belong in the balance sheet and those that belong in the profit and loss statement. The balance sheet in turn can contain only two classes of accounts, namely, assets and liabilities. By our favorite interpretation of accounting, the assets exactly balance the liabilities, because we make the business liable for the capital. Our capital, whether it be the amount originally paid in, or that which has been added to it, in the sense of accrued profits, is a liability of the business as we make up our balance sheets.

All the accounts in the profit and loss statement are comprised in two groups, namely, the expenses and the revenues, or income, or earnings, whichever you please to call them.

* * * * *

There can be very little difference in opinion between us as to what the assets of a cotton mill are. Cash, Accounts Receivable, Real Estate, Machinery, Tenement Property and items of that sort may be at once passed by, because no one would ever think of these things as anything else but assets. We are all agreed, likewise, that materials on hand are certainly an asset, but how about goods in process?

If we are going to have a perpetual balance sheet, we must know just how much material we have got on hand at every period, how much is in process of manufacture and also what we have got on hand in the shape of finished product.

Goods in process is an asset. It is not sufficient for our purpose to charge raw cotton into Materials Account. Materials Account may be debited with it, but only so much as goes into the factory is used, and therefore Materials Account should be credited with what it gives up. It should always show by its balance what is on hand.

Charging our factory with the materials that go into it, charging it with manufacturing expenses, charging it with labor, and in turn crediting it with the product that is turned out from time to time, taken at actual cost, there will always be left a balance which represents the goods in process. Apply this principle, if you please, to every one of the several departments that have been maintained. In our balance sheet all may be condensed into a single account, or the accounts may be as numerous as the departments.

(By means of an analytical chart here displayed, the speaker illustrated the different groups of accounts necessary to maintain in a cotton mill, and also specifically described many of the individual accounts, always referring to the classification scheme underlying the chart and indicating how the going balance sheet and going profit and loss statement were thereby sustained.)

Perhaps by what has preceded, I have developed the thought in your minds that the accounting of a cotton mill is a large undertaking, a complex problem, a scheme difficult to work out and involving rules difficult to convey to those who are apt to be put in charge of the system. This would seem to be a fair conclusion, and yet, permit me to say that by the plans which my company by long practice has learned to employ, all this becomes much simpler than it appears. The erection of a modern building is a complex problem. Foundations, walls and floors, plumbing, heating, ventilation and lighting, decorations, signal bells, roof, etc., all these are intricate from the standpoint of the layman. But an architect knows how to write the specification, and a builder knows how to follow directions. We are applying that same plan to cotton mill accounting and to accounting in various other directions.

(The address was brought to a conclusion by a reference to the much-abused merchandise account and the exhibition of a complete specification of a cotton mill installation, illustrated by blanks and forms. Following the address, there was a brief discussion in which various members took part. After adjournment the larger part of the audience lingered for the purpose of getting a nearer view of the specification, the blanks and forms which were shown and other features of the exhibit.)

The Work of the Assay Commission

That the fitness and weight of the coin of the United States may be kept at the standard required by law, the President appoints a commission to examine and report upon every coinage. This com-mission consists of the Judge of the Eastern District of Pennsylvania, the Comptroller of the Currency and the Assayer of the Assay Office in New York ex-officio, with usually fifteen other persons selected by the Director of the Mint, representing the President. The mints of the United States, which are located at Philadelphia, San Francisco, New Orleans and Carson City, are obliged to take from each coinage one assay piece for each one thousand pieces or fractional part of one thousand pieces, if of gold, and one for each two thousand pieces or fractional part thereof, if of silver, and send them under seal quarterly to the mint at Philadelphia. Here they are carefully preserved till the commission meets on the second Tuesday of February. The samples are then submitted to a rigid examination by weight and assay, and a report of the result is signed by every member of the commission. It is esteemed a high honor among scientific men to be appointed on this commission, and some of our ablest chemists have acted in this capacity.

Durability of Paper

Will we be able fifty years from now to read the books and papers that are being printed to-day? is a question that is often asked by those interested in their preservation. The enormous quantity of paper called for to keep the printing presses in operation, and to meet the demands of commerce, has necessitated the use of some other materials than those formerly employed. The rag man and refuse from manufacture once furnished the larger part of the supply. Now the paper mills are devastating whole forests and turning them into pulp. The durability of paper manufactured from this is not equal to that made after the old methods. The British Society for the Encouragement of Arts, Industry and Commerce has had investigation made, and published a report in which the deterioration has been divided into two classes—disaggregation and alteration of color. The first is by far the most vital, and while all papers are subject to it, due largely to a chemical change in the fibres, that which is designed to last as long as possible should contain at least 70 per cent. of cotton, hemp or linen.

A New Coin

There has been a disposition of late on the part of the community to count not only cents but the half cents. This half cent, which is alluringly ' eld out as an inducement to trade, the buyer has learned by experience, works to the advantage of the seller. The Treasury Department has appreciated for some time that it may be expedient to turn out of the mints a coin of this denomination, and a bill has been prepared to authorize it. Should Congress determine upon such a measure, it would not be an innovation, for half-cent pieces were once issued by the Government. They are not familiar to the present generation, however, for they went out of use about fifty years ago.

What the Credit Men Are Doing

BY A. O. KITTREDGE.

The Convention of the National Association of Credit Men, held at Milwaukee on the 12th, 13th and 14th of June, was not only the most largely attended in the history of the association, but much business of an important nature was transacted. Every part of the country was represented, and the benefit resulting from thus bringing together prominent business men from different sections of the country was greatly appreciated by all those who were so fortunate as to be present. Secretary Prendergast, in speaking of the convention, says:

"It was a remarkably enthusiastic meeting, the delegates on different occasions giving vent to their feelings in rousing cheers. All the business of the convention was transacted with unusual dispatch. Among the most important matters were the Bankruptcy law and amendments thereto, the plans for the investigation and prosecution of fraudulent failures, and credit department methods. It is a gratifying and significant fact that the delegates at this convention were unanimously in favor of a national bankruptcy law, proving beyond a doubt that their belief in the necessity for a national bankruptcy law has not been undermined or shaken by adverse criticisms of the present statute. It is admitted that the national law now in force is faulty, but credit men believe that its defects can be eliminated and its efficacy materially strengthened by proper amendments, and that the interests of both debtor and creditor can best be served by such a national law. With regard to the plans for the investigation and prosecution of fraudulent failures, the scheme, as worked out by the committee in charge of the matter, not only received the unqualified support of the convention, but the directors of the association were instructed to do all in their power to secure the necessary funds for establishing and operating the proposed bureau. As the plan has now been indorsed by the entire association in convention, every effort will be made to start the bureau at the earliest possible moment. Committees will be appointed in different sections throughout the country, and as soon as the necessary funds are subscribed the bureau, the headquarters of which will be at the office of the national secretary, will be put into active operation. Another matter brought up at the convention which is particularly important was the report of the Committee on Credit Department Methods, and the resolution passed by the convention to the effect that a thorough investigation should be made of every application for credit, as to the practice of the applicant in regard to taking an annual inventory to the end that his fire insurance may not be invalidated by his failure to do so, and the extension of the credit fully protected in this respect."

More than 100 members and friends of the New York Credit Men's Association assembled at the regular dinner and meeting in the rooms of the Wool Club on the evening of May 24. President A. H. Watson introduced as the first speaker L. O. Koven, who discussed the right of the association to send out debtor lists. He cited a recent decision of Judge Davy of the Munroe County Supreme Court, in a controversy over the amount the plaintiff was owing for goods purchased, in which the Court said:

"Merchants have an interest in knowing, and have a right to know, the character of their dealers and those who propose to deal with them, and of those upon whose standing and responsibility they, in the course of their business, have occasion to reply. As a necessary consequence, they make inquiries of other merchants or other persons who may have information, and if such merchants or other persons in good faith communicate the information which they have, the communication is privileged.

"It is a general rule that confidential communications respecting the character and financial standing of another made to one who is interested in the communication, or desires the information as a guide to himself in the conduct of his own affairs and dealings with such other, are privileged, and are not actionable unless there be proof of express malice. * * * The extraordinary development and growth of commercial enterprise within the past few years and the distribution of our vast products of industry in every part of the world have made it necessary for merchants and manufacturers to organize for the protection of each other in their business."

Jacob H. Schaeffer took an opposite view, and Charles Biggs, indorsing the first speaker, closed the discussion. The success of the meeting was due, in a large measure, to the efforts of its efficient secretary, H. J. Sayres.

The Baltimore Credit Men's Association has obtained from the Maryland Legislature a new charter, which gives the organization enlarged powers and enables it to do the work of reciprocal reporting and investigation and prosecution which under the old form of social organization it could not do. The recent additions to the membership indicate that the usefulness of the association is being appreciated by the business men of the city.

The Detroit Credit Men's Association met at Hotel Cadillac on May 28. About seventy members and ladies indicated their interest in the association by their presence. President Hall, in opening the meeting, called attention to the fact that the Membership Committee, under the leadership of its very efficient chairman, George R. Pulfer, had succeeded in adding thirty new members within ten days. A musical programme occupied a part of the evening, and the Rev. S. S. Marquis of St. Joseph's Memorial Episcopal Church gave a very witty and pertinent address on "Credit," which was thoroughly enjoyed. D. C. Delamater read a paper on "What Can Credit Men Do?" full of good points, and W. C. Sprague gave a brief history of the Credit Men's Association, and showed how much had been accomplished in four years. The delegates to the Milwaukee Convention were elected as follows: Philo E. Hall, George B. Pulfer, O. R. Baldwin and O. C. Lake. Alternates, D. C. Delamater, J. J. Smith, H. B. Gillespie and Edw. Bland. Walter S. Campbell, the Secretary, was authorized to attend the meeting of the Presidents and Secretaries of local organizations, to be held during the convention.

A local organization of Credit Men was effected in San Francisco on May 15. The association begins its work with a membership of seventy-five and the following officers: M. Feintuch of the Wertheimer Co., President; S. W. Fuller of Heywood Bros. & Wakefield Co., first Vice-President; G. Brenner of the Brenner-Ulman Co., Second Vice-President; C. J. Lutgen of J. A. Folger & Co., Treasurer; Arthur Bray, Secretary. The Board of Directors is composed as follows: T. J. Parsons, Del Monte Milling Co.; J. J. Schutz, Haas Bros.; M. Feintuch, the Wertheimer Co.; G. Brenner, L. & G. Brenner; S. W. Fuller, Heywood Bros. & Wakefield Co.; C. L. Bonestell, Bonestell & Co.; Ferdinand Frohman, California Wine Association; W. C. McCloskey, Hiller, Sloss & Scott; C. J. Lutgen, J. A. Folger & Co.; D. A. Hulse, Hulse, Bradfold & Co.; H. P. Capell, Brandenstein & Co.; G. L. Cunningham, American Steel & Wire Co.; G. C. Nevin, Nathan, Dohrmann & Co.; F. B. Nelson, the Dairymen's Union.

At the monthly meeting of the St. Paul Credit Men's Association, held at the Minnesota Club May 25, the business session was preceded by the usual informal dinner. E. A. Young and A. J. Galbraith, as members of a special committee to propose amendments to the bankruptcy law, made a verbal report, pointing out deficiencies in the law and reviewing several amendments that had been suggested. An interesting discussion followed, which showed that the prevailing sentiment was that the present law had many faults, and, in view of some recent decisions of the courts, was a very undesirable statute. The reciprocal reporting system recently adopted by the association also came up for consideration, and received hearty commendation. The plan for raising a trust fund of $10,000 for the Investment and Prosecution Committee was approved, and a committee appointed to aid in raising the fund. The year has been a prosperous one for the association, and there is a general feeling of enthusiasm and hopefulness for the coming year.

We make our fortunes, and we call them "fate."—Beaconsfield.

The Monthly Statement

For many years the only opportunity for education in what belonged distinctively to business was afforded by the commercial and business colleges or schools. The instruction given in these, while in some cases good of its kind, was of the most rudimentary character. As the commerce and manufacture of our country have increased, the need of broader training has forced itself upon the attention of practical men. Much has been said and written upon the subject, and as a result institutions devoted to higher culture are making provision in their courses of study to meet the situation.

*

The New York Chamber of Commerce has resolved to unite with the Columbia University in the establishment of a four years' collegiate course, to be open to students of the grade of high-school graduates. Dartmouth College has made the preliminary announcement of a scheme of work preparatory to a business life. President Angell of the University of Michigan, a short time ago took the initiatory steps which have resulted in the establishment of courses in diplomatic and consular education, higher commercial education and instruction in public administration. Lectures in commercial law have been arranged in the law department as part of the same plan. The University of Wisconsin announces a School of Commerce, designed to furnish facilities for the training of young men who desire to enter business careers in the fields of domestic or foreign commerce, banking and branches of the public service. The University of California, in addition to a general business training, intends to give especial attention to the commercial relations between this country and Asia. There is hardly a school of prominence which does not at present offer instruction bearing more or less directly upon business of a public or private character. So much having been accomplished in the last few years, the outlook for thorough and efficient work along these lines in our educational institutions is most hopeful.

*

That in which our readers will be more interested than in any other is the effort which has been made recently by the New York State Society of Certified Public Accountants to secure a university course in accounting which will directly qualify for the C. P. A. degree conferred by the regents of the University of the State of New York. Two different plans have been under consideration. One anticipates the co-operation with the Chamber of Commerce of the City of New York and the Columbia University in a course in accounting which would cover four years' work and be eminently desirable for those who could devote so much time to it. The second plan has for its object a night course of two years, and in this the co-operation of the University of the City of New York has been secured. A tentative agreement has been reached and preparations are in active progress. The work will be confined to accounting, finance, commercial economics and commercial law. Instruction will be given both in classes and on the lecture plan. The professorships will be held by prominent certified public accountants. Negotiations, at the date of this writing, have so far advanced that the hope is entertained by those immediately connected with the effort that the course can be begun with the approaching fall term.

*

The political policy which recognizes the importance of the extension of markets and the advantages of close relations with foreign dependencies is leading the French government to open a colonial institute in Marseilles to prepare young men to fill positions in the French colonies. Instruction will be given in botany, zoology, natural history, colonial geography and history, which will be aided by a museum of plants and animals belonging to the colonies, and the expense of expeditions of the students will be borne by the state. Commercial houses will receive information of the results obtained so that they may be kept in touch with their markets.

*

Belgium has also undertaken the work of colonial training. At the Horticultural School at Vilvorde a special department has been established for the instruction of students who intend to find homes in the colonies. The necessity of some such opportunity for the young man preparing to take up a residence in the new lands now connected so closely with the United States will be realized by commercial houses looking for a representative in these countries. A knowledge of the language, habits and customs of the natives, the climate and physical geography, becomes invaluable to a man when he seeks to push the interests of his firm, either in dealing with the population or advising the home office as to the best manner to meet or create demands.

The Language Universal

Commerce has proven the greatest unifier of the human family, not excepting those primal forces, the religious and the governmental. This is particularly exemplified by its ability to carry with it and establish the language of the trading nation. A people dominant in the commercial sense wields a power which reaches beyond the confines of its own government, strikes into the everyday life of the nations with which it deals, and compels the recognition and adoption of a manner of expression which shall be understood by it. Attempts to establish arbitrarily a language which shall be common to the members of different races have been limited and artificial, and answered but a narrow purpose.

The Church felt her need of intercommunication, and the Latin tongue was made the medium in which her scholars and dignitaries could find a common expression, but at a recent convocation of the Catholic priesthood, gathered from all quarters of the globe, it was found that each man pronounced his Latin after a manner peculiar to his mother country, and was well nigh incomprehensible to his brothers.

The state wanted a medium in which the relations between the nations could be adjusted, and for centuries French was the language of diplomacy and of the circumscribed circle around the throne.

The great mass of the people who bought and sold, built ships and sailed the seas must have some speech recognizable by high and low, the capitalist and the laborer, the official and the sailor from foreign parts.

Some scholars came forward and suggested an artificial arrangement which was to supersede all existing tongues and be the medium for church, state and commerce, and to this world's language they gave the name of Volapük. The idea was so visionary that it met with no favor from practical men in any walk in life, and passed into a deserved oblivion.

Natural laws, which override the futile attempts of man in a contrary direction, are working out the solution of the difficulty. The language of those who are most active in carrying on commercial intercourse between the different parts of the world is becoming the medium in which business between the inhabitants of countries foreign to each other can be carried on. There is no people so persistent in pushing commercial enterprise into every part of the two hemispheres as the English speaking people. The words in which they conduct their business force themselves, from the very nature of the case, into use. Travelers find that even among savages of different tribes enough of English has been acquired to form a common speech in which they can make themselves understood. French officials in far-off lands speak it more or less, and are compelled to learn it in order to perform the duties of their position and conduct the business which foreign ships bring to their ports.

The matter came up for discussion at the International Commercial Congress, held in Philadelphia. Among the speakers was the Chinese Minister, who dwelt at some length on the confusion of tongues in the commercial world, and suggested that the body assembled should assume the duty of designating one that could be made common to all. The fact that the representative of a sovereign who counted a quarter of the globe's population as subjects had found it necessary to acquire the language in which he addressed his audience was another illustration of the aggressive power of English.

The two closely-knit Anglo-Saxon nations, England, with a firm grasp upon Southern Asia and the North and South of Africa, and the United States, controlling the richest portions of America and reaching out across the Pacific Ocean, encircle the globe, and hold between them the mastery of the commercial world. There can be no doubt in the mind of any thoughtful man that the language of these peoples is to be the language in which the business of the world will be transacted.

Internal reasons exist which adapt it to a world-wide popularity. It is not the speech of a solitary nation; it is a growth, an assimilation of various elements. Many people have helped to make it, contributing that which was most vigorous in their mother tongue. The ancient Latins gave of their strength and the modern French of their finish, and the Teuton added force. It gathered grace and usefulness from every country with which it came in contact, and now, holding within itself a power of expression suited to the wants of every land and every situation, it is ready for the great work it has been preparing through the centuries, and, following the law of the survival of the fittest, will take its place as the language universal.

What We Hear in the Telephone

The bell rings, and we go to the telephone. "Hello!" calls a voice we recognize. "Hello, John!" we respond, and the familiar tones come back to us over the wire so distinctly that we catch all the little inflections and peculiarities which characterize the speech of our friend. Yet here comes an electrician and tells us that it is not John's voice we are listening to, but an imitation of it, a sort of sound writing. We will let him give his explanation in his own words. "It is very hard," he says, "to realize that the voice one hears over the telephone is not the voice of the person who is speaking. It seems exactly like the real tones, drawn out thin and small and carried from a long distance by some mechanical means, but it is not. When one speaks into the instrument, a little diaphragm, like a drum-head, begins to vibrate, and each vibration sends a wave of electricity over the wire. These waves set up a mimic vibration in another diaphragm at the opposite end, which jars the air and produces an imitation of the original voice. That's not a very scientific explanation, but it's accurate. The autograph-telegraph, which makes a facsimile of handwriting, is a fair parallel. You write your message with a pen, attached to a special electric apparatus, and a little ink siphon at the other end of the line exactly imitates every dot and curve. The result seems like the real thing, but is merely a first-class counterfeit. It's the same way exactly with the voice in the 'phone."

Reviews and Criticisms

Corporation Accounting

Corporation Accounting and Corporation Law. A complete exposition of the science of corporation accounting, both in theory and practice, with a digest of the corporation laws of all the States. By J. J. Rahill. Large octavo, 200 pages, bound in cloth. Published by the author. Price, $2.00.

Every work on corporation accounting or corporation law, of necessity, reflects more or less of the environment of the author. It is not surprising, therefore, to find in the book before us special reference made to the laws of California, because the author's home happens to be at Fresno, in that State. A California corporation, a New York corporation, a Pennsylvania corporation and a New Jersey corporation are no doubt in many respects identical, and yet the method of organization and management, the laws under which they are formed and various other features differ materially in the several States named.

The author states in his preface that the compilation which follows took only four months to prepare, and that the work was performed chiefly at night. Perhaps if he had taken a higher standpoint from which to view the general subjects of corporation accounting and corporation law, it would have taken somewhat longer time to prepare the manuscript, and further that the work would not have all been done at night. And yet this is not intended as an adverse criticism of the book in itself. There are many excellent features about it, and the author is evidently clearheaded in his definitions and statements in general.

"Stock Exchanges" is the title of a special chapter in the work, and is introduced, as we are informed, because stock exchanges are so interwoven with stock companies that they necessarily form a part of the general subject under discussion. The latter part of the work embraces a digest of the corporation laws of the various States and Territories throughout the Union. This digest, unfortunately, is not dated, and therefore the reader will be at a loss in the near future to know whether the laws referred to are at present on the statute book or have been amended or repealed. The abstract, however, is so thorough—that is, the statements are reduced to such a small compass—that there is less danger in this regard than would have existed had the author gone more into details and minutæ. For example, just eight lines are devoted to the corporation laws of Ohio. The eight lines constitute a sentence setting forth that there is a liability of stockholders in the State named to an amount equal to the stock owned by them, or, as it is very commonly expressed, a double liability exists. That is all there is on Ohio corporations. Nearly a page is devoted to New

Jersey, and about a half page to New York.

The author has succeeded in presenting his ideas on accounting, so far as they relate to corporations, on a plan more satisfactory to the general reader than that which is generally followed in the text books on bookkeeping. The forms of the general books are presented with sufficient entries to illustrate their purpose. Columnarization is used in journal, cash book, etc. The ledger forms are shown upon advanced lines, and altogether the work is one which the average accountant will examine with interest and satisfaction, even though he does not find anything decidedly new in it. As before mentioned, the text holds to the usages which obtain in California, and therefore is less instructive to the general reader than would otherwise be the case.

Professional Education

Professional Education, being No. 10 of Monographs on the United States, edited by Nicholas Murray Butler, Professor of Philosophy and Education in Columbia University, New York. By James Russell Parsons, Jr., Director of the College and High School Departments, University of the State of New York.

This pamphlet is one of a series of nineteen prepared by the Department of Education for the United States Commission to the Paris Exposition of 1900. It is one of several that were contributed to the United States educational exhibit by the State of New York. The author says in his preface that the object in view has been to show the development of professional education in the United States, from colonial times to the present year. The several professions considered are theology, law, medicine, dentistry, pharmacy and veterinary medicine. The statistics are tabulated, and are also shown graphically. With nine professional schools only in this country in the period prior to 1800, with thirty-five established in the first quarter of the century, sixty in the second quarter of the century, 146 in the third quarter, and 283 in the last quarter, gives a total at the present date of 533. Of this considerable number 165 are devoted to theology, 87 to law, 156 to medicine, 56 to dentistry, 52 to pharmacy, while 17 are veterinary in character. Two hundred and eighty-six of these schools reported in 1898 property amounting to nearly $50,000,000, of which one-third was located in the State of New York. Two hundred and sixty-two of them reported receipts exceeding $5,000,000 annually, and of this amount 31 per cent. was in New York, from which it will appear that the Empire State holds no mean position in this regard. Comparative statistics show that in matter of students the State of Illinois ranks first, having 7,231 students in professional schools in the year 1899. New York reported 6,777, Pennsylvania 5,988, while Missouri, Ohio and Massachusetts each reported over 3,000, Maryland, Tennessee and Michigan each over 2,000, Kentucky, District of Columbia, Iowa, California, Indiana, Minnesota and Virginia each over 1,000. Thirty-eight States and Territories have professional schools, and the total number of students attending all of them is reported at 55,669. The above are only samples of the very interesting contents of this work.

Packard's Bank Bookkeeping

In the November issue of ACCOUNTICS we presented a brief review of "Packard's Bank Bookkeeping," and in the notice mentioned the names of some of those who were associated in the work with Mr. Packard, in compiling and preparing the manuscript for this volume. Inadvertently we omitted the name of Edgar M. Barber, to whom the author gave credit for important assistance in the detail presentment of the matter. We very much regret this omission, for it was in nowise an intentional slight upon Mr. Barber.

In a letter received a short time since, Mr. Barber, who was formerly a teacher in the Packard school, calls attention to this omission, and presents certain statements, to which we are glad to give space in this connection, since they indicate in an authoritative way the scope of the work and the effort that was put forth in its preparation. Mr. Barber says:

"I made a careful study of all American commercial school text books, including Williams & Rogers', Powers', Musselman's, Goodyear's, Sadler & Rowe's, Bryant's, the Practical Text Book Company's, and several others. I decided that the plan of those works was not adapted to the needs of a great metropolitan school, whose students were to go directly into the largest banks of this city. I spent nearly a year thereafter mastering banking and familiarizing myself with the best text works on bank accounting published in this country and in England. With that kind of foundation I entered the Fourth National Bank and actually worked through every department. A similar plan was pursued at the National Union, Chase National, the Second National, the State, the Fifth Avenue and the Standard National Banks. * * *

"The old idea of commercial text-book authorship was that the author should imagine how business was done and evolve from his inner consciousness a theoretical scheme of instruction. It seems to be more sane for the author to find out first how business is done and then confine the authorship to the actual facts. It is one thing to speculate as to how bank bookkeeping ought to be done, but it is an intensely more vital thing for the student in this day and age to know how bank bookkeeping is done. The principles upon which bank accounting is based do not differ from the principles upon which sound accounting

is based generally, and these principles students thoroughly understand before they begin the study of bank accounting."

From these statements the reader will perceive that the point of view of this author in the preparation of the book and the point of view from which our criticism of it proceeded are radically different. The object of the first was to produce a text book generally acceptable in the schools. On the other hand we pointed out wherein certain things contained in the book are at variance from good accounting principles. If it is to be inferred that this writer urges the practice of certain banks as justification for what the book contains, then our reply is that even the banks may be wrong, and that this author, as well as others in the past, has missed an opportunity which might have been improved. As a fact, bank accounting is not without its blemishes and defects. As practiced, it does not approximate the ideal by a very large majority. While it may be sufficient for compilers of text books to stop when they have reflected actual practice, it is not enough for the accounting critic to know that current practice has been described so long as it is evident that the practice indicated is not in strict harmony with the best interpretation of principles.

Mr. Barber's letter to us is accompanied by testimonials and extracts from articles in different papers, referring to his technical standing and the reputation in which he is held by his associates in the business educational world, all of which are eminently satisfactory.

Compulsory Honesty

A belief in the honesty of mankind is a fundamental principle without which the transaction of business would be impossible. Watchfulness to guard against the mistakes and dishonesty of the few is a safeguard which every careful man will take in the conduct of his affairs. The means which will best subserve that end are important considerations to thoughtful business men.

A short time since several questions were submitted to Charles W. Haskins, President of the Board of Examiners of Public Accountants, appointed by the Regents of the University of the State of New York, with a view to obtaining his opinion on the subject of compulsory honesty. That the readers of ACCOUNTICS may have the benefit of such opinion, based as it is on a long experience in a line of business affording unusual opportunities for the observation of the effect of checks and guards against peculations and embezzlements, we publish these questions together with Mr. Haskins' answers.

Question 1. What methods have you found most effective in preventing the misappropriation of money among trusted employees?

Answer. The adoption of the most approved modern methods of accounting and bookkeeping.

Also, periodical, independent audits of

the accounts by certified public accountants of character and standing.

Q. (2) Is the average cashier and bookkeeper a man of absolute integrity, or is he prevented from stealing by fear of exposure or the sacrifice of his bond?

A. The average cashier and bookkeeper is undoubtedly selected after a thorough investigation of his character, and our opinion is that he is, on the average, a man of integrity. The causes of defalcation or dishonesty are usually traced to some particular temptation to which the man has been exposed or from a pressure of circumstances peculiar to his case, and these have usually been the cause of his act rather than an inherent dishonesty.

Q. (3) Does the periodical examination of a firm's books by an expert accountant, called in for the purpose, act as a beneficial check upon men who might otherwise pilfer?

A. Yes, undoubtedly. A proper examination by independent auditors is bound to discover any irregularity, and as this is known to clerks or officials, it must act as a moral check upon any dishonest purposes.

Q. (4) Have you found, in your experience, that most men are to be trusted without recourse to any kind of preventive or detective aids?

A. We think that the majority of men are honest, but we are not familiar with cases where men are intrusted with responsibility without any checks. Whatever the opinion might be of the owners of a corporation or business, it is extremely unwise to place any more reliability upon the honesty of men than can be avoided.

Q. (5) How would you advise a young man holding a position of trust to conduct himself so as to win the utmost confidence of his employer?

A. To be modest, energetic, zealous in the service of his employer, and at all times to work for the interest of such employer rather than to be too eager for his own advancement.

Q. (6) Will you kindly cite some instance (without the use of names, of course), in which a defalcation or an embezzlement, large or small, was prevented by a good system of "keeping tabs" on an employee?

A. We know of no case in which a defalcation or embezzlement has been prevented by a good system of "keeping tabs," as it necessarily could not be known until the defalcation had taken place. As an instance, however, of the discovery of irregularities by an independent audit, we refer to the case of the Atlanta & West Point Railroad and the Western Railway of Alabama. The auditor of these roads had been in collusion with certain of the agents, and had been covering up his defalcations during a period of six or seven years. The quarterly audit of these accounts, which was instituted in the month of October, 1899, brought to light these irregularities, and the auditor was shown to have been able to manipulate the accounts so that the company had lost from $40,000 to $45,000.

Accountics

The Office Magazine.

Published Monthly.

A. O. KITTREDGE. F. I. A., C. P. A., Editor.

E. R. KITTREDGE, Associate.

Accountics is devoted to the Science of Accounting, to the Art of Bookkeeping and to the advocacy of Improved Office Methods.

Subscription.—One dollar a year, payable in advance.

Postage is prepaid by the publishers in the United States, Canada and Mexico. For all other countries in the Postal Union, subscribers must add 50 cents a year.

Discontinuances.—In the absence of specific orders to discontinue at the end of the subscription term the magazine will be continued and a bill sent.

Remittances should be by Draft, P. O. Order or Express Order, payable to the order of the Accountics Association. Money and postage stamps are at the risk of the sender, unless sent by express or in registered letters. Add 10 cents each to checks on local banks to defray collection charges.

Advertising Rates will be quoted on application.

Official Journal.—This publication, by resolutions duly passed, has been made the official publication of the following organizations:—

The Institute of Accounts.
The New York Chapter of the Institute of Accounts.
The Washington Chapter of the Institute of Accounts.
The Hartford Chapter of the Institute of Accounts.

Accountics is the accredited medium of intercommunication between members of the Institute of Accounts wherever located.

ACCOUNTICS ASSOCIATION, Publishers,

Lancashire Building, Pine Street, near Nassau, New York.

Copyright 1900 by the Accountics Association.
Entered at the Post Office New York as Second Class Matter.

Publishers' Desk

The Association of American Advertisers, with general office at 18-29 Park Row Building, New York City, are out with a very attractively printed and nicely illustrated circular on the post-dollar bill constructed on the post-check money bill was introduced to the Senate by Senator MacMillan of Michigan, and to the House of Representatives by Representative Lentz of Ohio, in March last. The title of the bill is as follows: "A Bill to Prevent Robbing of the Mail, to Provide a Safer and Easier Method of Sending Money by Mail, and to Increase the Postal Revenue." The cover pages of the pamphlet before us illustrate a two-dollar bill constructed on the post check plan, and also a fifty-cent piece (fractional currency). The illustration inside of the book also refers to the fifty-cent piece. The essence of the scheme is that the bills and pieces of fractional currency shall be payable to bearer until such time as there is a name inserted in the face of the bill with an address. Whenever a payee has been thus nominated the currency becomes payable only to his order, and the postal check, as it is called, is then bankable in the usual way. The advantages of this scheme, which we have previously alluded to in these columns, are numerous. It would save the necessity of going to the post office or express office for a money order, for one who desired to remit a small sum would only have to go to his own pocketbook or money drawer and select such a bill or bills as would answer the purpose. He would then insert the name and inclose it in his letter. Making the post-check payable to the person nominated renders it entirely safe for transmission through the mail. A letter which the Association

of American Advertisers sent out with this pamphlet alludes to some of the advantages which would follow upon the use of this device, and asserts that it would greatly increase the mail-order business throughout the country.

———

We are indebted to P. Moutier of Rue Pillore 15, Rouen, France, for a copy of his pamphlet entitled, "Theorie Algebrique de la Comptabilitie," in other words, the "Algebraic Theory of Accounting." This little work seems to be the first number of a series of essays on the fundamental principles of double-entry bookkeeping. A casual examination of the work will lead to the thought that while perhaps it is less involved and much briefer in its presentation than anything that has appeared in the way of logismography, still there is a resemblance between it and the treatment usually accorded the latter topic. The fact that there has been no American translation limits the usefulness of this work to those who are able to study it in French.

———

The city of Boston has been making an investigation of its books to ascertain the amount of worthless bills it is carrying. Harvey S. Chase, Secretary of the Massachusetts Society of Public Accountants, was appointed Examiner, and he found that bills amounting to nearly $2,000,000 were of no value, and could not be collected. Upon receipt of the Mayor's message, which accompanied Mr. Chase's report, the Board of Aldermen ordered that the City Collector be authorized to cancel the bills considered by him uncollectible.

———

Blotting paper, now an indispensable adjunct of every writing desk, is a commodity general use of which does not date far back in the past. When it first appeared in small quantities it was made to serve a long while before it reached the waste basket. So completely has it superseded the sand-box, which once held a place by the side of the ink-stand, that that article has come to be valued as a curiosity. It was made something like a pepper box, with a concave instead of a convex cover, so that the sand, after being shaken over the writing, could be poured back upon the cover and fall through the perforations into the box again. The vicinity of Lake George furnished the sand, which was fine, black and of uniform grain. The gathering and preparation of this for market was the means of livelihood of a considerable number of people.

———

The Remington typewriter gets some free advertising in the following story which we clip from an exchange:
As Frederic Remington, the artist, who lives in New Rochelle, stepped from his train in the Grand Central Station one morning a thin man, with an alert expression, who was standing near the waiting room saw a fat, red-faced man from Chicago, caught sight of him.
"Hello," he said, "there's Frederic Remington."
"Where?" asked the Chicago man, with great interest.
"There he comes, the big fellow. Would you like to meet him?"
"You can gamble on it that I would," said the Chicago man. "I don't know a citizen of your town that I would rather meet than Remington."
"I didn't know that you cared for his work, but I will be glad to introduce you."
"Care for it!" exclaimed the Chicago man. "It's the best thing in the market."
The thin man greeted Mr. Remington

as an old acquaintance, and then presented the Chicago man as a great admirer of his work.
"Indeed I am, Mr. Remington. I am proud to meet you. Remington is a household word with us," said the Chicago man.
"Indeed," said Mr. Remington, looking as any modest man might at such a tribute from the West.
"It is, for a fact," said the Chicago man, "and when I tell my wife that I have met Frederic Remington she will want to know all about you. She was my stenographer before we were married, and she used only your typewriter. I wouldn't have any other machine in the factory, and"—
Mr. Remington walked away abruptly, and the thin man gasped and then explained to the Chicago man.
"Artist, did you say?" asked the latter. "Why, I thought he invented the typewriter. Now, isn't that enough to freeze your feet?"

———

It requires as much talent to spend as to make.—Whipple.

———

Poverty treads close upon the heels of great and unexpected wealth.—Rivarol.

———

Sovereign money procures a wife with a large fortune, gets a man credit, creates friends, stands in place of pedigree, and even of beauty.—Horace.

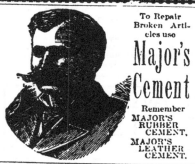

Accountants' Associations

Convention of the Institute of Accounts

The fourth annual convention of the Institute of Accounts was held at Morrello's, New York, Thursday evening, June 7. Delegates were present in person and by proxy from the Washington Chapter, the Hartford Chapter and the New York Chapter. The principal business was the election of officers and the choice of members to fill vacancies occurring in the Executive Council. John R. Loomis, accountant of the International Paper Co., was elected President, and Charles Dutton was re-elected Secretary and Treasurer.

The following were chosen to fill vacancies in the Executive Council occurring by reason of expiration of terms: George Soule, New Orleans; Charles W. Rohne, Hartford; Thomas S. Whitbeck, New York; Samuel D. Patterson, New York.

At the conclusion of the convention the delegates were entertained by the New York Chapter of the Institute of Accounts. After a very satisfactory dinner had been disposed of, short addresses were made.

Charles W. Haskins, Fellow of the Institute of Accounts and President of the New York State Society of Certified Public Accountants, gave some account of his recent trip abroad, in which he visited London, where he was the guest of the Institute of Chartered Accountants. His journey was also continued up the Mediterranean. He interested his audience with accounts of the business customs of the Orient, and entertained them with apt quotations from the Koran bearing upon accounting matters.

W. P. Plant acted as toastmaster, and in succession called upon nearly all the members and guests present for remarks. Henry R. Hovey, President of the Hartford Chapter, gave interesting particulars concerning the purpose of that Chapter. Leon Brummer, Secretary of the New York State Society of Certified Public Accountants, gave expression to the good will existing between the several organizations in the accounting field, and called attention to the initials of F. I. A., saying that they stood for "Foremost in Affiliation." Samuel D. Patterson entertained the company with a song in place of a speech. His skill as a vocalist was greatly admired and heartily applauded. Addresses were also made by Messrs. Child, Dutton, Kittredge, Vedder, French, Selis, Althers, Whitbeck, Sargent, Glardon and others. It was at a late hour that the company dispersed.

New York Chapter of the Institute of Accounts

The members and guests of the New York Chapter of the Institute of Accounts met on May 24 at the Waldorf-Astoria and listened to an address by James G. Cannon, President of the Institute of Accounts and Vice-President of the Fourth National Bank. President Cannon's subject was "The Relationship of the Bank to the Merchant," and he employed in illustration of it more than fifty lantern slides.

The interior of a bank was first thrown upon the screen, with a would-be depositor presenting his letter of introduction. That was really a very important document, Mr. Cannon said, although some poor specimens were at times received by the banks. The correct form, stating what the depositor was going to do, where he came from, and what the introducer knew of him, was given. Then followed the letter of the introducer to the bank direct, supplying additional particulars concerning the depositor's business and estimated financial worth. After that the signature was taken, an affair of much importance, which should be properly done; signatures to checks ought always to be written in the same way. As an old paying teller, Mr. Cannon could remember many signatures that recalled hundreds of men who had long since passed away, but whose signatures would always remain familiar to him.

When an account was opened certain information was filed by the bank, stating title, business, character of the account, whether there would be any borrowing, probable balance, other bank accounts, the depositor's references, who he had been introduced by, and who had accepted his account. The head of various departments in the bank had to initial this statement. Name, maker and amount of the first checks presented were also data of importance which it was well for a bank to preserve. Deposit books were then explained, and the intricacies of the exchange system described, to show how checks were put through the clearing-house and what was done to trace each separate item. Methods of getting at a depositor's daily and average balance gave an idea of the mass of detail work incident to the proper handling of a bank's business. Mr. Cannon then interested his hearers with full details attending the negotiation of loans, showing correct forms for discount collateral notes, discount collateral slips and discount collateral envelopes, so familiar to Wall street borrowers. The collateral note was the form approved by the best attorneys who had given long study to the subject, and was in all respects an ironclad document, so

worded that the borrower signed away practically his "wife, children and friends."

The devices used for tracing the rise or fall of each stock on which a bank loaned money, so that the lender could be sure of ample protection in having at all times a sufficient margin, were illustrated by the screen. Commercial agency reports, statements by retail dealers' protective associations, profit on account, checks correctly drawn, checks incorrectly drawn, cashier's check, foreign check and a sight draft were the subjects of further slides and running comment. Mr. Cannon then described the process of negotiating single-name paper, telling exactly how a bank ascertained the real strength of a borrower and the actual value of his account. The life of a country check with the process of its collection (the cause of so "much trouble and tribulation") provoked laughter.

In closing, Mr. Cannon told about the clearing-house system, showing the method of effecting exchanges and the business done at the "head centre of the entire financial institutions of the city." The slides gave an excellent idea of how the business of the clearing-house was done, showing all stages of the proceedings, even to Mr. Sherer's signal for the actual work to begin. Mr. Cannon paid a tribute to the whole system, saying he did not believe there was a man connected with a New York bank who did not feel "proud of the clearing-house, the members of the clearing-house committee, and all connected with that splendid organization."

Massachusetts Society of Public Accountants

The members and guests of the Massachusetts Society of Public Accountants met at Young's Hotel on June 14 for the closing meeting of the season. After the regular dinner, during which there was an interesting but informal discussion of municipal accounting and affairs, Secretary Chase read a paper by Prof. J. W. Jencks of Cornell University upon the New York Business Companies' Act. Prof. Jencks' absence from the meeting was occasioned by his immediate trip to Europe.

President Albee then introduced Charles W. Haskins, President of the New York State Society of Certified Public Accountants, who gave an address on the history and development of accounting. Mr. Haskins' treatment of his subject was such as to merit and receive the closest attention of his hearers. As members of the profession, they felt a new enthusiasm as he set before them the broad field that it had covered in the past and the place it should occupy in the future. The next meeting of the society will be held on the second Tuesday of October.

Associated Accountants of New Orleans

The eighth anniversary of the organization of the Associated Accountants of New Orleans was celebrated on the 12th of May by a reunion at the Capitol Hotel, West End, Lake Ponchartrain. The committee charged with the duty of providing entertainment had a most bountiful table spread on the balcony of the hotel overlooking the lake. Music and tasteful decorations added to the enjoyment. Toasts were responded to as follows: By President Hart, for the Association, and by Mr. Soule, for the ex-president. Messrs. Sherwood, Fowler, Farquhar, Dudley Watson, R. Lee Edwards, John Huffman, F. Ernst, E. J. Ficken, Nicholas Cuney, E. P. Barrierre, J. E. Elizardi, L. R. Jauquet and H. Daspit also spoke. G. E. Duclaux gave an able talk on the relation between accountants and credit men, and I. J. Fowler, by his constant fire of humorous remarks, and E. J. Ficken, with his witty sallies, kept the company in a continuous uproar of merriment. In memory of the "good old times," the evening was closed with the singing of "Auld Lang Syne."

Illinois Institute of Accountants

Through the courtesy of the Secretary, W. S. McKinney, we received the programme for the regular meeting of the Illinois Institute of Accountants, which was held on June 14. There was an address by George A. S. Wilson, expert insurance adjuster and counsel, on "Insurance Accounting and Adjustments," a paper by William G. Adkins of Adkins & Arnold, accountants, on "Provincialisms" and some special musical features.

New York State Society of Certified Public Accountants

The last meeting of this organization before the summer vacation was held at the Waldorf-Astoria, on Monday, June 11. Contrary to the usual rule heretofore prevailing in this society, invitations were extended to the members of the other accountants' organizations, including the American Association of Public Accountants and the New York Chapter of the Institute of Accounts. A considerable number of the latter were present. The regular routine of business was dispensed with, and attention was given to an address by President Charles W. Haskins, in which he contrasted the state of accountancy in Great Britain and other countries of Europe, as observed by him in his recent trip abroad, with that prevailing in this country. He dwelt particularly upon the courtesy extended to him by English accountants, and mentioned with gratification the interest that British accountants feel in what is being done on this side of the water in the way of legalizing the profession and establishing it upon a proper foundation. At the close of Mr. Haskins' address brief remarks were made by various members and guests, among whom may be mentioned H. H. Todd, A. O. Kittredge, W. P. Plant, Charles Dutton, Samuel D. Patterson and others.

So much satisfaction was expressed with the result of this experiment in inviting members of the different societies to the session of the New York Society of Certified Public Accountants that after adjournment, in an informal way, it was suggested that, commencing in the fall, a union meeting should be held whenever there are public addresses or discussions of interest to the business community. This idea was heartily indorsed by all the members of the different organizations present, and no doubt it will be tried after the summer recess.

New Bookkeepers' Organization

An association has been recently formed by a number of accountants and bookkeepers of New York City, the object of which is to promote and encourage the investigation, study and discussion of matters of advanced accounting and improvement in methods. It is intended to have addresses made at the regular monthly meetings, which shall be interesting to laymen as well as of practical benefit to the members, giving demonstrations of improved systems in use in many of the largest establishments throughout the country. A complete library is to be maintained, consisting of books and magazines from all countries upon matters relating to accountancy. The New York Association will become a branch of the National Association of Accountants and Bookkeepers, and will be represented by delegates at their annual convention. We shall watch the development of this latest addition to the list of accounting organizations with great interest.

Chinese Logic in America

Some one, in writing of the difficulties of introducing modern inventions into the Chinese Empire, thus describes the arguments with which a Chinese dignitary would guard the exclusiveness of the Flowery Kingdom:

If a railway was proposed, and it was shown a Chinese mandarin that it might earn £500,000 per year, he would immediately exclaim that you proposed to rob China of half a million per annum. You might point out that there was no robbery about it; that people need not use the railway unless they liked, and could, if they preferred, travel or send their goods by boat in the old way. "That is just what I say," the mandarin would reply. "You are robbing the boatmen." You might next point out that a large proportion of the earnings would be paid in wages, and was, perhaps, your most effective argument; but even here the mandarin would assert that you were taking your employes from agriculture, which was, he would claim, much better for the nation. As for the money paid for materials imported, that, the mandarin would hold, was lost to the country. You might point out that the money need not necessarily leave the country, being paid into a bank, and being finally exported in the shape of silks, tea, etc., but the mandarin would reply:

"That is just what I say. You steal the money in the first place, and then use it to buy silks and tea, which had much better stay in the country." Finally, you would try to get round him in another way. The mandarins holding the most important positions, necessarily involving heavy expenditure, are paid the most inadequate salaries, say £150 per annum. A mandarin must, therefore, take fees; he does not call them bribes, or consider them so. You set to work to make the desired arrangement in the best way you can, and the mandarin does the best he can for himself. As a foreigner, you are considered a rich man and thus fair game. The mandarin, if honest and patriotic, wants to do the best he can for his country, but interprets this inversely, namely, by making things as bad as possible for the other side. He cannot believe that a bargain may be profitable to both parties. In fact, the more honest the mandarin the more difficult it is to transact business.

A like spirit is shown by many of our citizens and at times a Chinese aversion to change, a Chinese dread of innovation, and a Chinese distrust of modern improvements seem to bar the advance of the nation to broader usefulness and wider fields of action. That it was not the doctrine of our fathers is accounted sufficient argument against a new policy. That the merchant of the past generation conducted business on a small scale, with a few clerks, and used an archaic system of keeping accounts, thereby supporting his family in moderate circumstances, is deemed a satisfactory reason against the department store which has forced him to abandon his business, because it can afford to sell goods at a lower price. Meanwhile the fact that the community is better served and a greater number of individuals are given employment has no effect upon the mandarin-like obtuseness of the objector to the new order of things.

The Chinese disposition comes to the front when the subject of trusts is under discussion. The objector forgets that he might be lumbering over muddy roads in the ancient stage coach if combinations of capital had not provided a means whereby he can swiftly and comfortably be carried from one part of the country to the other. He quite overlooks the fact as he settles his grocery bill that the delicacies with which his table is daily covered would be unaccustomed luxuries did not like combinations of capital so far cheapen the manufacture and distribution of such merchandise as to bring its purchase within his means.

Again, the mandarin obtuseness in the matter of foreign commerce has its counterpart here in those who fail to see in an interchange of goods with other nations, and in the increase of facilities for such interchange, an impetus to internal trade, manufacture and agriculture and a source of wealth to the country. Like the mandarin, they cannot believe that the bargain can be good for both sides. In fact, they would like a Chinese wall around the country, but, in spite of such Old World policy, the spirit of progress will move on dragging these worshippers at the shrine of the past along with it, while they continue to protest against the advance, though profiting from the advantages which follow in its train.

The Department Store

The department store has long been an object of attack on the part of the demagogue, the newspaper that truckles to certain classes of our citizens and politicians who intend thereby to gain favor with the masses. But no matter how virulent the attack, the department store thrives because it meets the wants of the community and serves it better than it ever has been served before. As is frequently the case, the persons who have gained the most from the introduction of this new feature into mercantile industry belong to the classes which these pretended friends are striving to arouse to opposition. If goods are sold at a low price, no one appreciates it so much as the workingman. If fresh avenues of labor are created in which the different members of his family can find employment, the home of the workingman is the first to feel the benefit. Are opportunities for investment of small savings thrown open, it is to the workingman's advantage much more than any other.

A defense of the department store by Lawrence M. Jones, or the Jones Dry Goods Co., of Kansas City, Mo., was recently contributed to one of the local papers. Mr. Jones sums up the beneficial result flowing from the introduction of department stores as follows:

It has banished the old haggling or two-price system from the commercial world.

It has provided every comfort for the customer while shopping, and for the employes while at work.

It has reduced the hours of labor and increased the wages of the laborer.

It has dealt a hard blow to the old credit system, and, by selling cheap for cash, has encouraged habits of thrift and industry.

It has encouraged employes to save their earnings, and, by investing them in the stock of the concern, enabled them to become partners in the undertakings.

It has reduced the prices of merchandise, thus increasing the purchasing power of all the people.

It has placed business on a high plane of honor and integrity, and has thrown around every transaction the strongest guarantee.

It has placed the newspaper in the hands of all the people, by reason of the large amounts paid to the newspapers for advertising, just making the cheap paper possible, • • • and one of the most important of all is the enlarged field of employment it has created for women. Until the department stores became prominent, the opportunities for the employment of women were few. The department stores now offer and furnish the largest field for the employment of women of any industry in the country.

Men may second Fortune, but they cannot thwart her.—Macchiavelli.

The highest excellence is seldom attained in more than one vocation.—Bovée.

Not only is Fortune herself blind, but she generally causes those persons to be blind whose interests she has more particularly taken in hand.—Cicero.

Preparation of Mail

Out in the Philippines a soldier scrawls the story of a battle on a bit of coarse paper and tosses it into a pile with hundreds of others. It passes from hand to hand, travels by sea and by land, till some morning a white-haired old lady finds it waiting for her at the breakfast table.

A man goes on a hurried business trip up and down the country, and the day after his departure starts a letter from the home office. It follows him from place to place as he doubles upon his track, and at last is laid on his desk the day after his return bearing stamped on its worn surface a record of his journeyings. Back in the fatherland a man sends a misspelled, misdirected message to his brother away off in America, and in a lonely farmhouse out on the broad prairie, or at the mouth of a mine among the hills, or up at the top of a crowded tenement house in a big city, it finds him. Thus it is that these little, white packets fly back and forth across the country and drop each one at its own proper place. We are so accustomed to a marvelous activity and vigilance on the part of the Post Office Department that we do not even note when it accomplishes what seems the impossible in the execution of the service imposed upon it.

The chief difficulties in the way of promptness and speed in the performance of its duties arise from the ignorance or carelessness of those who wish to employ it as a medium of communication, and frequently the very class of men who are most interested in the efficiency of its workings are those who hamper its operations. By the exercise of ordinary judgment and care the speed with which mail can be delivered will be much enhanced, and the advantages which flow from promptness secured. It is another illustration of the old adage that what is worth doing at all is worth doing well. If it is no consequence whether your letter or parcel goes to-day or to-morrow, don't send it till to-morrow. Use the time to-day for something that needs doing to-day, but if you wish delivery at the earliest moment possible, mail in such a shape and manner that this will be accomplished without hindrance through neglect or carelessness on your part.

Here are some suggestions that may be of use; at least they touch upon points that are frequently cause of criticism on the part of the Post Office Department, and doubtless many a reader will recognize his own deficiencies:

Wrappers should be employed that are not so flimsy as to break or become torn in carriage. Who has not received mail stamped by the office as injured when received? If a paper is valuable do not trust it to ordinary wrappers. Very strong envelopes are manufactured especially for such purposes, and should invariably be used when such matter is sent.

Write the address with extreme legibility. Postal clerks can decipher very blind writing, but of course plainly ad-

dressed matter will take precedence with them, and be sent forward first. Illegibly addressed mail will be thrown one side to be given to men or women in the department skilled in deciphering peculiar handwriting. Still another form of trouble arises from improper or insufficient address. The street and number are requisite for immediate delivery. Railroad mail clerks don't know firms—only streets, numbers and stations—and the mail properly addressed is in condition, when it leaves their hands to be instantly delivered. Don't depend upon the name of the firm or building or street corner to locate your correspondent. Mail improperly or insufficiently addressed, if it be first-class matter, is sent to the directory and searching department, where it awaits its turn, while, if it be second, third or fourth-class matter, it is sent to the dead letter office, or the addressor is notified.

A wise precaution, when the name of the town of the person addressed is one which occurs in more than one State, is to give the county and to write the name of the State in full. In using an abbreviation for the name of the State, be careful not to employ such as can be easily confounded with that of some other state. Thus, Vt. for Vermont and Ct. for Connecticut are frequently misleading. Conn. is a better abbreviation for the latter State. "Col." for Colorado and "Cal." for California are a like instance, and the number of examples might be greatly increased. Mail addressed vaguely and not to a definite individual is never delivered, as, for instance, "To the Most Prominent Hardware Dealer."

After the letter is addressed, see that it is fully stamped if you would avoid the detention which will be necessary for collection at the other end. Affix the stamp at the upper right-hand corner. Custom has made this imperative, and the postal clerk looks for it there, and if he does not see it, your letter may get sidetracked. To avoid the loss of mail, in case from any cause it cannot be delivered, the careful business man will not fail to put a return card on every piece that leaves his office. Many men will look carefully to the addressing, stamping and sealing of their mail and then hand it over to the office boy and dismiss it from their mind. The office boy lets it lie on his desk till his inclination or some other errand takes him to the street, when he drops it in the nearest letter box. The post office may be but a few blocks away, and had the letter been mailed as soon as it was written, it would have been on its way hours before the postman in his rounds took it from the letter box.

Do you really care that the papers and parcels you send reach their destination? Then see that they are not left on the top of the letter box. This is not mailing, and it affords an easy opportunity for theft, either for the contents or stamps. Again the collection from the package boxes are not as frequent as from the letter boxes, and there is an almost certain gain in time by mailing

parcels at the office. It may mean hundreds of dollars to a business man that his advertising matter gets to his customers before his competitor's reaches them.

It will be well if he sees to it that it is intrusted to some one who will attend to its proper mailing.

Here is still another way in which he can assist the postal department and insure a rapid delivery. The saving of time would be sufficient to pay for the extra expenditures in clerk hire. Let all pieces going in one direction be tied together and properly labeled. If a large number goes to one city, have that also indicated. No business man needs to be told that on his alertness, quickness and thoroughness depends his chance of success, and he will not fail to recognize the tendency of the above suggestions to the furtherance of the end sought, namely, the rapid communication between his customers and himself.

Money Making

The making of money, not on "change," but in the Government Bureau of Engraving and Printing at Washington, is interesting to the crowd of visitors at our national capital. The manufacture of bills for circulation would be a very simple process were it not necessary to guard against counterfeiting. For this reason it is of prime importance that the paper used be difficult of imitation. A silk-threaded article is made expressly for the Government, under a close supervision, at Dalton, Mass. The sheets are of a size to be cut into exactly four bills, and in the Bureau of Engraving and Printing record is kept of the amount given out for manufacture into bills. No employee is allowed to leave the building at night till every sheet has been accounted for and returned. The paper passes through the press three times in the process of printing, and then goes to the Treasury Department proper for an impression of the Government seal, in order to exercise a check upon the bureau.

Municipal Bookkeeping

By John H. Blacklock.

Correct financiering lies at the basis of economical government. An indispensable aid to a sound financial system is an advanced and correct system of bookkeeping. That a municipality should have a correct system of bookkeeping is a matter of importance to every citizen, for upon correct bookkeeping depends, in a large measure, the fixing of the rate of taxation.

An examination of the auditors' reports from various cities shows a wide divergence of opinion as to the fundamental principles of municipal accounting. Cleveland, Ohio, Boston and Cambridge, Mass., and Providence, R. I., are examples of what may be done in the matter of reports of municipal auditors, and valuable contributions have been made to the literature of the subject by such men as Prof. Leo S. Rowe of the University of Pennsylvania, and Prof. Clow of the State Normal School of Oshkosh, Wis.

To financial men, particularly to owners of, and dealers in, municipal securities, a uniform and correct system of municipal accounting is of immediate importance. What may be accomplished in this respect is shown by reference to the advance in railway accounting which is now practically uniform throughout the United States. The fundamental principle in municipal accounting, as to receipts and disbursements, is to make a classification into four groups, namely, ordinary and extraordinary receipts and ordinary and extraordinary disbursements.

Ordinary receipts, including receipts

from such sources as taxes, licenses, etc.; extraordinary receipts from such sources as the sale of municipal bonds. Ordinary disbursements include the operating expenses of the municipality and extraordinary disbursements include expenditures for public buildings, redemption of loans and the like. A full inventory of city property, corrected annually, is a valuable and, indeed, a necessary feature of correct municipal bookkeeping. But the essential principle, the most valuable of all, may be summed up in the statement that public accounts should at all times be open to public inspection.

A Parcels Post

Suggestions that the Government incorporate in the Postal Department some system of a domestic parcels post come from various quarters. A method by which business houses and private parties may send merchandise C. O. D. by this means is a growing need. The convenience and economy of trading by sample has resulted in an enormous increase in the number of parcels transmitted from one part of the country to the other, and the merchant and buyer both feel the necessity of some provision in the Post Office Department by which it could be made the medium, not only for the transmission of goods, but also for the receipt of payment for the same in behalf of the sender.

Some such arrangement as this might be provided: A customer orders from a merchant certain goods; the merchant forwards the goods by parcels post, and at the same time mails a letter to his customer, saying that he has done so, and that the goods will be delivered by the postmaster on receipt of the price

named. A letter of advice is sent to the postmaster, instructing him to deliver the parcel to the customer on receipt of the sum specified, after which the postmaster may deduct a fee, and remit the remainder to the merchant. The amount of the fee could be made dependent upon the sum collected.

That some such method will be adopted before long there can be no doubt, as it is called for by the situation, and a plan like the above is certainly feasible.

Designations of Cities

Certain of our cities, by reason of their physical peculiarities, have acquired another designation than the one which legally belongs to them, as that of Crescent City applied to New Orleans, Elm City to New Haven, and Forest City to Cleveland. Others have acquired such distinctive name by reason of the occupation of their inhabitants. Thus Joplin, Mo., since the development of zinc mines in its neighborhood, has come to be known as the Zinc City. Cincinnati has long borne the unpoetical name of "Porkopolis," on account of the important part which pork-packing has in its industries. Milwaukee is generally known as the Beer City; Wheeling, W. Va., as the Glass City, and Minneapolis, as the Flour City. Denver leads other places in the number of bicycles in proportion to its inhabitants, and hence is called the Bicycle City. Grand Rapids has a right to the name of Furniture City; Kalamazoo to that of Celery City; Pittsburg claims pre-eminence as the Steel City; Danbury, Conn., as the Hat City, and Salem, Ore., as the Hop City; South Bend, Ind., may well be called the Wagon City; Wilmington, Del., the Match City, and Haverhill, Mass., the Shoe City. There are but few places of importance which do not lead in some industry, either through natural advantages for production along a certain line, or because facilities for distribution of manufactures have drawn capital to the locality.

Composition of the Lead Pencil

A small proportion of the number of persons who use a lead pencil for hours each day know that there is not a particle of lead in its composition. The misnomer arose from a popular mistake on account of similarity in appearance, and can be traced back to the discovery of graphite mines in England in the reign of Queen Elizabeth. The first pencils attracted a great deal of attention, and these mines were considered of inestimable value. Originally the graphite was sawed into thin sheets, which were afterward cut into strips and covered with light wooden slips. From these crude pencils, by continued improvements, the modern article has been developed. In 1795 a Frenchman introduced a method of pulverizing graphite and mixing it with clay. This process permitted the manufacture of pencils of different degrees of hardness which were uniform throughout the entire length.

Volume VII, Nos. 1 to 2
July 1900 to August 1900

Volume VII
Number 1 | JULY, 1900 | Monthly, $1 a year
Single Copy, 10 cents

The Accountant as a Man*

By Y. B. Haagsma

much has been said with a view of phasizing the importance of proper tine and system in accounting, and so h less value appears to have been ..ached by the public to the qualifications and character of the accountant, that an effort toward describing the qualifications of men who would be fitted for responsible accounting work may not be out of place, and if, coupled therewith, some attempt were made at reciting the reasons why many accounting men fail to reach positions of responsibility, important and interesting results might ensue.

I heartily indorse efforts toward the establishment of proper routine and system in accounting, because an accounting department that is not governed by proper system and run in proper grooves will have its work in a chaotic shape. I think, however, that we underrate the value of the accountant when we compare his importance with that of accounting methods. Railroads require tracks for the easy propulsion of cars, but the tracks are of little use without the equipment, and behind the equipment there must be trained men. The man at the lever, of course, is of more importance than the machinery; the great gun is of little value without the experienced artillerist, and the best telescope is practically useless without the trained astronomer. The average employer understands all of this very fully. He knows that proper systems are of much value, but he also knows that the accounting man must be of more importance than the accounting machinery. Nevertheless, it is probable that most employers do not fully value the importance of the accountant himself, and it is natural that the accountant should feel, now and then, that to his brain work and to his persistent plodding a full measure of recompense is not meted out. In this connection, I hold, however, that in very many cases the accountant himself is at fault, and is responsible for this condition. The accountant usually forgets that his value may depend upon considerations other than his experience and his work, which other considerations frequently tend to sway the judgment of

(*A paper read at the meeting of Illinois Institute of Accountants, Chicago, April 12, 1900, by Y. B. Haagsma, General Auditor of Republic Iron & Steel Co.)

the employer in estimating the value of the accountant's services. It may be an immoral thing on the part of the employer to look upon the accountant as a mere part of his machinery, but is it usually true also that the employer is not alone to be censured for the existence of these views, for no manly man of clean character and good ability as an accountant will fail to obtain proper recognition. If he fail, then I hold that the reason very likely lies either in the nature of his efforts, or in his own character and habits. It is often the case that the accountant is so persistent in the exploiting of his views concerning proper methods and systems and routine, before he has established the fact that his knowledge and his ability are such as would make his views of value, that his persistence in this direction may come to be regarded as a nuisance. No man should expect his views to be valued at a high rate until he has demonstrated in some way that his ideas are entitled to consideration. This failure to obtain immediate indorsement and ratification of his ideas often engenders in the accountant a spirit of personal antagonism to the management, whereby he stultifies himself and stifles the opportunity for inauguration of what he deems to be necessary. If, instead of cherishing this feeling of personal antagonism, he would cultivate a likeable disposition, deference to the views of the men who are responsible for the conduct of the business, and readiness to accord to them all the respect to which their positions and financial interests entitle them, the accountant would certainly sail in smoother waters.

We cannot expect men to coincide with our views unless they are presented in a manner at once pleasing and convincing, and with due deference to those most interested. The attempt to force one's particular views upon those who are not thoroughly conversant with accounting requirements usually accomplishes little. To the practical man, any additional outlay in dollars and cents on systems and extra routine must be shown to be justifiable. On the other hand, if the efforts of the accountant lie in the direction of introducing innovations which are expected to effect economies in the accounting work, then the accountant must be able to demonstrate that nothing is lost by laying

aside old methods, and that a gain will follow. He should be willing to believe that old methods have existed because they had some value at the time when they were inaugurated, and it will not do to discard them without consideration. It is natural that a man, not fully conversant with the requirements, should hesitate to permit the introduction of what is called labor-saving accounting machinery, even if large economies may be expected therefrom, when these changes involve laying aside methods and systems that have been in vogue for years. I wish to emphasize that the personality of the accountant, his habits of thought, his manner, his disposition and the details of his personal life are of the first importance, if he would put into effect changes of this kind, and I therefore, wish to impress upon every young accounting clerk the great necessity of studying himself, and it will be well in the same breath to urge that the accountant study his employer.

It is difficult to say what sort of a man an accountant should be in order to obtain the best success. It would be useless to say that he should have the qualifications of an angel. This is earth, and not heaven, and we can expect neither the accountant nor his employer to be perfect.

As to character and habits, I should certainly draw the line at men who are guilty under any one of the four points which cause a man to be ostracised at West Point, and which are as follows:

First, personal uncleanness.

Second, personal cowardice.

Third, lying.

Fourth, tattling.

Young men in large cities often have the view that these points are of secondary consideration and importance. In this I am sure they are mistaken. Employers watch their men, and when they observe, for instance, personal uncleanness, either in the care of the person or in any respect which could be properly classified under this heading, the employer will be on his guard. If the employer observes personal cowardice, such as, for instance, the inborn or cultivated hesitancy on the part of a clerk to stand his ground in an argument, when he knows himself to be right and when a profit to the business is involved, or when that species of fear is manifested which would cause a man to report only part of a transaction and not all, in order to hide the fact that he has made a mistake, the employer will take note of such conditions. If the employer ever has occasion to find the employee guilty under the third heading, viz., lying, either by indirection or by straight prevarication, the employee will never again be trusted. If a man tattles the employer knows very well that such a man will create discord in the best regulated office. These things, therefore, are to be avoided.

Whatever sentiment may exist against it, I am prepared to defend the proposition that there must be, above all things, the determination to do right at any cost, both to the employer or to the employee. In this connection, it may be well to remember that one of the most brilliant statesmen of our day lost his Senatorship by the alleged declaration that the decalogue has no place in politics. It is possible that some accountants may have permitted themselves to be so far mistaken in their views as to suppose that the decalogue has no place in business. The accountant who is not the embodiment of personal integrity can never hope for influential connection or advancement. If he is not absolutely truthful and does not tell all of the truth about transactions, he will be regarded as unreliable and unworthy. He might, by these unworthy processes, occasionally find temporary advantage, but he cannot expect success in the long run. He must be ready to do right even if it costs him his position, and the man who loses a position for such reasons will not be long finding a better one, if he has manhood and the necessary qualifications in the way of knowledge and experience. I know that these sentiments are not generally entertained, but it is easy to see that one cannot expect an employer to place confidence in the statements made by an accountant concerning his business if the accountant's character, habits and general views of life are such as do not inspire all who know him with implicit confidence in his integrity.

The accountant must always be ready to put more of value into the business than he gets out of it, because the employer is entitled to a profit on the money expended for his services; the employer takes all the risks of the business, the employee none. It should be the special study of the accountant to so transform himself into a necessary part of the business machinery that he cannot be readily duplicated, and if an employee will persist in giving more value than he receives, he will make reputation somewhere, and often in unexpected quarters, and the time will come when he will be sought out for greater responsibility. It is obvious that if the man's habits are not correct, if he is not regular in his hours for sleeping and rest, he cannot expect to give to the business the full strength that the business requires, and he cannot be in full command of all his mental faculties. Further, if a young man so little respects himself as to enter upon an immoral course of living, he should not expect his employer to respect and trust him. If a young man is inclined to gloat over the imperfections of others, he will not

find much mercy and consideration when his own imperfections are discovered. If a young man spends his leisure hours in an unsatisfactory way the employer may be inclined to conclude that the time devoted to business may also bear as little fruit in the way of unsatisfactory work.

A young man should either learn to love his business or leave it. Many an accountant shows a disposition to be sour and sore and sad and disappointed. Such an unhappy temperament injures him far more than he thinks, and should be banished. If it be part of his nature, then he should "throw away the worser part." The world has no sympathy with nor respect for disappointed people. "Laugh and the world laughs with you; weep and you weep alone." A woman who persistently shows the effects of disappointed love will not readily find a suitor, and the man who continually exhibits to his employer and his co-workers nothing but sourness, soreness and sadness, and who does not make every effort toward making life pleasant for others, will not receive very much comfort in the association of others. He may be tolerated for a time on account of his ability, but even that will gradually begin to be underrated and his real value to the business discounted.

I advocate very strongly the cultivation of nobility of the mental equipment. The mind of the accountant should be so trained as to be capable of instantaneous change of thought from one subject to another. In this connection I think that a young man entering an office should, first of all, acquire great rapidity of bodily movement. This will stimulate rapidity of the operations of the mind. I have found that when young men receive a preliminary training in a large mailing department, where great rapidity of movement in handling papers is required, they will, in later years, show the benefit of that training; they will dispatch papers and perform general work more rapidly than men without such training. Rapidity of thought comes almost intuitively with rapidity of physical action. It is of great importance that the young man be impressed from the beginning with the necessity of cultivating the power of concentrating his mind on the matter in hand and on excluding everything else from his thoughts. That power of concentration can be developed and become one of the strongest features in a man's value. It not only teaches him to think, but also to marshal all his mental forces on the business in hand. This power of concentration of the mind is really the secret of the success of the most valued office men. Of course, if a young man is in the habit of centering his mind on matters other than his business, and particularly in foolish play, and more especially on play to which a certain hazard is attached, he is likely to fail at the time when he most needs to think, and it is my observation that the young man who spends much time with cards shows more or less abstraction of mind during the day. This card-playing habit, as we all know, usually brings late hours. Fur-

thermore, when a young man permits himself to be drawn into games of chance, it is reasonable to expect that his work may be more or less unreliable because his mind is not fully on his business. If the young man would spend the time so used in an effort to inform himself concerning matters directly or indirectly connected with his business, or in the acquisition of other useful knowledge, he would soon become master of his business, as well as an agreeable companion to men of cultivation, and he would find a charm in this mental cultivation such as would not only bring him solace in the lonely hours, but also afford him enjoyment far beyond anticipation. If some of the time usually spent without special purpose were given to memorizing the best sayings of great men and to the study of the thoughts of great men, life would soon feel a companionship with these great men and find himself elevated to a higher plane of thought and living. If we may not have the companionship of the great on earth we may have the companionship of the thoughts of the great ones of our present day and of those who have gone before. The young man who is content with limiting himself to such information concerning his business as happens to come before his eyes, and who does not pursue a persistent course of observing all that surrounds him, and who shuts himself off from the many avenues of cultivation of mind and heart that are open to us all, will find himself poor indeed in the declining years, wealth and affluence to the contrary notwithstanding. The man who finds his diversion in the lines indicated herein will steadily grow stronger in judgment and in value to his employers, and will feel within himself the steady growth and ripening of a nobler and higher life.

Above all, I would advocate a constant recognition of the thought expressed in the two French words, "Noblesse oblige," meaning that our rank or station or position imposes obligation. The very fact of communion with other men imposes obligation—every possibility for the enlargement of heart and mind brings responsibility. To the extent that a man fails to make use of opportunities for improving himself, he degrades himself, and every opportunity for development that is not improved precludes the chance for using that development for the betterment of mankind. The failure to make the best of these opportunities will certainly have a deleterious effect on his possibilities for advancement in business. I am entirely satisfied that young men do not appreciate this as fully as they should. It would be a great blessing if these matters could be brought forcibly to the attention of men when very young. Because these facts are not brought to their attention they give, perhaps, little thought to such things. "Noblesse oblige" means a friendly hand and a real interest in the welfare of others; its real lesson is that man's responsibilities are measured by his possibilities. It means what is expressed in the following:

"We need, each and all, to be needed,
To feel we have something to give
Toward soothing the moan of earth's
     hunger;
And we know that then only we live
When we feed one another, as we have
     been fed,
From the hand that gives body and
     spirit their bread."

In this connection I cannot forbear quoting from James Whitcomb Riley what he says about the friendly hand, as follows:

"When a man ain't got a cent, an' he's
     feelin' kind o' blue,
An' the clouds hang dark an' heavy an'
     won't let the sunshine through,
It's a great thing, oh, my brethren, for
     a feller just to lay
His hand upon your shoulder in a friend-
     ly sort o' way!

It makes a man feel curious; it makes
     the tear-drops start,
An' you sort o' feel a flutter in the re-
     gion of the heart.
You can't look up and meet his eyes;
     you don't know what to say,
When his hand is on your shoulder in a
     friendly sort o' way.

Oh, the world's a curious compound,
     with its honey an' its gall,
With its cares and bitter crosses; but a
     good world after all,
An' a good God must have made it—
     leastways, that's what I say
When a hand rests on my shoulder in a
     friendly sort o' way."

In this attempt to measure and prescribe what the accountant needs to be as a man it has not been my purpose to burden your minds with a moral disquisition, but rather to outline the results of my experience and observation concerning man's ordinary faults, failures, weaknesses and victories, and their effect upon his career in life. If I have impressed upon you what we should be if we would be truly successful, then I shall feel that some of the great lessons of life have been imparted, which usually come to us by experience only, and are therefore often learned too late to be of the greatest benefit.

Railway Blanks and Forms

We are in receipt of a circular from W. B. Brockway, secretary and treasurer of the Street Railway Accountants' Association of America, in which he draws attention to the fact that the value of the Department of Blanks and Forms can be greatly enhanced from year to year by the addition of new forms issued by the different companies and the refiling of blanks re-issued. An appeal is therefore made to the members of the Association to keep the secretary well informed of any changes in their blanks and forms.

A separate book, it is announced, is to be devoted to rubber-stamp impressions, and there seems to be every reason to believe that in future exhibitions this last feature will prove an interesting and useful one. Electric lighting blanks will also be included among the collection, inasmuch as electric lighting is in many instances managed in the offices of street railway companies. The members are requested to observe the following regulations in forwarding blanks to the secretary:

Impressions of rubber stamps should be made on white paper, four inches wide by six inches long, each impression on a separate slip of paper. Blanks should be rolled and not folded.

Names of companies should be written in ink on all blanks where they do not appear in the printing.

Two copies of all forms (excepting rubber-stamp impressions) should be submitted.

The term "blanks and forms" covers everything in the way of books, circulars, rubber stamps, tickets, transfers, statements and reports, and all printed matter.

A Mortgage 1800 Years Old

Every business man is acquainted with the appearance of the conventional mortgage. A mortgage which is 1800 years old must, however, be regarded in the nature of something unusual. Such a document was found among some old Egyptian papyri, recently discovered at Oxyrhynchus. It is surprising to note the similarity of this ancient document to the mortgage of the present day. The paper sets forth the contract of loan from Thonis, son Harpaesis, etc., received by Caecilius Clemens, the loan consisting of 400 drachmae. The security given was the third part of a house, situated in the Gymnasium Square Quarter, by the Temple of Osiris and the Treasury. From the document it would appear that the registrar of that time was called Agoranomous. Here is the wording of the document in full:

```
CAECILIUS CLEMENS TO THE
AGORANOMOUS (OR REGIS-
TRAR) GREETING:
REGISTER A CONTRACT OF
LOAN FROM THONIS, SON OF
HARPAESIS SON OF PETSERO-
THONIS. HIS MOTHER BEING
PETOSIRIS, DAUGHTER OF HAR-
PAESIS, OF THE CITY OF OXY-
RHYNCHUS, CHIEF BEARER IN
THE TEMPLE OF THOERIS AND
ISIS AND SARAPIS AND OSIRIS
AND THE ASSOCIATED MOST
MIGHTY GODS, ON THE SECUR-
ITY OF THE THIRD PART OF A
HOUSE IN WHICH THERE IS A
HALL, WITH THE COURT AND
ENTRANCES AND EXITS AND
APPURTENANCES, SITUATED IN
THE GYMNASIUM SQUARE
QUARTER BY THE TEMPLE OF
OSIRIS AND THE TREASURY,
WHICH WAS MORTGAGED TO
HIM BY HIS FULL BROTHER
THOMPHICAS IN RETURN FOR
AN ACCOMMODATION IN AC-
CORDANCE WITH A NOTE OF
HAND AND A PAYMENT
THROUGH A BANK OF 400
DRACHMAE.
```

A Trust That Did'nt Kill Competition

It is a generally accepted fact, even among those who claim to see compensating advantages in the existence of so-called trusts, that the chief source of danger of these vast combinations of capital lies in the fact that their very existence depends upon their ability to stifle competition. This being the case, the fact that one of the largest industrial combinations in the United States has recently gone out of existence on account of too much competition, should come as a comforting piece of news to those who entertain no friendly feelings toward these organizations. The corporation in question is the so-called Wall Paper Trust, with a capitalization of many millions. What is most surprising in this instance is the fact that the competition was not furnished by other trusts, but by independent individual manufacturers. With all its superior facilities of improved methods and other advantages of enormous capitalization, this concern could not meet the competition of the smaller companies, and confessing itself to be beaten, has had to dissolve.

The president of the corporation has openly stated that the above is the reason for this unlooked-for step. In view of the fact that this was one of the most powerful industrial organizations in the country, it would seem doubtful whether these combinations are, in fact, the terrible invincible monsters they have been time and again asserted to be.

Organization of Reciprocal Reporting Bureaus

At the convention of the National Association of Credit Men, held at Milwaukee, Wis., June 12, 13 and 14 last, among other interesting proceedings was the report of the Credit Department Methods Committee, from which we extract the following:

"In Portland, Ore., a system which practically amounts to reciprocal reporting is conducted by the Credit Department of the Merchant's Protective Association. The operations of this department are regarded by the members of the Portland Credit Men's Association as being very effectual in shutting off excess credits. The method employed requires the use of four forms. When a member desires to make an inquiry regarding any party in business, he fills out a slip prepared for that purpose and sends it to the central office. The name of the party inquired about is immediately circulated among the trade, and a sheet left with each house, upon which the house answering records its number, the amount of total indebtedness (which must include notes and secured accounts), past due indebtedness, and notations as to whether the account is new, discounts are prompt, fair, slow, very slow, C.O.D., or whether the terms are of a special character. A report is then prepared for the inquirer which contains a notation as to the number of people who have responded, the total indebtedness, the amount of such indebtedness past due, etc. In addition to this, however, besides the special report that is sent to the party making the inquiry, a report is also furnished to every member, whether he has made an inquiry or not, this being done on a sheet containing eleven different reports, so arranged that each report may be clipped and filed separately.

The Committee urge, in their report, that a determined effort be made to create local reciprocal reporting bureaus, similar to the above, and call attention to the fact that such institutions are already in existence, in the Minneapolis Credit Men's Association, the Sioux City Bureau of Credits and the St. Paul Credit Men's Association.

The Monthly Statement

The political issues of the two great parties in the Presidential campaign that is just opening have been clearly joined and their consideration is fast becoming the matter of first importance whenever men meet in conversation, as well also as on the editorial pages of the daily papers. Sound money, free silver, expansion, anti-trusts, imperialism and a few other high-sounding words and phrases are fast becoming trite, if not commonplace. This, very fortunately, is not a political paper and therefore we are saved the necessity of joining in the discussion. All our readers, however, are interested in the outcome of the contest. We may, therefore, be pardoned for an occasional word as the campaign proceeds. At this time we shall offer a single thought, and that is that no accountant, trained as he is to compare values and obtain proof by balance, can have any sympathy whatever with a depreciated currency, nor in the interests of business can any accountant favor any monetary scheme which would disarrange values and produce confusion in exchanges. It is as impossible for an accountant to favor two standards of value as it would be for him to favor two yard sticks of different lengths. The rule of his life is that every debit must have a credit, and that the debits must balance the credits. To have the funds received measured by one value and the funds paid out measured by another, would be an absurdity. To extort from debtors the amounts they owe in one currency and to discharge liabilities in another, would clearly be a violation of principle, as well as morally wrong. We venture to believe that accountants in general, whether under ordinary circumstances they are Democrats or Republicans, are now and always advocates of a single standard in monetary affairs. We doubt very much if so-called free silver would ever show its face again if the question could be left to the vote of the accountants of the country for a decision. The majority against it would be overwhelming.

The "man behind the accounts" is of late coming into more prominence than ever before; first, because he is getting to be better understood and his real importance in the community appreciated, and second, because instead of being any available person able to write a fair hand and cast up a column of figures, he has become by the course of business selection a skilful specialist. The man behind the accounts, and the man behind the gun (as in naval parlance) give character and quality to whatever is done. As is the skill of the man behind the accounts so, in a large measure, is the efficiency of the business work of the establishment. The man behind the accounts at the present time, we regret to say, is in many instances one altogether unworthy of the place he occupies. He is out of date and unprogressive. He

represents the old school that is gradually disappearing from the business world. In the near future he will be supplanted by the man of the modern school, whose characteristics include a trained eye, skilful hand, a steady brain, a willingness to learn and to adapt, and, best of all, sound, practical business sense. In the future, more than at present, and very much more than in the past, will the man behind the accounts be a force to be reckoned with in the general economy of the business establishment. How secure in its position and how safe in its operations is that business venture which has a competent and up-to-date man behind the accounts.

We alluded in these columns, a short time since to the preparations that are being made by the University of the City of New York, co-operating with the New York State Society of Certified Public Accountants, in respect to a course in accountancy, commercial law and business economics. We now have the pleasure of announcing that the arrangements have reached such a stage that there seems to be no doubt that the new school will be open to students at the approaching fall term. The course of study is to be two years in extent. The branches taught will be the theory of accounts, practical accounting, commercial law and commercial economics. The two branches last mentioned will be in charge of professors of the University who have already achieved distinction along these lines in other branches of educational work. The theory and practice accounts, including auditing, will be managed by prominent practicing accountants.

The immediate object of the course is to qualify young men who propose devoting themselves to the practice of accountancy for the C. P. A. examination. It is also designed to meet the requirements of those who are now in active work in the profession, and who desire to prosecute their studies in a way to secure the degree at the earliest possible moment. To this end, the instruction is to be evening work entirely. It is believed that there are many who, while not at present active in the profession, will yet take the course at the earliest opportunity for the purpose of qualifying themselves for the examination to that extent, even though the practical work demanded is not taken up until a later date.

We frequently hear it said of one man that he is a most excellent business manager, and of another that while he can perform almost any class of work which he undertakes, still he fails as a manager. It would seem that some men are born managers, just as some men are born soldiers, while others are born without the essential qualities of manage-

ment. A little examination into facts shows that for every man who is able to manage or direct there are many who need constant supervision to enable them to earn even a bare living. As just stated, some are natural managers or leaders. Others, however, deficient in natural endowment, have to acquire whatever managerial talent they exercise. To paraphrase roughly, some are born to management, others have management thrust upon them and still others achieve management by hard work. Some are by nature directors of affairs. Others, as we have intimated, are called to management before they have had the chance to demonstrate their skill in this regard. Heirs to estates and going businesses and those who happen to be situated where an emergency occurs requiring some one to take charge of affairs instantly are examples in point. Great is the success of the man who, when management is thrust upon him, is able to rise to the occasion. On the other hand, mortifying in the extreme is the failure of the man who, under these circumstances, is unable to meet requirements.

Finally we come to the class of those who achieve management by thorough drill and careful training. Every captain must have his lieutenant; every principal has in fact an understudy. The opportunities of achieving management by careful attention to detail and honest effort at following example are far more numerous than would be supposed by any one who has not given careful thought to the subject.

Every young man starting out in business naturally desires to devote himself to that which will pay best. The most cursory examination of business institutions reveals the fact that management is much better paid than performance. It shows that the director of affairs has a more lucrative position than any of the subordinates under him who execute his orders. The so-called business man, if, perchance, he is successful, makes the fortune that he aspires to, not alone by the detail work that he does, but rather by the skilful management with which he handles the men he employs.

These thoughts lead up to the broad question of the theory of business administration and the science that underlies business management. It must be admitted that there is no school at present teaching business administration save only the expensive school presided over by dame Experience. Further, there is little or no literature referring to the theory or science of business management. It is true that there are odd volumes referring to salesmanship, to commercial credits, and upon finance, and also certain works on accountancy, all of which should be included in a library relating to this general subject, but after all they treat of business administration only in a general way and leave the main part of the subject untouched.

*

We do believe, however, that in the course of time, and that at a not very distant date, business administration will be taken up by some of the schools, and further, that business management will be discussed by some of the ablest economic writers of the period in a way to supply in part, at least, the want which manifestly exists for such literature. There is so much in the way of material prosperity dependent upon the adequate direction of business affairs that the welfare of the nation demands the establishment of schools which will train men for business administration and make them sufficiently skilful in the management of affairs to avoid the losses which are occurring constantly, due to ignorance and incompetence. Just as insurance companies find it profitable to exercise a proper supervision of the construction of the building they insure, so will the financial interests of the community discover sooner or later that it is profitable to train men to management for the sake of reducing the risks incidental to business ventures.

* * *

The Present of Accountancy from an English Point of View

Recent issues of this journal have contained a full report of the very interesting address recently delivered before the New York Chapter of the Institute of Accounts by C. W. Haskins, C. P. A., F. I. A., president of the New York State Society of Certified Public Accountants, entitled "The Past and Future of Accountancy." This effort has been read by accountants and business men everywhere and has attracted a very large amount of attention. It has been reproduced in full or in part in various trade and technical journals and has been commented upon therein.

In the issue of our London contemporary, "The Accountant," for the week ending June 13, there were nearly three pages devoted to Mr. Haskins's address, and in the belief that our readers generally will be interested in what the organ of the Institute of Chartered Accountants in England and Wales has to say upon this subject, we propose at this time to present a few excerpts and accompanying same with such remarks as seem appropriate. At the outset our contemporary says:

"Our readers will doubtless have noticed that even when American accountants are dealing with a subject of no special intrinsic interest, their treatment of the matter is well worthy of attention on account of the (to us) novel point of view from which the subject is approached. And these general remarks apply with perhaps more than usual force to Mr. Haskins's presidential address."

From the last clause it would appear that our contemporary assumes that the address in question was delivered before the society of which Mr. Haskins is pres-

ident. This appears also in what follows in the succeeding paragraph, for in all the comments upon the address references are made to public accountants and the laws existing in this country relating to public accountants. There is no reference to the Institute of Accounts, the only society which devotes itself to the advancement of accountancy in the broadest meaning of the word, of which Mr. Haskins is an honored fellow, and before which the address was delivered.

We are naturally much interested to learn what is the novel point of view from which this subject was treated. We again quote:

"In the case of so new an institution as the New York State Society of Certified Public Accountants it necessarily follows that the president would have to deal with the accountancy profession as a whole, rather than with an exclusive history of the body over which he presides."

From this we are allowed to infer that in England the officials of societies which have sufficient history to make that course possible are in the habit of confining their addresses to the glorification of the bodies to which they belong. Or to put it still more plainly, that it is customary in England to take the narrowest possible view of the subject, and that, therefore some explanation is necessary of the course of action followed by an officer of a society of the new world who is so bold as to take a comprehensive view of the subject. We quote further, bearing upon the same point:

"This is also fortunate from the view point of our readers who are thus presented with a record of the early history of accountancy, which is more complete than any which has recently appeared in these pages, while the references which are appended at the end of the paper will also prove of value to those who wish to follow the subject further."

This is a neat way of saying that from the English point of view the profession of necessity depends upon the efforts of new organizations and recent additions to the societies devoted to accountancy for all progressive and valuable work.

With this much of introduction, our contemporary proceeds to make a brief digest of the information contained in Mr. Haskins's address which, it would seem, is, in most part, new to it. The various historical references in the address are alluded to. Finally coming down to recent times, special mention is made of what was presented in the address on the subject of education. Mr. Haskins's reference to the reports of the American Bankers' Association, commenting on commercial education in England, in which it is suggested that it is deviating from the proper order of things to establish examinations without first founding schools where the various subjects to be dealt with may be learned, and wherein he quotes: "When a school here and there finally decided to open a commercial department, it was found that in all England there was no properly qualified teachers for this work," draws from our contemporary the frank admission that the reference is not recognized. "Presumably," it says, "this refers to various technical and commercial colleges which have been established during the past ten years; but if so there would not be, and there never has been, the least difficulty in finding qualified persons willing to teach accountancy subjects. Naturally, however, such teachers are somewhat expensive, and in most cases the governing bodies have preferred to work upon more economical lines, even when efficiency has been thereby impaired."

This appears to give us the information that commercial schools in England are of recent date. However this may be, we are still further informed by it that the commercial colleges of England prefer to work upon extremely economical lines, even though efficiency is thereby

impaired. As to this we are free to declare that our American commercial colleges parallel them, notwithstanding they have the advantage of fifty or sixty years in age.

We continue to quote from our contemporary:

"When a scheme of education is being considered it is of course more important to provide the means of learning than to establish examinations upon subjects which are comparatively unknown. But in connection with accountancy it must be borne in mind, in the first place, that the English Institute does not profess to be an educational body, and in the second place that no school could possibly be designed at which any one could learn to be an accountant."

We are at a loss to know why the reference to the English Institute is brought in at this point, for, as it happens, the association referred to is only one of several influential bodies representing the accountancy profession in Great Britain. The subject under discussion is education broadly, and it is absurd for the organ of the English Institute to suppose that all the responsibilities rest upon the devoted shoulders of the single organization for which it speaks.

We think that accountants generally will agree with our contemporary that there is no school at which it is possible to learn to be an accountant, and we also believe that the majority of the profession will agree with Mr. Haskins that schools might be established which would successfully teach many things which professional accountants ought to know, and which, supplemented by actual experience in the field, would make a man a broader accountant and a more useful business adviser than would be possible if his training were to be confined to an apprenticeship in an accountant's office.

We are much interested in the frank admission of our contemporary that the progress that has been made in New York State in the way of statutory recognition places New York accountants in a better position than that at present held by English accountants. We again quote:

" . . . Accountants have already secured a reasonable statutory recognition in . . . the United States. The general position of accountancy in this country (England), however, is little better than it was prior to the granting of the Charter, save that the influence of the Institute has caused the average standing and ability of practitioners to be very considerably higher. This, of course, is a great advantage to the public, and from that point of view the English Institute must be regarded as an unqualified success; but as much has not been obtained from membership of the Institute as might have been the case if the scheme and constitution of the Institute, as laid down by the charter, had been on broader lines."

The article closes with a column or more devoted to that paramount topic in all discussions of accountancy in its page, namely, the relative position of the English Institute among the various accountants' societies which now exist in Great Britain. Particularly hostile does our contemporary appear to be toward the Association of Accountants and Auditors, which, it says, is successfully conferring the privileges of its membership on practitioners abroad, a matter in which the English Institute is conspicuously deficient. It says:

"Unless chartered accountants are prepared to look forward with equanimity to the time when the Institute shall cease to occupy numerically the premier position among associations of English-speaking accountants (they will no doubt continue to occupy the premier position in other respects) it is important that their powers should be enlarged while there is still time to stem the tide of coming events."

A Debilitating Strain

By B. LEBAHR.

Bills, bills, nothing but bills, is the wail
of the penniless man;
Bills, bills, from morn to night, and it's
dodge them whenever you can.
They come with the milk, and they come
with the coal, and they're poked
through the crack in the door,
It is, "Please, Mr. Debtor, won't you settle at once,
We need cash, and can't wait any more."

And what boots it to toss them right
into the fire,
When to-morrow they haunt you again?
In daylight from every corner and nook,
Peers a bill with a horrible leer,
And when Morpheus appears, relief com-
eth not,
For e'en in one's dream they appear,
And the bills then take forms, as of
horrible birds,
Big ones and fat ones and sleek,
But no matter what shape, for every
bird,
Has an obtrusive, cruel cut beak.

A NIGHTMARE OF BILLS

Bills, bills, at every turn. One's hair
grows gray from strain.
Butcher's bills, baker's bills, big bills
and small,
And the old ones keep coming again.
And talk of Nemesis, of the man with a
Past,
Of the spirit avenging that thrills.
Was man's spirit e'er tortured for im-
provident act,
As it is by the horror of bills?
Bills, bills, what an endless pile,

How they sear on a man's weary brain;
And the bills of the birds eat into one's
flesh,
'Till he wakes in a horrible sweat,
But the peck of those bills is not nearly
so sore
As the bills that the debtor beset,
Bills, bills, of every kind,
Save one solitary kind I don't know,
And, oh, for a few U. S. Government
bills,
And less of the bills that I owe.

Accountants' Associations

Corporation of Accountants of Australia

Australia, which in matters of enterprise and public improvements, is probably able to hold its own with any other
country, has recently incorporated a new
association of accountants. This organization has been founded to enlarge upon
the good done by the Sydney Institute
of Public Accountants, established in
1894. The new association has its home
in New South Wales. Sir W. P. Man-
ning is the president. The society proposes to hold regular meetings at which
papers will be read and discussed. We
also learn that a monthly magazine is
to be published. Numerous representatives of banks, insurance companies and
commercial houses, we are informed, are
in support of the movement, and the association bids fair to prove a success.

Illinois Institute of Accounts

The regular meeting of the above organization was held at Dewey Hall, Chicago, Ill., on Thursday evening, twelfth
instant. Several invited guests were
present and a very interesting programme was gone through. Careful attention was paid to the address of L. A.
Goddard, cashier of the Fort Dearborn
National Bank, who chose for his sub-

ject "Banking and Currency." He succeeded in arousing the interest of his audience by the pithiness and pertinency
of his remarks. The audience were also
treated to "An Analysis of the Building
Trades Strike," by C. Milne Mitchell, a
member of the Chicago Bar. There were
also several musical features on the programme and altogether a very profitable
and enjoyable evening was passed.

To Avoid the Use of Initials

From the official organ of the Society
of Accountants and Auditors, we note
that there is a movement on foot in that
organization to substitute for the present method of appending initials after a
member's name, denoting membership in
the society, some other means conveying
equal honor but which is free from am-
biguity.

At present it is the custom for members to place after their names the initials F. S. A. A. (Fellow Society Accountants and Auditors). The association has now come to the conclusion
that these letters have not enough sig-
nificance with the general public to warrant the continuance of their use. It is
held that they serve neither to identify
the society or the member in the public

mind. Business firms who require the
services of a public accountant, while
surmising that a "F. S. A. A." indicated
some degree or honor, are, in the majority of cases, quite ignorant of what
that degree consists. It is proposed,
therefore, to drop the use of these initials altogether and to make use of the
term "Incorporated Accountant" for denoting membership in the society. As
this organization is generally known
throughout England as the "Incorporated Society," the use of this term will
give the members greater prestige and
at the same time keep the society constantly before the public.

Organization of Women Bookkeepers

In a recent issue of ACCOUNTICS, we referred to the fact that certain bookkeepers of Chicago were organizing under the name of the "Chicago Society of
Accountants and Bookkeepers," and that
the movement was attracting considerable attention. The success of this venture has aroused the interest of the
women bookkeepers of Chicago, and the
latter have given evidence of their enterprise and ability to look after themselves by forming an auxiliary society
to the Chicago Society of Accountants
and Bookkeepers.

At last accounts the membership of the
women's organization consisted of sixteen,
and their platform was declared to be
"equal wages for woman and man." Efforts, it is declared, will be made to in-
duce every woman bookkeeper in Chicago to enroll herself under the banner
of the organization. As there are several hundred in the class all working for
comparatively small wages, it is expected that the roll of the organization
will be rapidly filled.

The new members of the organization
mentioned are said to look with favor
upon this new movement on the part of
their sister bookkeepers. President
Hindley is reported to have expressed
himself as being anxious to have women
become the fair competitors of men and
to place them where they could demand
a "man's salary for a man's work." Nor
are these sentiments to be set down
only as the manifestation of a spirit of
gallantry. It is well known that a
woman bookkeeper's willingness to cut
the rates is the cause of many a good
man bookkeeper finding himself out-
classed. He has found it impossible to
meet the competition of his more easily
satisfied sister bookkeeper. Thus, a determination upon the part of the women
to make a strike for equal wages with
the men, it is believed, will redound
greatly to the advantage of the latter.
We shall watch the progress of the
movement with interest.

A correspondent writes to an exchange
as follows: "Why are paper makers the
greatest of magicians?" To which the
editor replies: "Because they transmute
the rags of beggars into sheets for ed-
itors to lie on. We might add that some
of the sheets escape this low office, being
those on which accountants spread their
balances.

Accountics

The Office Magazine.

Published Monthly.

A. O. KITTREDGE, F. I. A., C. P. A., Editor.

E. R. KITTREDGE, Associate.

Accountics is devoted to the Science of Accounting, to the Art of Bookkeeping and to the advocacy of Improved Office Methods.

Subscription.—One dollar a year, payable in advance.

Postage is prepaid by the publishers in the United States, Canada and Mexico. For all other countries in the Postal Union, subscribers must add 50 cents a year.

Discontinuances.—In the absence of specific orders to discontinue at the end of the subscription term the magazine will be continued and a bill sent.

Remittances should be by Draft, P. O. Order or Express Order, payable to the order of the ACCOUNTICS ASSOCIATION. Money and postage stamps are at the risk of the sender, unless sent by express or in registered letters. Add 10 cents each to checks on local banks to defray collection charges.

Advertising Rates will be quoted on application.

Official Journal.—This publication, by resolutions duly passed, has been made the official publication of the following organizations :—

THE INSTITUTE OF ACCOUNTS.
THE NEW YORK CHAPTER of the Institute of Accounts.
THE WASHINGTON CHAPTER of the Institute of Accounts.
THE HARTFORD CHAPTER of the Institute of Accounts.

ACCOUNTICS is the accredited medium of inter-communication between members of the Institute of Accounts wherever located.

ACCOUNTICS ASSOCIATION, Publishers,

Lancashire Building, Pine Street, near Nassau, New York.

Publishers' Desk

The address by C. W. Haskins, C. P. A., F. I. A., president of the New York State Society Certified Public Accountants, entitled "Accountancy; Its Past and Its Present," delivered before the New York Chapter of the Institute of Accounts, Thursday evening, January 25, 1900, has been reprinted from the pages of ACCOUNTICS in a very attractive twenty-four-page pamphlet with deckled edge cover. The interest aroused by this address, manifested by the extensive correspondence it has called forth, merits the effort to give it a special circulation. In another column we refer to the comments upon this address made by our London contemporary.

Fear lest a new concern, calling itself the "National Credit Men's Association," which seems to be a private collection agency, shall in any ways be confounded with the National Association of Credit Men, on account of the great similarity of the names, has caused the latter organization, through its secretary, to issue a circular strenuously and emphatically denying any connection with it. In this circular it is stated that dunning circulars are being sent to merchants throughout the country by the new concern which have created the impression among the recipients of such circulars that they came from the National Association of Credit Men. Inasmuch as the National Association of Credit Men is not a collection agency, and does not even run a collection department, the fraud is palpable. In the circulars of the dunning concern no specified address is given, but they bear the names of thirty-three cities. The organization calls itself, as above stated, The National Credit Men's Association.

In reporting the address on the subject of "Accounting for Cotton Mills," delivered by A. O. Kittredge, editor of ACCOUNTICS, before the New York Chapter of the Institute of Accounts some time since, the "Furniture Trade Review" of recent date says:

We reproduce the address in substance because the system of accounting described therein is applicable not only to cotton manufacturing but to the making of carpets, upholstery goods, and, in fact, all manufacturing business. The general system of accounting referred to in the address is one that has recently been put into operation by two very prominent cotton mill corporations in the northern part of the country and by another in the South. The system has been adapted to the requirements of various other industries, and is in use in many of the largest establishments throughout the nation, from bicycle factories to engine works, and from publishing concerns to department stores.

Tecumseh Swift, writing in the "American Machinist," makes the following comparisons between trade papers and technical books: The book writer deals mostly with what has been, while the trade journal has to do much more with what is and what is coming. The trade journal cannot be made by one writer, as the book can, but needs the active co-operation of the many, and it must be in touch with many more. I can understand much better how a live mechanic can get along without many technical books than I can his living and thinking he can know what he ought to know without his trade paper. I have an idea that the trade papers are to become more important and useful and necessary as the years roll on, and that no one can keep the run of progressive development and attainment without them.

He Found Out

He was a city man.

He raved loudly against monopolies every time he paid his gas bills.

He declared himself in favor of municipal ownership of public utilities.

He used to write letters to the papers on the subject.

One day he saw an advertisement in the daily paper.

The advertisement read, "Send a dollar and learn how to save your gas bills?"

He hastened to send his dollar, immediately.

He went around the next few days with a happy smile.

He was eager to get square with the company.

In course of time the answer came.

He opened it eagerly and read:

"Dear sir, your inquiry and fee received.

"How to save your gas bills? Paste them in a book, and keep the book in a safe place."

Then he swore. He swore long. He swore ardently.

The Novelty Inkstand

Much inventive skill has been displayed in the matter of inkwells, and, if the truth were told, the market has been flooded with many contrivances of this character. Some of them, while reflecting the ingenuity of the inventor, are devoid of practical use to the consumer. Therefore, we can readily understand why the business man turns impatiently aside at the mere mention of a new idea in inkwells. If, however, such a one will glance for a second at the cuts on this page, illustrating the Novelty Inkstand, we feel sure that he will find his attention held for a moment at least, in spite of his prejudice. The Novelty Inkstand is constructed on the same principle as a certain kind of bird trap. The ink well proper is rectangular in form, and at the top, is a hollow cover, the front side of which is hinged and yields inwardly whenever the slightest pressure is brought to bear upon it. The swinging side of this cover is made of glass, and when the pen point is pushed against it, it falls back, allowing the pen to enter the ink. As soon as the

General View

pen is withdrawn, it closes the space by gravity.

The inkwell is made in two separate pieces. The base is of ornamental glass and the top of white metal, full nickel plated. The fact that the swinging front of the top or cover is of glass prevents the spoiling of the pen by friction. One of the chief advantages of this inkwell, to which the manufacturers direct attention, lies in the fact that the top attachment or cover can be lifted off the base, and the well itself, as well as the top, cleaned with perfect ease. The manufacturers also direct attention to the

Sectional View

fact that there is no rubber to rot and no springs to get out of order.

In the illustration, Figure 1, shows the inkstand complete and ready for use, while Figure 2 is a sectional view, showing the manner in which the pen is inserted into the ink and the action of the swinging glass side.

The Novelty Inkstand is manufactured by the Philadelphia Novelty Manufacturing Co. of Philadelphia, Pa.

The Thoughtful Boy

"That office boy of yours has a thoughtful cast of countenance."

"Hasn't he? He's thinking up some new excuses for getting away to the ball games."

A Legal Wonder

The great lawyer was just ready to go home when his office door was rudely pushed open by a tall, shabby look'ng man who entered, leading by the hand a remarkably impudent-looking, twelve-year-old boy. The man sank into a seat without being asked, while the boy went over to the bookcase and gazed wistfully at the calf-bound volumes.

"Well, sir," said the lawyer, with some asperity, "what can I do for you?"

"Say, mister," said the man, speaking

in a low tone of voice, "I want you to take my son Willie into your office"—

"Very sorry," began the lawyer, half rising.

"Wait a minute, wait a minute," sa'd the man, hastily. "Willie ain't like other boys, Willie ain't. He'd be a treasure to any first-class lawyer, Willie would. Knows more law than some men three times his age, Willie does."

"Really, I don't care to hear any more about Willie," interrupted the lawyer. "I tell you, that I have no vacancy in my office just at present."

"Make one—make one," whispered the man, hastily. "It'll pay you. Why, Willie has been a lawyer ever since he was born. As soon as he could talk, he told his ma he'd apply to the courts for an injunction if she didn't take the pin out of his swaddling clothes. When he got a year or two older and learned how to print, that boy drew up a constitution and by-laws for the regulation of the nursery and pinned them to the wall."

"Really, you must excuse me," muttered the lawyer, wearily.

"Wait a little," said the man, feeling in his pocket and pulling out a soiled scrap of paper, "this is his latest. The other day I told him to give his brother an orange. He did it, and gave him th's along with it; wait while I read it:

"'Brother Georgie Adolphus, I hereby give, grant and convey to you all my interest, right, title and advantage of and in said orange, together with its rind, skin, juice, pulp and pits; and all rights and advantage therein, with full power to bite, suck or otherwise eat the same, or give away with or without the rind, skin, juice, pulp or pits; anything hereinbefore or in any other deed or deeds, instruments of any nature or kind whatsoever to the contrary in any wise notwithstanding.'"

"That's all his own work," said the man, proudly, "and I thought if I brought him over here, you'd find him a position as manager or something. That boy is too bright to be at school any longer. What do you say?"

But the lawyer had fled, leaving the office in possession of the applicants.

Trials of a Bank Clerk

Bank clerks are often regarded as exceedingly lucky and fortune-favored mortals. A few such experiences as a clerk of a certain down-town savings institution recently went through would cause even the most patient of them to disgust. An old woman, of undeniable disgust. An old woman of undeniable Celtic origin, entered the bank and walked up to the desk.

"Do you want to draw or deposit?" asked the gentlemanly clerk.

"Naw, I doant. Oi wants ter put some in," was the reply.

The clerk pushed up the book for her signature, and, indicating the place, said:

"Sign on this place, please."

"Above it or below it?"

"Just above it."

"Me whole name?"

"Yes."

"Before Oi was married?"

"No, just as it is now."

"Oi can't write."

The Nation's Accounts

It would be impossible in a single article to describe all of the accounts that the National Government is obliged to keep in order to know its financial condition and the general progress which the development of the country is making. At best not more than one class of accounts could be treated in a single article. It is very generally admitted that the statistics of an enterprise are an essential part of its accounting. Therefore, we may reckon the statistics of a nation as part of the accounting of the nation. Included in the statistics of the nation is the census. How the census is taken, so far as the enumerators are concerned, is already known to our readers, who have been put to the trouble of answering the various pertinent questions asked by these agents during the past few weeks; but how the data so gathered is compiled into tables and a faithful count made out is something upon which perhaps a little information would be acceptable.

As a rule, the census of the United States has been very slow in compilation. Not only months but sometimes years, have transpired before the work of the enumerators has been got into final shape for public use. In late years, however, remarkable progress has been made in matters of this kind. The last census, ten years since, was brought through much more rapidly than any of its predecessors, and the present one is being put into shape with a speed that is extremely creditable.

This is due to the adoption by the government of certain unique machines which render possible the performance in a few hours of work which, without their use, would entail a great amount of labor. The New York "Sun," in the head lines of an article dealing with this subject, facetiously puts into rhyme the method of counting the census now employed, as follows:

"Each person's card is punched with care,
With all the facts that should be there,
Then fed to a machine and pressed—
And electric currents do the rest."

The employment of punched cards and electric currents herein referred to is not entirely new to practical statisticians, but the employment of such machines as at present are being used in the census office has never been attempted before. To give an idea of the efficiency of these machines it is said, for example, that Chicago's population of two millions of people could be counted by means of the machines in five days.

The machines employed are of two varieties or classes, and are known as the punching machine and the electric tabulator, respectively. The punching machine is technically known as the keyboard punch and is something like a typewriter in appearance. It has in front a perforated keyboard made of celluloid. Over this keyboard swings freely a sharp index finger whose movement, after the manner of a pantograph, is repeated in the rear by a punch. The keyboard has twelve rows of twenty holes and each has its distinctive letter or number, which corresponds to the inquiry or answer respecting a person. Hence, when the index finger is pressed into any one of these holes, the punch at the back says ditto by stamping out a hole in a manila card.

Dr. Fred H. Wines, Assistant Director of the Census, describes the punching machine in this way:

"The punching machine is something like a typewriter in appearance. The punch is attached to a movable key, which plays over a perforated keyboard arranged like the keyboard of a typewriter. It contains 288 symbols, and is an exact duplicate of the cards employed to contain the statistics of each person. For the most part, these symbols consist of figures and easily understood abbreviations, and the labor of learning to operate the machine is hardly any greater than that of mastering the ordinary typewriter."

Director Merriam has disposed of the punching apparatus even more briefly. He says in a recent article:

"This transcript from the original returns of the enumerator to the punched card will be done with small machines, something like typewriters, called keyboard punchers. About 1,000 of these will be used, and the entire work of transcribing the 75,000,000 or more individual records will be done in about 100 working days, or nearly four months."

There are 100,000,000 of these manila pasteboards hoarded away and in use at the Census Bureau. Director Merriam has figured out that though each card is only 7-1000 of an inch thick, the total supply of cards on hand will form a stack nine miles high and will weigh over 200 tons. Each card looks like a Chinese puzzle, containing as it does various figures, abbreviations and symbols. Each figure, abbreviation or symbol means something, and when punched tells some sort of a tale about a certain citizen of the nation, for every man, woman and child in this broad land has a card to the twelfth census of the United States.

In a semi-technical way the tabulator may be said to consist of three main parts, namely, the press or circuit-closing device, the dials or counters and the sorting boxes. The press consists of a hard rubber plate, provided with 316 holes or pockets, the relative positions of which correspond with those of the holes in the keyboard and gang punches. Each of these pockets is partially filled with mercury, and they are thus in electrical connection, when the circuit is closed, with the binding posts and switch board at the back of the machine.

Above the hard rubber plate swings a reciprocating pin box, which is provided with a number of projecting spring-actuated points, so hung as to drop exactly into the center of the little mercury cups below. These pins are so connected that when a punched card is laid on the rubber plate against the guides or stops and the box is brought down, all the pins not stopped by the unpunched surface will be pressed through, close the circuit and count on the dials. The circuit is really closed first through platinum contacts at the back of the press. In this way no difficulty is experienced from the oxidation of the mercury from the spark, as would be the case without this precaution.

The dials of the tabulator are not the least important part of the machine. The front of each dial or counter is three inches across, and, as now made, consists of paper ingeniously coated with celluloid, insuring a smooth, bright, clean face. Each dial is divided into 100 parts, and two hands travel over the face, one counting units and the other hundreds. The train of clockwork is operated electrically, by means of the electro-magnet, whose armature, as it moves each time the circuit is closed, carries the unit hand forward one division, while every complete revolution actuates a carrying device, which in turn causes the hundred hand to count. In this way each dial will register up to 10,000.

A noteworthy feature of these ingenious little dials is that they can quickly be set at zero, while they are also removable and interchangeable. The electrical connections are made simply by slipping them into frames and clips.

As fast as they are punched and sorted according to sex, nativity or color the punched cards are taken to the machine room and run through the electric tabulating machines. To take off all the information contained on the cards they are run through the machines four or possibly five times. Each instrument is capable of disposing of about 10,000 cards per day, and it will, therefore, take from ten to fifteen of them to finally keep pace with the punchers.

Concerning the electric tabulator, Director Merriam says: These punched record cards are then counted or tabulated in the electrical tabulating machines. These machines are provided with a circuit-closing device, into which the cards are rapidly fed one by one. The holes in the card control the electric circuits through a number of counters, which will, as desired, count the simple facts, as to the number of males, females, etc., or the most complicated combination which the statistician may ask for. After the cards for a given district are thus passed through the tabulating machine we know the number of native-born white males of voting age, the number of white children under five years of age born in this country, with both parents native born, or the number of such children with one or both parents foreign born, or any other information contained in the enumerators' sheet which the statistician desires tabulated. In short, it is only necessary for the statistician to decide upon the information wanted and for the electrician to make the proper connection from the counters and relays to the circuit-controlling device into which the cards are fed.

The methods employed for checking the proper workings of the machines are ingenious and interesting. If the card is not completely punched or not properly fed to the machine or is placed upside down, or if some item has been over-looked, or, in fact, if everything is not all right, the machine refuses to work and the card is rejected. Neither will the machine work if the circuit-controlling device is operated without a card in place. Such a machine also has the advantage that it will not make mistakes because it is tired or does not feel well, or because the weather is warm, or by reason of the thousand and one causes which will upset the human machine.

Another description of this interesting device—and no two persons can say the same thing of it—is by the Assistant Director, Dr. Wines, who says:

"Roughly described, the electric counting apparatus consists of a box of needles set on spiral springs. These needles descend on each card as it passes through the machine. Where there are holes in the card the needles pass through and dip into a cup of mercury placed underneath. This completes an electric circuit and sets in motion an indicator upon a dial, which moves forward exactly like the second hand of a clock, the various dials thus enumerating all the facts and combinations of facts wanted. From the indicator dials the figures are copied off on 'result slips' and filed for the tabulating clerks. It is estimated that each of the tabulating machines compiles and registers information that would require the services of twenty clerks under the old system of tally sheets. A consideration of even more importance is its greater accuracy. The machine automatically throws out any card that is wrong. For example, if one of the required facts, say sex, has not been indicated on the card, the plunger will not register, and the bell at the side of the machine, which rings to indicate the correctness of each card, remains silent. It is then a comparatively easy matter to go back to the schedules and supply the missing information, whereas on the tally sheets such a mistake would hardly be discovered."

Disadvantages of Paying Cash, or, How to Establish Your Credit

The advantage and advisability of always paying cash for his purchases has been so well drilled into the young man with the future before him that if he were to be questioned as to what, in his opinion, is the golden rule he must observe in business, he would, in nine cases of ten reply, "Never take credit." Successful business men, as a general rule, deem the adoption of this advice to be of paramount importance, and, although they recognize the fact that if the young business man is progressive, he is bound to seek credit to a certain extent in order to increase the scope of his operations; still they impress upon him the fact that, unless at the start he adheres to a system of strict cash payment, and thereby earns the respect and confidence of people he deals with, he will never reach that stage where he will be able to borrow. This seems to be the generally accepted theory, and its propagation has

certainly done much to establish good business habits in young men.

Now, however, a well-known business man of such standing as to enable him to speak authoritatively, comes forward with the statement that, in his opinion, a young man is ruining his own prospects by paying cash where he can get credit. He deems the golden rule of business for the young man to be "Never pay cash where it is possible to obtain credit." In order, however, that his advice may not be suspected of savoring of dishonesty, he adds the important supplementary injunction, "Always see that you are in a position to meet your bills."

"In my opinion," says this writer, "it is folly on a young man's part to have such a dread of falling into debt. Every business man with any enterprise about him is bound to need additional capital in his business sooner or later, and the man who has been borrowing little amounts all the time and paying them back promptly and without any trouble stands a much better chance of getting financial help when he needs it than is the man who scrupulously refuses to take a cent's worth of credit until he actually needs it.

"The reason for this is easily apparent. It is one of the traits of human nature to go on trusting until suspicion is awakened. The young man who keeps on borrowing and borrowing and always takes care to maintain a reserve fund sufficient to meet all his bills and obligations on time, will never awaken that suspicion, but will, on the contrary, obtain a splendid reputation for thrift and industry among his little world. The young man who pays cash will, on the contrary, be trusted only as long as he continues to pay cash, but as soon as he seeks credit he will awaken suspicion on account of his change of policy and will probably meet with a cold refusal, although he may be of greater integrity than his credit-seeking brother. People will say to each other, 'Young M—— must be doing well, he pays his bills with the regularity of clock-work and never asks for an extension. He seems likely to succeed. Let's deal with him.' Thus this young man's creditors become his best advertisers, and when they have tried him for some time and find he never fails them they will be only too willing to accommodate him any time he needs a financial loan.

"Now let us see how the cash-paying young man is going to fare. I cannot do better than to narrate to you the case of a young country merchant I know. He has always paid cash for everything he bought (and did a correspondingly small business). He determined finally to enlarge his trade, and to do this required the credit he had never before asked for. When he came to town and asked the men to whom he had always paid cash to let him have goods on time they one and all became suspicious of him and refused. The very fact that he had always paid cash made them think, when he finally asked for credit, that he wasn't a safe man to trust. Moral: Never pay cash for anything if you would avoid suspicion."

New York Credit Men's Association

We are in receipt of a communication from Secretary Sayer, of the New York Credit Men's Association, in which he asks us to call the attention of our readers to the struggle that this organization is making to "improve the laws bearing on the rights of creditors and the punishment of rascals who prey on commerce." In this work the association claims to have been largely successful in the past, in spite of the inadequacy of the laws that prevail. As an evidence of the good work done, we give below an abstract of a circular just issued by this organization, detailing some of the proceedings of the National Convention of Credit Men, held at Milwaukee in June. At that convention, says the circular, the following measures were recommended:

Increased exertion to be made by each local organization to punish dishonesty and to prevent the benefits of the bankruptcy act being obtained by those who are evidently guilty of fraud. Renewed efforts be made to have a fund of ten thousand dollars available and in the hands of the National Committee for the prosecution of those who have perpetrated fraud on its subscribers.

The legend "Member of the —— Credit Men's Association" be printed on all business stationary so that fellow members may recognize it and be more ready to answer inquiries.

Credit men to be recommended to take the precaution to ascertain if applicants for credit take an annual inventory so that fire insurance may not be invalidated by their omission to do so—some companies making that a condition of their policies.

Where Taxes Should Be Placed

From W. G. M., Buffalo, N. Y.:

In your December issue you extend an invitation for other communications upon this subject. It would seem to me that much of the discussion which is likely to follow from such questions might be set at rest if there were a better understanding of the meaning of many of the terms used in accounting. I would be very much pleased to see some bright accountant take up the whole subject of accounting nomenclature, formulate an "Interpretation of Business Terms Bill," and have it presented to the State Legislature. It would further raise the standard of the profession, harmonize the technical terms used by accountants, and be an invaluable aid in fixing the equitable tax to be paid by those corporations which are so soon to be asked to pay a tax upon their public franchises. Even accountants do not agree upon what constitutes "net profits." And some of them seem to be a little wide of the mark in forming a correct interpretation of some easier problems.

It is freely admitted by modern pedagogues that the use of diagrams when at all possible produces the best results. And it seems to me that the proper disposition of any item of income or expense can best be shown by illustrating a specimen sheet, with the item placed where it properly belongs. Herewith you will find a specimen of a railway profit and loss sheet, showing what I have conceived to be the proper disposition of all taxes which are not properly classified as a permanent increment to the property taxed. I might state here that taxes are divisable into two very distinct classes. First, those by which the property taxed is permanently improved. The first cost of a sewer, a pavement or a sidewalk is properly included as part of the cost of the real estate benefited thereby, and is part of the investment just as much as the buildings erected upon the land. But (second) the repairs upon that sewer, pavement or sidewalk are maintenance charges, because they merely restore the property to its former condition, and therefore must be included with the constantly recurring expense of keeping the property up.

It has been suggested that taxes which are admittedly maintenance charges should be eliminated from the general expenses, and in lieu thereof be deducted from the income. That plan seems to me to be quite as void of good reasoning as the pernicious system of eliminating from both the assets and liabilities of business concerns the amount of all customers' notes (bills receivable) which have been discounted at the bank. It is true it makes a better showing, but the business man who likes that kind of a statement is like an ostrich.

If the taxes charged in the specimen profit and loss account, submitted herewith, had been left out of the cost of maintaining the way and structures, the net profits upon the investment would have been $900,000, which would have

been misleading. Profit and loss sheets are prepared for the information of two classes of investors—the bondholders and the stockholders. The bondholders want to see the amount of the fund out of which they are to receive their interest, and the stockholders want to see the amount of the fund out of which they are to receive their dividends. And neither of them want any figures given them which are subject to further deductions.

Uniform Accounting and Municipal Ownership

J. B. Cahoon, in speaking before the National Electric Light Association a short time since, referred to the fact that a year ago the League of American Municipalities had been challenged to a comparison of the costs of production in private and municipal gas-lighting plants. He declared that all public utilities must in the end submit to public regulation, and stated his opinion that resistance against this course on the part of public utilities would mean municipal ownership in the end. "The number of agitators who are crying municipal ownership of public utilities," he declared, "is constantly and rapidly increasing, and their attacks will be stronger and stronger as time goes on. Our plan of defence must lie in the correct determination of costs, and in showing that, while exercising the functions of a monopoly, we are only attempting to realize therefrom a legitimate profit for the capital we have invested in the enterprise. To do this, we must have uniformity of accounting in order that we may present a solid front and be able to disarm the agitators by showing to the people at large that we are following fair business methods and only obtaining a fair return on our investments."

Mr. Cahoon is of the belief that the question of the accounts themselves, entering into the cost of the product, would not be raised until the class known as capital accounts were arrived at. In order that the true cost of the product may be ascertained, it is necessary to include these latter as part of the operating expenses and not to classify them as deductions from income. In the Street Railway Accountants' Association, the speaker pointed out interest on bonds, interest on current liabilities, investment insurance and reserves for sinking funds, as well as taxes, are not considered parts of the operating expenses, but instead, are treated as deductions from income. This system is criticised by Mr. Cahoon in the following words:

"If we do not charge off each year and expend as an investment in renewals and minor extensions and betterments, a certain portion of the original investment, the time comes, in the course of seven to ten years, when we have got to borrow thousands and thousands of dollars to renew the plant and it may be at a time when that will be very inopportune. The best policy for ourselves, laying side the whole question as to whether or not it is better as a source of protection from the public, is to recognize this factor and include it in our cost of operating expenses.

"We are not private companies in the strict sense of the word. We are operating public utilities, and the public de-

mands to know what it costs us to deliver our product to the consumer and what our profits are. Certainly a part of our costs is taxes, and again, before we can declare a dividend, we must take care of the interest on our bonds, and on our current liabilities. As regards a reserve for sinking fund, the only true way is to recognize the fact that the bonds must be redeemed at maturity, and to make provision for their redemption by setting aside each year such a reserve as will take care of the bonds at their maturity, charging this reserve as part of the operating expenses, or in other words, as one of the factors in the cost of production."

"We may thus see," concluded the speaker, "that the cost of the product is legitimately represented by the four groups of accounts, namely, manufacturing, distribution, general and capital."

The Relationship of Accounting to Economics

By J. THORNTON

There is a close connection, as it seems to me, between economics and bookkeeping. This is only natural and inevitable. Economics is the science of exchanges. Bookkeeping is the art of recording those exchanges. The recognition of this connection enables the theory to be stated in an exceedingly simple form. Every exchange involves of necessity a coming IN and a going OUT. Therefore, every exchange (or transaction) may be clearly and accurately understood as an instance of value IN versus value OUT, and may appropriately be recorded in the books by a reference to this principle. The terms Dr. and Cr. are often employed in bookkeeping in a forced and highly artificial way, and I have found the substitution of the simpler terms IN and OUT, when explaining the principles of the science, a great gain to clearness and accuracy of thought.

Mottos of the Rothschilds

When a man attains anything like success in this world, his opinion on "how to get there" is always eagerly sought by the thousands who are anxious to do likewise. If the great men of any age were to answer every call made upon them to say a few words on the basis of their successes, they would have no time for anything else and would soon be reduced to a state of nervous and physical exhaustion. To the credit of successful men, however, it is to be said that the majority of them are quite ready to give profitable advice to the world at large, if they are only allowed to do it in their own way. Some regard the daily press as being the most suitable medium for the purpose, others favor the rostrum, while still others write and publish books.

It remained, however, for the late Alphonse de Rothschild to put into epigrammatical form a statement of the elements upon which he based the success of his famous house. As being the utterances of this famous member of perhaps the richest family in the world, the following are well worthy of careful consideration:

"Carefully examine every detail of your business."

"Be prompt in everything."

"Take time to consider, but decide positively."

"Dare to go forward."

"Bear troubles patiently."

"Maintain your integrity as a sacred thing."

"Never tell business lies."

"Pay your debts promptly."

"Make no useless acquaintances."

Can any one question the usefulness of the advice thus presented? Will any young man go astray from following this guide to success?

Whereas they have sacrificed to themselves, they become sacrificers to the inconstancy of Fortune, whose wings they thought, by their self-wisdom, to have pinioned.—Bacon.

An Attempt to Elevate the Accounting Profession in England

The professional accountants' bill, which has been recently introduced into the English Parliament, and which counts among its sponsors Sir Arthur Rollitt, ex-president of the London Chamber of Commerce, has for its object the organization of the profession of accountancy on lines similar to those on which the legal and medical professions are now run.

If this bill becomes a law its enforcement, it is claimed, will drive out of the profession all those who are not qualified to practice. The public will thus be protected against the dangers of employing incompetent and disreputable practitioners in the confidential relations of an accountant. This will be done by the establishment of a register, by which recognition will only be given to qualified accountants. The bill also aims at establishing a uniform system of apprenticeship, examination and admissions, throughout the United Kingdom.

This bill is fathered by the Society of Accountants and Auditors (incorporated). The raison d'etre of the bill lies in the fact that this society has viewed with alarm the constant recurrence of cases where the professional prowler and trickster has, by glaring and apparently bonefide advertisements, won himself into public confidence and succeeded in wrecking small companies and in plundering insolvent estates, to the disgrace of the entire body. The passage of this bill, it is claimed, will elevate the profession of accountancy, and at the same time greatly benefit the business public.

Gambling is a mode of transferring property without producing any intermediate good.—Dr. Johnson.

Two English Investors of Note

American securities find purchasers among our friends on the other side of the water, and as is only to be expected, it happens that these foreign investors in American stocks sometimes experience heavy losses, due to injudicious selection. Such calamities are not calculated to increase the faith in the American market. Cases have been known where an unfortunate English speculator who has invested heavily in unsafe American securities and thereby suffered loss, has conceived a mistrust of the people at large and has reached the conclusion that the nation is only a pack of thieves. Such a case is furnished us by Matthew Marshall, the able financial writer of the New York Sun, who amusingly tells the experience of the Rev. Sydney Smith in American investment.

It appears that this famous divine on one occasion bought some Pennsylvania State bonds, on which interest payments were afterwards temporarily suspended. When Mr. Smith learned of this he "set up a howl against the entire American people," accusing them of being a nation of bunco steerers and sharps of the first water. To quote his own words: "I never meet a Pennsylvanian at a London dinner without feeling a disposition to seize and divide him. To allot his beaver to one sufferer and his coat to another, to appropriate his pocket handkerchief to the orphan and to comfort the widow with his silver watch, Broadway rings, and the London Guide, which he always carries in his pocket."

Lord Macaulay, however, did not have equal cause with his contemporary to cherish resentment against our countryman, for he seems to have exercised more sagacity in his investments, both American and other. In his biography it is told that he once found himself with $20,000 which he was free to invest. He inquired first about Spanish bonds, and when he was told that there were several different classes of these and the nature of each class was explained to him, he said:

"I think I catch your meaning. Active Spanish bonds profess to pay interest and do not. Deferred Spanish bonds profess to pay interest at some future time and will not. Passive Spanish bonds profess to pay interest neither now or in the future." He therefore decided to "have none of them," and invested his money to better advantage and in a safer channel

---

Much learning shows how little mortals know; much wealth, how little worldlings can enjoy.—Young.

Golden roofs break men's rest.—Seneca.

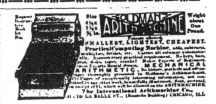

Accountics:—
THE OFFICE MAGAZINE

Volume VII Number 2	AUGUST, 1900	Monthly, $1 a year Single Copy, 10 cents

Shall the Measure of Values be Changed ?

By THOMAS HITCHCOCK.*

Money is anything which serves by common consent, and with or without the help of law, as a measure of the values of commodities and a means for making exchanges of them easy.

We measure the length of cloth by the yard, and the weight of sugar, flour, butter, etc., by the pound, saying that a piece of cloth is so many yards long, and that a particular quantity of sugar, butter or flour weighs so many pounds. In like manner, since these commodities have different values, we express the value of each of them by saying that cloth is worth so many dollars and cents per yard, and sugar, flour and butter so many cents, or hundredth parts of a dollar, per pound. Dollars and cents are the common measure of value, as the yard and its fractions are of length, and pounds and ounces are of weight.

To be a measure of value, money must itself possess value, just as a measure of length must itself have length to measure length, and a measure of weight must have weight to measure weight. If a yardstick had no length we could not use it to measure cloth with, and if a pound had no weight we could not weigh anything with it. In the same way, if a dollar had no value, a million dollars would be worth no more than one, and no one would accept a million of them in payment for his commodities any more willingly than he would one.

The dollar which, with its fractions called cents, is the measure of value in this country, consisted at first both of 371¼ grains of pure silver and of 24.75 grains of pure gold. This made the silver in the silver dollar weigh fifteen times as much as the gold in the gold dollar; and hence it is said that the ratio of the two metals was 15 to 1. Afterward, in 1834, we reduced the weight of gold in the gold dollar to 23.2 grains of pure gold, or 25.8 grains of gold nine-tenths fine, leaving the silver dollar at 371¼ grains of pure silver, or 412½ grains of silver nine-tenths fine. This changed the mint ratio of the two metals to about 16 to 1, at which it has ever since remained.

The reason for the change was that at 15 to 1 gold was undervalued in compar-

* Mr. Hitchcock is widely known by his nom de plume, "Matthew Marshall," over which name his Monday articles on financial topics have appeared in the New York "Sun" for a long time past.

ison with its value in Europe, so that it was all exported and left us only silver dollars for use as money, but the ratio of 16 to 1 was too much in favor of gold, and undervalued silver. Hence, silver became worth in Europe more than we allowed for it, and was in turn exported, leaving us only gold coin.

From 1834 down to 1873 the silver dollar was worth $1.06 in gold, and consequently ceased to circulate as money, so that in 1873 we repealed the law authorizing its coinage, supposing it would never again be wanted.

In 1878, however, silver had so fallen in value that the 16 to 1 ratio overvalued it, and then we recommended coining it on government account and have continued it, until now we have coined 500,000,000 silver dollars, of which 66,000,000 are in actual use and the rest are in the Treasury, being represented by certificates payable in silver dollars on demand.

It has been shown that whatever is used as a measure of value must itself possess value, because, if it did not possess value nobody would give in exchange for it anything valuable. More than this, the things used for money must not only have a value, but they must be generally acceptable. They must pass readily from hand to hand, because if a man could not get rid of them when he wanted to, he would not take them. This was the trouble with cattle, iron, brass, tobacco, skins and wampum; and it is now the trouble with silver.

Tea circulates in Asia and salt in Africa, because everybody can use these commodities; and, therefore, everybody accepts them. Their defect is that they are liable to damage by keeping. Tea loses its flavor in time and salt is injured by dampness. They are, besides, bulky and take up a great deal of room.

Gold, now, besides possessing value, is acceptable all over the civilized world. It loses nothing by keeping, it is of small bulk in proportion to its value, it can be cut up into small pieces and then melted together again without loss of weight, and it can be buried in the ground for centuries and come out as good as ever. Silver has some of these qualities, but it is bulkier than gold in proportion to its value, it tarnishes more quickly, and latterly it has been produced so abundantly

that its value, as we know, has fallen more than one-half from what it was formerly. Hence it has been discarded as a measure of value by all European nations and by the United States. As has been said, we discarded it really in 1834, and by Act of Congress in 1873. Since 1873 gold has been in this country, as it is in Europe, the only recognized standard by which the values of other things are reckoned.

The Democratic party does not deny that, since 1873, the gold dollar has been the only measure of value in use in this country, and that since 1879 all contracts for the payment of dollars have been virtually made for the payment of gold dollars. Even during the suspension of coin payments, from 1862 to 1879, the country repeatedly promised to redeem the greenbacks in gold, and everybody who took and gave greenbacks did so with the knowledge that they would, as soon as possible, as they were in 1879, be made as good as gold.

It is true also that, as has been already said, the government began in 1878 to coin silver dollars at the ratio of 16 to 1, and to make them a legal tender the same as gold dollars, but it coined them slowly and under a pledge to keep their value equal to that of the gold dollar. Thus far the pledge has been redeemed, because the amount of silver dollars is comparatively small, and they are received, like gold dollars, in payment of dues to the government, which in one single year more than equal them in amount. While there are altogether only 500,000,000 of them in existence, the government collected from the people last year $600,000,000.

The Democratic party propose now to throw the coinage of silver at the old ratio of 16 to 1 open to everybody, and let everybody who chooses bring to our mints what is now 47 cents worth of silver and get back for it a silver dollar. There is in the world already enough silver to make 4,000,000,000 of our dollars. The Bank of France alone has enough for 250,000,000; Germany enough for 100,000,000, and the silver mines in various countries are already producing 165,000,000 ounces a year, which would add over 200,000,000 dollars to the mass, to say nothing of the increase of their output which would follow the offer to coin the metal without limit into dollars as available for the payment of debts as gold dollars are.

That the effect of the coinage of this immense amount of silver dollars would be to reduce their value to that of the metal in them, that is to say, to 47 per cent. of the value of the present dollar, is evident.

The man who had lent out $1,000 in gold, or taken notes to that amount for property sold by him, would get back $1,000 in money which would enable him to buy no more than he could have bought with $470 when he lent the $1,000 or sold the property on credit for $1,000. In the same way the mechanic, the laborer, the clerk and every man, woman and child receiving pay for services would find his or her compensation, though apparently the same, really cut down by the rise in the prices of everything that they had to buy—food, fuel, clothing, especially—to less than one-half of what they had been. In order to live as well as they did before they would have to insist on higher wages, and though they would get them in the end, would have to fight for them and go through all the misery and turmoil of strikes.

The immensity of the values which the unlimited coinage of the silver dollar would destroy can hardly be computed. The government bonds alone, which would be payable in silver amount to $700,000,000; the bonds of railroad companies to $3,000,000,000; the bonds secured by mortgages on real estate to $4,000,000,000; the notes held by banks to $5,000,000,000, besides book debts and things of that kind to an unknown extent. Above all, the $2,500,000,000 of deposits in savings banks due to 5,000,000 depositors would be reduced more than one-half, sweeping away the savings of years. What privations, suffering and general misery would follow, any one can judge for himself.

The unlimited coinage of the silver dollar would, therefore, benefit no one but those who happened to owe money when it began, and even these, as soon as their debts were paid, would be in the same condition as the rest of the community. Creditors and wage-earners would, on the other hand, be robbed of millions and never get them back. While the change, too, from gold to silver was going on business would be in confusion, there would be no end of quarrels between debtors and creditors, and we might even have a financial panic, worse than any which the country has heretofore experienced.

Opportunity

By JOHN J. INGALLS

Master of human destinies am I!
Fame, love and fortune on my footsteps wait;
Cities and fields I walk; I penetrate
Deserts and seas remote, and, passing by
Hovel and mart and palace, soon or late
I knock unbidden once at every gate!

If sleeping, wake—if feasting, rise before
I turn away. It is the hour of fate;
And they who follow me reach every state
Mortals desire, and conquer every foe
Save death; but those who doubt or hesitate,
Condemned to failure, penury and woe,
Seek me in vain and uselessly implore.
I answer not, and I return no more.

Depreciation

By CHAS. KER, C. A., Glasgow

When many articles are put together to form the unit called a factory, the parts lose their individuality and become atoms in a whole, whose value is determined not by its cost but by its profit earning power. If there be no demand for the whole because its profit-earning power is nil, its value is the aggregate of the values of the component parts—the break-up value, as it is called. How then is profit to be determined? What test must be applied to ascertain that the fixed capital is intact. Is it to be considered that a factory has made no profit until its works are written down at break-up value? Or is the life of its works, as a whole, to be estimated, and the value to be written down by instalments over that period? Or are the probable lives of the separate items to be taken and written down by instalments? Or are the works to be revalued each year as is the stock, and if so, what is to be the basis of valuation? How are repairs, renewals and outlay on extensions to be treated? The problem is to find out if the original capital is represented by assets of equal value, when it is not possible to bring that value to an accurate test. The usual practice is to estimate the lives of the different assets, and write off yearly instalments from their book value for their estimated depreciation for the year.

It is not, however, always possible to estimate the ultimate break-up value of the assets. In the first place, it is not enough to say there has been use, therefore, there has been depreciation. There is a tendency to depreciation, that is all. Land used as a works site may steadily improve in value. Buildings deteriorate in time, but the period is so long that annual depreciation of buildings kept in repair is practically nil. So it is with machinery. Considering all such different kinds of property, it appears that the physical life of the subject is not of much practical use in determining a rate of depreciation. Secondly, even if one could determine how long it would take to use up the asset, that is only one factor in the question. Buildings in use for many years may become more valuable, owing to advances in material or wages making them more costly to replace. Examples might be multiplied, but it seems clear that depreciation is not necessarily to be inferred from the fact that a subject has been in use for some time. Property in patents and copyrights, and in leaseholds does, of course, depreciate from efflux of time and mines and quarries are gradually worked out; but even in such cases, the statement that the use of an article tends to lessen its value must be qualified by the consideration that at any given time the age or condition is only one element of value, and that the market value—what the thing will realize—is regulated by the law of supply and demand.

There are, thus, disadvantages in attempting to provide out of profits, for

capital used in earning them by estimating the lives of the different assets, and writing their value down by instalments.

In English law there is no provision in the Companies Acts that depreciation shall be provided for. The Acts do not seem to recognize it in any way. There is an article in the Act of 1862 which says that no dividend shall be payable, except out of profits. That does not help one to decide what profits are. All that the courts seem to require is that floating assets should be valued.

By a decision in the case of Lee v. Neuchatel Asphalt Company, Ltd., the partners in a limited company are left to decide, as a question of internal management, what are profits. There are many decisions bearing on the subject; all seem to indicate that, so long as there is a surplus of earnings over disbursements, it may be provided as profits without making any provision for lost capital.

In the recent case in the English Court of Appeals, National Bank of Wales v. Cory, the Court even went so far as to say that the surplus of earnings over disbursements might be divided without providing for bad debts. But while providing for depreciation is a matter within the shareholder's discretion, in England, and while there is no compulsion on the part of directors or shareholders to set aside annually a sum to replace capital so that in a winding up the shareholders may receive the face value of their shares, the auditor is within his province in pointing out to shareholders that, in the absence of such provision for redeeming the capital through writing off for depreciation, they cannot expect to get their capital back in the winding up—that they cannot eat their cake and have it.

German mercantile law lays down definite rules to be adhered to in preparing balance sheets, and inter alia prescribes: "Plant and such articles as are not intended for sale, but on the other hand are intended for carrying on the trade of the company, may be put down at purchase price or cost of producing the same without deduction for deterioration in value, provided that an equivalent amount for wear and tear has been deducted, or that a relative renewal fund has been opened." This is a good working rule to follow in balancing. It is one which, as a matter of fact, most companies in England adopt, but it is not statutory.

Repairs are, of course, a direct working charge on profits. Renewals are a charge to profits of the nature of a depreciation allowance. A direct charge for depreciation, while in theory a provision for exhausted capital, or for future renewals, is in practice only an expedient (though an excellent one) for keeping in hand a portion of the earnings which might, without it, be withdrawn and spent; or, in other words, an expedient for keeping intact the working capital.

This is especially true of limited companies. The limited capital is the life blood of the company, and it is in this essential that the limited companies are limited. They cannot draw on their partners beyond a certain amount. Private partnerships, where each partner is liable for the whole debts, need not, and do not, as a rule, concern themselves much with depreciation, and many a successful business is being carried on without any attention being paid to it. But where success is attained in such private concerns, one finds due regard paid to keeping up the efficiency of the business by spending money in replacing assets which have served their turn, and are, for one reason or another, out of date.

The books of a certain prosperous concern were kept in single entry, no ledger accounts but those of debtors, creditors and bank. The test there of the year's profit was the rough and ready one of the increase for the year of money on deposit receipt. That concern prospered, one might say, because of its rudimentary bookkeeping, which showed the fixed idea that it is only free money not required for the business that is truly divisible profit. So when the concern had to spend $25,000 on extensions, that sum came out of the bank account and consequently out of the profits for the year.

We see the other side of the question in private partnerships in which the personal drawings of partners have led them to dispense with repairs and renewals in order that they may spend the last penny of profits which have been arrived at, without any attempt being made to retain in their businesses, by depreciation or reserves, the cash required to keep the business alive. And as in private partnerships personal extravagance is one of the most common causes of bankruptcy, so in limited companies one of the most serious risks run is that shareholders may not realize the importance of keeping working capital intact, or may elect to ignore it.

The exact form in which capital necessary for assuring continuity in a business by maintaining the working capital should be reserved out of profits is not of much moment. Providing for depreciation is favored, because by this method the profits set aside are put out of reach and cannot be brought back into account, as sums in reserve account can. The main thing is to adhere to a policy of laying by. The whole thing, therefore, amounts to this: Provision for depreciation is necessary, not specifically to meet anything that is accurate and scientific and definable, but to prevent the dispersion among shareholders of funds which may be required to meet the various contingencies and perils of trade, so that the company may keep abreast of the times, vigorous and well equipped against home and foreign competition. It is not, however, to be understood that sums voted for depreciation should not be applied to the assets in a discriminating way according to a plan based on the estimated life of each asset so as to provide for its future renewal. The main thing is that such sums should be voted and if there is any error at all, it should be an error on the side of fulness.

When It's Hot

When it's hot—mighty hot—
Don't believe it if your neighbor says it's not
    Very hot;
Always keep your old thermometer located at a spot
    Where you'll not
    Fail to notice that it's hot;
And be sure your every thought
Shall be centered on some subject that is hot—
    That is boiling, seething hot—
    Hot, hot, hot, hot, hot!
Take your coat off and your collar off and swat
Any man who tries to tell you that it's not
    Half as hot
Here as where the happy, happy Hottentot
    And a lot
Of your other fellow creatures have to squat
In the shadows of the palms, where ice is never, never brought—
    Where a cold is never caught—
Fan yourself and keep a-going on the trot.
    Keep complaining that it's hot;
    Keep declaring that it's rot
    To imagine that it's not
    Beastly hot—
Hot, hot, hot, hot, hot, hot, hot, hot—
Always fume and fret and bother when it's hot!

The Boston Bank Ledger

A contemporary in discoursing upon the Boston bank ledger, along with other misinformation, credits the invention to a Boston bank bookkeeper by the name of Lane, with date 1852. The facts are that the form of ledger named originated in the Park Bank, New York, several years prior to the year above named. It is called the Boston ledger, because it was Boston that saw a good thing, promptly adopted it and in the exploiting which followed very generously gave the device its own name.

Wages and Salary

"Pa!"

"Well?"

"What's the difference between wages and salary?"

"If a man is working for $5 a day running a machine of some kind, or laying brick or doing something else that makes a white collar and cuffs uncomfortable, he gets wages. Do you understand what I mean?"

"Yes, sir."

"But if he sits at a desk and uses a pen and gets $11 a week and has soft hands, he receives a salary. Now do you see the difference?"

The possession of wealth is, as it were, prepayment, and involves an obligation of honor to the doing of correspondent work.—George Macdonald.

Many fortunes, like rivers, have a pure source, but grow muddy as they grow large.—J. Petit-Senn.

Managing the Good but Slow Customer
By MYRON CONOLLY

To the business man with outstanding accounts the question of how to deal with the class of customer described in the title of this article is a constant and perplexing puzzle. For all other classes of debtors he has his methods of treatment. The customer whose payments are prompt and on time of course affords no trouble whatsoever. For the bad accounts, while the chances of getting what is due to him are slight, at best the merchant at least has a course of action well defined. He has merely to put the account into the hands of his attorney or of a collection agency, as the case may be. The "good, but slow customer," however, is not to be thus summarily dealt with. His case is one demanding the exercise of the utmost amount of ingenuity and tact. He must not be approached in an abrupt or offensive way or he is liable to flare up and withdraw his trade. The self-consciousness that he is perfectly good will render him exceedingly susceptible to taking offense. To let him alone altogether, however, is equally unsatisfactory, inasmuch as he never will volunteer to pay unless his memory is somehow jogged along. The merchant, therefore, in his treatment of such a customer, finds himself in a very difficult position.

Some merchants, appreciating these difficulties, prefer not to have such customers on their books at all. Others, deeming that they cannot afford to display such independence, try various methods of coping with this difficulty. Some business men instruct their collectors, when calling on such a customer as above described, to appeal to his sympathies by informing him that the firm is in need of all the money it can raise. This step, however, is not advisable when it is taken into consideration that such a statement, however groundlessly made, is liable to spread abroad and place the firm under suspicion, or at least in a bad light. Other merchants again try to persuade the slow, but good customer, to give them a note, while still others declare that the very suggestion of such a course would lose for them their customer and their account, and advise, where possible, that the debt, or part of, be taken out in trade, and in that manner the debtor may be successfully reminded that his account is not "squared."

Still another class of merchants favor the demanding of payment on instalments, deeming that the mere demand will cause the customer to awaken to the fact of his indebtedness and forward a check in full immediately. A business man of considerable experience in this direction has a thoroughly systematic method of dealing with the good but slow customer, and his advice is certainly worthy of note. Therefore, I append what he says:

He advises, in the first place, that a draft be made upon the customer. If the draft comes back marked unpaid there is generally a few words marked on the back explaining the reason for non-payment. These excuses take such forms as "not due" or "amount incorrect," or any plausible reason for not honoring the draft that may suggest itself to the mind of the man drawn upon at the time the draft is presented. In the event of such an excuse being given, a letter is then sent to the tardy customer, expressing, in mild terms the greatest surprise that the draft was not honored, refuting the reasons given for failure to honor and expressing the intention to again make draft a few days hence, and not failing to end up with a desire for "further valued patronage."

A second draft is then made and should this also come back, not honored, a quite severe letter is despatched expressing the writer's great surprise that the account, long past due, has not been paid. Gently but firmly intimating that most drastic measures must be taken, if payment is not made at once, or giving the debtor a short extension, and insisting upon the honoring of the draft that will then be made. At the same time an appeal is made to the sense of justice of the customer, and he is assured that the taking of stringent methods will be a matter of great regret to the merchant. A hope is expressed that the customer will appreciate the position in which the creditor finds himself, and that the relation of merchant and customer in the future may be of the most pleasant and cordial nature.

In the majority of instances a really good customer will not let the matter go further, but will "pay up" even though he should grumblingly request to know "whether they think he is going to run away," or if "Mr. Blank thinks he's going to fail." If, however, the next draft is not met, the account is placed in the hands of an attorney for collection, and a letter sent to the customer informing him of the action that has been taken. This invariably brings the money, providing the customer has it, and has no just reason for withholding payment. If this correspondence throughout has been managed properly, care being taken neither to be too aggressive nor too weak, even the fact that legal steps have been taken does not always mean the losing of the customer; but if the latter should happen, our merchant comforts himself with the reflection, "It matters not how good a customer may be, if he don't pay his accounts I don't want him on my books."

When the desire of wealth is taking hold of the heart let us look round and see how it operates upon those whose industry or fortune has obtained it. When we find them oppressed with their own abundance, luxurious without pleasure, idle without ease, impatient and querulous in themselves, and despised or hated by the rest of mankind, we shall soon be convinced that if the real wants of our condition are satisfied, there remains little to be sought with solicitude or desired with eagerness.—Dr. Johnson.

The good things of life are not to be had singly, but come to us with a mixture—like a schoolboy's holiday, with a task affixed to the tail of it.—Lamb.

The Monthly Statement

The school of "Commerce Accounts and Finance," to which allusions have been made in these columns in several recent issues, is now an accomplished fact. It opens in the University Building, Washington Square, New York, October 1 next, and from every indication will from the very start be a useful addition to the means of acquiring professional knowledge. It will be conducted under the auspices of the City University, as it is familiarly called, and managed by a faculty composed in part of regular professors connected with that institution and in part by volunteers from the New York State Society of Certified Public Accountants. The latter, whatever may be their handicap as teachers, from lack of training in that particular field, will commence upon their work with earnestness and enthusiasm, combined with a very clear idea of what they believe the young accountant ought to know. Or, perhaps, it were better put in this form—with a very clear idea of what they would have found advantageous to know when they commenced upon practical accounting. Other columns in this issue contain extracts from the comments of the New York newspaper press upon this most important departure in educational work.

❧ ❧

All those who have occasion to make or receive remittances for all small amounts have noticed long before this the new postal money order, which, during the last few months, has gradually superseded the old form. In shape the new postal order closely resembles a bank draft or check and in this respect is more acceptable for handling than the old, particularly when the orders are deposited in bank. Another feature that is to be noticed in the new form is that the plan of tearing or cutting against amounts printed in the margin in order to show on the face of the order and the stub from which it is detached the number of dollars for which it is drawn, has been omitted. A bit of history attaches to this feature of the old form of money order.

❧

Some years since, when the accounts of the government were being revised by a commission appointed for that purpose, it was found that the auditing of the money division was greatly in arrears; in some departments the work was over three years behind. Up to that time the form of money order employed was equivalent to a common bank check with a stub for recording necessary particulars. If a fraud had been committed by a postmaster, for instance, by filling out the order for a large amount and the stub which went to the treasury for general adivce for a smaller amount, the discrepancy would not be discovered perhaps until the postmaster were either out of office or dead. His bondsman could not be released until the accounts had been audited. The tearing and cutting against amounts was introduced by the

commission for the purpose of preventing further frauds, and also of avoiding the necessity of tedious auditing. The stub and order were bound to agree by this device. The saving of labor was very great. As a fact, the force in the money order division was greatly reduced. With the new order economy of labor is also served. The notification to be sent by the issuing postmaster is a reproduction of the order by the use of carbon or manifold paper. This is simpler and cheaper than the zig-zag tearing plan. Another improvement is that the purchaser of the order gets a receipt for the amount he pays from the issuing postmaster. In all respects the new form of order is to be commended, and it is not surprising that the business public is well pleased with it.

❧ ❧

There are numerous progressive establishments all over this broad land, the accountants in which are proud of the fact that they employ no journal. Of course they have the equivalent of the journal, in that the credits are balanced by the debits, but aside from the book containing cross entries between the groups of accounts comprised in the system and provision for the correction of other errors, there is nothing that bears any resemblance to the conventional journal. A contemporary commenting upon the gradual release from the bondage of the journal discourses as follows:

❧

"In the beginning there was a journal. Everything that was, or had to be, went through the journal. The journal was the summary, or recapitulation, of every transaction. Nothing could be posted until it had first been deposited in the journal. The journal was the guarantee of double entry and the assurance of mathematical accuracy. It was the key to the system. In the journal every debit had a corresponding credit—every credit a corresponding debit. Sales, purchases, expenses, cash transactions—everything went through the journal. The debits and credits were equal in the journal, therefore they must agree in the ledger. The enfranchisement from the bondage of the journal has been gradual but is still incomplete."

❧

A combined manufacturing and jobbing business to which our attention was recently called is getting along very nicely without journal, without cash book, without check book and without sales book. The sales are up in the millions and a more complete daily, weekly and monthly showing than the accounts in this case present would be hard to conceive. Of course something takes the place of each of the elements discarded, and that something, as may be inferred, is progressive, labor-saving and up-to-date in character, as well as adequate for the purpose.

The New York Newspapers on the New School of Accounting

Almost every daily paper published in New York had something to say about the new school of accounts on the day succeeding the public announcement by Chancellor MacCracken of its establishment. This we take it is indicative of the general appreciation of its usefulness by the business public. We have space for only a few brief extracts:

The Reason for the School
From the "Sun."

The trustees of New York University have decided to establish in connection with the university a school of commerce, accounts and finance. This departure, Chancellor MacCracken said yesterday, has been decided upon only after a careful consideration of the advisability of such a school by a special committee composed of representative business men of New York. The committee found, so the Chancellor said, that professional accountants all over the State were persistent in their demands for such a school in which could be taught the theory of accounting and commercial law. This demand, it was also found, was one of the results of American expansion and the complexities of foreign trade. The new school will be practically the only one of its kind in the country by reason of the fact that it is to be a purely professional one, having the same relation to the university that the law school has. The University of Wisconsin and the University of Pennsylvania have schools for higher commercial education, but both are open to undergraduates and are made parallel to the regular college course, and are not strictly professional schools in any sense.

The Organization Committee
From the "Evening Sun."

The committee which has had the organization of the school in charge is composed of James G. Cannon, vice-president of the Fourth National Bank; W. M. Kingsley, William F. Havemeyer, William S. Opdyke and Chancellor MacCracken. The school is to be placed in the University Building in Washington Square. The faculty is to consist of eight professors of the university's law school, and eleven new professors of recognized proficiency in all kinds of business and accounting. Seven of the professors have already been obtained. The school is to open in October.

Evening Sessions
From the "Commercial Advertiser."

The trustees of New York University, at a meeting yesterday, held in the office of W. F. Havemeyer, established a new school, to be called the School of Commerce, Accounts and Finance. The classes will meet in the evening from 8 to 10 o'clock, five days each week, beginning

October 1, in the Washington Square Building. The purpose of the school is to give a scientific business education of an advanced type, leading possibly to the recognition of graduates as certified accountants. The principles of business, economics, trade, commercial law and accountancy will be taught by experts. The school was established after consultation with the Society of Certified Public Accountants, who desired the university to undertake the work.

The Faculty
From the "Evening Post."

The faculty will be as follows: Henry M. MacCracken, president; Charles Waldo Haskins, Dean, and professor of auditing and of the history of accountancy; Clarance D. Ashley, Dean of the School of Law and professor of law (contracts); Charles E. Sprague, professor of the theory of accounts; Thaddeus D. Kenneson, professor of law (Trusts); Dr. Ernest L. Bogart, professor of economics (public finance and banking); Ferdinand William Lafrentz, professor of auditing; Frank A. Erwin, professor of law (sales and agency); Arthur E. Rounds, professor of law (partnership); Anson O. Kittredge, professor of theory of accounts; Henry R. M. Cook, professor of practical accounting; Leslie J. Tompkins, professor of law (bills and notes); Leon Brummer, secretary of the faculty and professor of practical accounting; Alfred Opdyke, professor of law (international law); Francis W. Aymar, lecturer on insurance.

The Object in View
From the "Times."

Chancellor Henry M. MacCracken of New York University announced yesterday the establishment of the School of Commerce, Accounts and Finance. The purpose of this new school is to train men for practical business.

"No American university," said Dr. MacCracken, "has undertaken such a step. In various institutions there are departments that teach subjects similar to those we plan to have in the new school; but in every case those departments are regular parts of the collegiate course. We propose to make ours a professional school, separate and distinct, just as are the courses in law and medicine.

"A committee of trustees was appointed to formulate the plan, public demand having called our attention to the necessity of an orderly pursuit of business studies. On the committee were James G. Cannon, William M. Kingsley, William F. Havemeyer, William S. Opdyke and myself. The faculty of the school will consist of nineteen members, part of whom already occupy chairs in the university law department."

International Law
From the "Sun."

One of the features of the new school is to be a course in international law. This is aimed at fitting men for the consular service. The plan of the school is elastic as regards the more general higher commercial education, and the course in economics and law will probably be enlarged eventually if patronage warrants it. Provision has been made for the financial part of the undertaking so that it will not be a burden on the university for several years. Chancellor MacCracken and the rest of the faculty believe that in that time its success will have been such as to warrant endowments being sought for it. The new school is founded in the belief that business education to meet adequately existing and future conditions of civilization should be placed upon a scientific basis. The school will fill a long-felt want in this respect and that eventually no large university will be without one.

Business on a Scientific Basis
From the "Tribune."

The school will open October 1 and will occupy rooms in the new University Building, in Washington Square, which has been selected for the purpose of securing the services of practical business men and public accountants as instructors along lines in which they have become prominent. The classes will meet evenings to permit the attendance of young men employed during the day in business houses. The hours will be from 8 to 9 and from 9 to 10 o'clock, five days in the week. It is expected that arrangements will be made so that a graduate of this school may obtain the degree of Certified Public Accountant without a further examination before the proper State authorities. The school offers many advantages to the clerk who is ambitious to become a manager of finance, a bank president or the holder of an office of public trust. The aim of the school, therefore, will be chiefly to equip a man with the power to grasp the details of great commercial enterprises and carry them to a successful issue. The aim is a practical one.

The school is a result of the present general movement in Europe and the United States in behalf of the higher commercial education. Its establishment is due to enthusiastic action on the part of the professional accountants of the State of New York. Accountancy was raised to the dignity of a legally recognized and safeguarded profession in New York by the Certified Public Accountants' Act of 1896. Under this act certificates of qualification to practice as Certified Public Accountants, with exclusive right to use the initials C. P. A. as a professional designation, are granted to those only who have had three years' satisfactory experience in the practice of accounting, one year in the office of an expert public accountant, an examination in the theory of accounts, in practical accounting, in auditing and in commercial law.

This school differs from the several schools of finance or commerce recently established by prominent universities in America in that its entire instruction is intended to be professional in character. It is in no way to be confounded with or substituted for the course of liberal culture in a college of arts and science. It is founded in the firm belief that business education, adequately to meet existing and future conditions of civilization, must be placed upon a scientific basis; that traditional methods, office routine and procedure of control must be traced to their underlying principles; that native genius for trade and finance must be reinforced by a well-grounded knowledge of economics, accountancy and commercial law; that not only administrators of affairs, but, in due proportion, their assistants, ought each to understand the philosophy as well as the art of his calling and be able intelligently to adapt himself and his work to the exigencies of the commercial and financial world.

The Eighth School

From the "Evening Post."

The school has originated partly from a suggestion on the part of the Chancellor that the university celebrate in some signal manner the completion of its seventy years of educational activity; partly from an appeal on the part of the scientific accountants of the State, represented by President Haskins of the Regents' Board of Examiners in Accounting, for the founding of a school or college of accounts, auditing, commercial law and kindred subjects. Students will be prepared to pass the examination established under the Public Accountants' Act of 1896 for the granting of the certified accountant's certificate. The seven existing schools of the university roughly represent the seven completed decades of its corporate existence; and it was believed that a most fitting memorial of its septuagesimal would be an eighth teaching department. The new school will differ from all the schools or departments of finance, or of commerce, recently established by a few other universities in Europe and America, in that its courses of study are intended to be strictly professional in character. "We propose," said Chancellor MacCracken, "to make ours a professional school, separate and distinct, just as are the courses in law and medicine." It is intended that graduation shall result in the degree, already conferred by the University of Wisconsin, of Bachelor of Commercial Science.

Another American Innovation

From the "Evening Sun."

A curious innovation is to be made at New York University this fall. A professional school, corresponding to the medical school or the law school, with a faculty of nineteen professors, is to devote itself to the higher commercial education. Among the subjects taught will be accounts, and the theory of accounting, auditing and certain other things of a strictly business nature. In addition, economics and international law will be dealt with seriously. And no doubt in due time the mercantile course will involve the study of certain foreign languages to which much attention is given in German business schools. Indeed, it is this peculiarity of business education in the Fatherland to which much of the recent success of the Kaiser's subjects in the markets of the world has been attributed.

A short time ago, when plans were making for the English University of Birmingham, in which Mr. Joseph Chamberlain, the British Colonial Secretary, is interested, a deputation of experts was sent to this country to try and pick up some hints as to modern requirements in scientific education. These persons in their report admitted the superiority of the training in our colleges, in the matter of enabling men to apply scientific knowledge to industrial needs. And they hinted that unless their own countrymen realized the need of just that sort of method in their scientific schools, Great Britain would be seriously handicapped in trying to hold up its end in the industrial struggle. But if special training is needed in actual production it is also necessary in distribution. And here again the English have had to admit that they are woefully handicapped. From time to time there have been complaints about the bungling methods which interfered with successful trade. If the school of commerce established here is successful it will be followed by similar institutions at our big colleges, not to give instruction to undergraduates, as is the case at the University of Wisconsin and the University of Pennsylvania, but regular professional schools apart from the studies in the arts departments of the various seats of learning.

We can afford to lose no trick in the game of competition. And it isn't likely that we shall lose any. The world is coming to realize more and more every day that the adaptability of Americans to circumstances is one of the most dangerous things about them when they are encountered as rivals.

Commerce in the University

From the "Times."

One cannot but admire the University of the City of New York under the lead of Chancellor MacCracken. What it lacks in fame and antiquity compared with Columbia University it more than makes up through its energy and enterprise. Now grave, now gay, now lively, now severe, it makes at one time the grave mistake of pulling down a picturesque college on Washington Square and substituting therefor a commonplace stack of offices; then it adds to the gayety of nations by its Hall of Fame; next we find its liveliness expressed by the seizure of a commanding hill beyond the Harlem, where its fine buildings vie with those of Columbia, and now, to show that it can be serious also, it is about to establish a School of Commerce, Accounts, and Finance for the City of New York.

The boldness of this move is apparent when we remember that the Commissioners of Schools of the city were stirred up long ago by the Chamber of Commerce to consider the founding of a School of Commerce, and that in consequence a committee was designated, which remains a designation to the present day. Facts have been collected by this committee; but we seem no nearer the end desired than we were before. So the City University steps in, takes the wind out of the School Commissioners' sails, and announces that the school will open next October in its building on Washington Square.

The course in the School of Commerce is fixed at two years and it is proposed to grant a sheepskin to graduates which will permit them to tack B. C. S. or Bachelor of Commercial Science to their names. Although Leipsic University has a department of commerce, and commercial schools have been founded in Switzerland, Belgium and France, perhaps the City University would be still hesitating were it not for the impulse given by the professional accountants of the State who received the aid of the Legislature in 1896 and became a duly legalized body.

The school will be essentially a night school at first, in order to meet the requirements of young men in business. Theoretical science of commerce will go hand in hand with business itself, as the law student works in a lawyer's office downtown and still keeps up his studies and lectures in the law school. As a preparatory course for positions involving complicated affairs and financial responsibilities the school will meet a need. The expansion of American manufactures calls for a more specialized education in those who must look after the interests of our merchants and manufacturers abroad. Incidentally the graduates of a professional school of the sort will furnish good material for consuls, after they have added foreign languages and foreign travel to their collegiate education. The City University may be congratulated on its timely push. The school is needed in New York, and New York is the place for the school.

Time Reckoning

The artificiality of our system of time reckoning is clearly set forth in the following extract from a daily paper, the item having been published during the first week in January last:

A child born in this city about 12:30 o'clock last Sunday night will hereafter date his birth January 1, 1900. Another child born at precisely the same time in Chicago will date his birth December 31, 1899. The two will not be able to celebrate their birthdays in the same year, the same month or on the same day. That is one of the many curiosities of our time reckonings.

What better argument could be offered for uniform time the world over? Why should it not be the first hour of the new year at the same instant in America, Europe, Asia and throughout the width of the Pacific Ocean? It was a great step in advance when the railway companies established the present system of time belts or sections from which we derive what is called standard time. But it was only one step in the direction of ultimate perfection. Every business need will be served by having universal time, and clocks arranged, not to show two 12-hour periods to the day, as at present, but with 24-hour dials.

Accountics

The Office Magazine.

Published Monthly.

A. O. KITTREDGE, F. I. A., C. P. A., Editor.

E. R. KITTREDGE, Associate.

Accountics is devoted to the Science of Accounting, to the Art of Bookkeeping and to the advocacy of Improved Office Methods.

Subscription.—One dollar a year, payable in advance.

Postage is prepaid by the publishers in the United States, Canada and Mexico. For all other countries in the Postal Union, subscribers must add 50 cents a year.

Discontinuances.—In the absence of specific orders to discontinue at the end of the subscription term the magazine will be continued and a bill sent.

Remittances should be by Draft, P. O. Order or Express Order, payable to the order of the Accountics Association. Money and postage stamps are at the risk of the sender, unless sent by express or in registered letters. Add 10 cents each to checks on local banks to defray collection charges.

Advertising Rates will be quoted on application.

Official Journal.—This publication, by resolutions duly passed, has been made the official publication of the following organizations:—

THE INSTITUTE OF ACCOUNTS.

THE NEW YORK CHAPTER of the Institute of Accounts.

THE WASHINGTON CHAPTER of the Institute of Accounts.

THE HARTFORD CHAPTER of the Institute of Accounts.

ACCOUNTICS is the accredited medium of intercommunication between members of the Institute of Accounts wherever located.

ACCOUNTICS ASSOCIATION, Publishers,

Lancashire Building, Pine Street, near Nassau, New York.

Copyright 1900 by the ACCOUNTICS ASSOCIATION.
Entered at the Post Office New York as Second Class Matter.

Publishers' Desk

An Accountant's Typewriter

With the number of typewriting machines now before the public, each one being guaranteed to be better than all its competitors, it would seem almost useless to look for further improvements. At the same time it appears as though the typewriter inventor was not yet through with his job, and that good work in this direction is being done in other countries as well as our own. Here is a description of a typewriter, said to be ready for introduction in England, that we find in one of our exchanges. Unfortunately, no names are mentioned. It is a device by which vertical columns of figures can be written as readily as they could be set by type. A special line space-key enables the operator to write on either the whole width of the paper or in narrow columns. He does not have at the end of each line to adjust the machine for the next line, but the paper goes forward automatically and his writing proceeds without a break, his hands not being lifted from the keyboard. There are the usual claims of durability, efficiency and general appearance, but the feature which will attract the attention of the public is the fact that it is operated entirely from the keyboard without adjustment of either carriage or paper.

Foolscap Paper

Peculiar names usually have a history back of them. Every one knows in a general way what is meant by foolscap paper, but of the many thousands who handle it daily there are but few persons who could tell why it is so called. We find in one of our exchanges the following story, which will be interesting to those who like to know the reason for things: It was the custom in England in olden times to have as the watermark upon paper of this size the King's arms. After the trial and execution of Charles I., in front of his own palace of Whitehall, London, in January, 1649, the Parliament party, to throw contempt on royalty, changed their watermark to that of a fool with cap and bells. This mark ceased when the Stuarts returned to the throne, but paper of the particular size on which it had been placed still retains the name of foolscap.

A Handy Desk Device

In these days of humidity and heat, when the thermometer is apt to register 100 in the shade and the least exertion, either mental or physical, is apt to plunge one into a perfect bath of perspiration, the unfortunate hard-working business man is reduced to a state bordering on nervous prostration by the rapidity and constancy with which such little trifles as important papers, business cards which bear important names, and other memoranda which must be kept constantly in sight, manage to lodge themselves in places where it is impossible to lay hands on them just at the time when they are most required. There is not a business man anywhere, be he never so methodical, who has not experienced this unpleasant state of affairs at some time or other, and, therefore, in placing on the market the "Crystal Upright Clip" the makers are conferring a boon upon every man who sits at a desk. The Crystal Upright Clip, as its name implies, consists of a nickel-plated clamp with a glass base, and, unlike ordinary clips, it clutches the matter to be held in an upright position, thus keeping it constantly before the business man's eye. By applying pressure with the palm of the hand to the lever the clip releases its hold with ease. Accordingly, there is absolutely no danger of the papers held therein being torn or mutilated. The spring of the clip, which is constructed on new lines, is about as strong as it is possible for a spring of its size to be. It is of such a form that wear and tear cannot decrease its resisting powers.

Not only can the article be used for the purposes stated, but it can be used as a holder for photographs, or, in fact, for any perpendicular article of a similar character which requires a base. It is strong and wide enough to hold a small memorandum book in an upright position. The article is very attractively gotten up in ornamental glass and is supplied to the trade by the Philadelphia Novelty Manufacturing Co., Philadelphia.

What to Do with Unused Railway Tickets

Some men with unused railroad tickets on their hands sell them to scalpers, while others go to the railroad company that issued them and obtain their value in money. Most persons, however, do neither and accept the loss when the ticket is worth less than a dollar. Indeed, many persons do not realize that the railroad companies stand ready to redeem unused tickets even of small value, so that the companies must be richer by many thousands of dollars a year through this ignorance.

Every railroad ticket bears the name of the general passenger agent and of the general manager of the road. It is a simple matter to inclose the ticket with a letter directed to the general passenger agent asking him to refund the money paid and explaining the reason why the ticket is left unused in the hands of the purchaser. It is courteous to inclose a stamped envelope in which the money may be returned.

When all these things have been done the company generally acknowledges the receipt of the ticket holder's communication and promises to investigate the matter. The investigation consists in the proper identification of the ticket by the agent who sold it, and a little bookkeeping to set the accounts right. Then the purchaser receives a check for the amount due from the railroad company, along with a letter requesting acknowledgment.

Total Fire Loss

The Supreme Court of Ohio has recently been called upon for the first time to determine what constitutes a total loss under a policy of fire insurance. Some portions of the burned building remained in place and undestroyed, and were of some pecuniary value, although not capable of being utilized in the process of reconstruction or for purposes of repair. The court holds that this does not prevent a loss from being total. "It seems to be agreed," says Mr. Justice Minshall, "that it is not necessary, to constitute a total loss, that all the material composing the building should be destroyed. It is sufficient, though some parts of it remain standing, that the building has lost its identity and specific character as a building; the insurance not being upon the material composing the building, but upon the building as such." The loss is

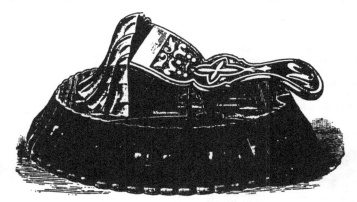

The Crystal Upright Clip

regarded as total, even though something might be realized for the material by removing it.

If we command our wealth, we shall be rich and free; if our wealth commands us, we are poor indeed. We are bought by the enemy with the treasure in our own coffers.—Burke.

Women Accountants in Australia

It will be observed with interest that the Incorporated Institute of Accountants, Victoria, whose report for 1899-1900 will be found in this issue, says the "Incorporated Accountants' Journal" for August, has had the question of the admission of women as members under consideration. The council of the Victorian Institute adopted the course followed by the society some years ago and referred the question to the members for decision, the result being similar, a large majority

voting against the proposal. The report states that each of the other Australian Institutes has come to the same determination. The matter is not, however, likely to rest so far as women accountants in England are concerned, as they have again been bringing their position under notice in connection with the Professional Accountants' Bill.

Good Credit
By W. H. PRESTON

There is nothing that helps a fellow out so much
    As keeping his credit good.
He need not be looking for some one to touch,
    If only his credit is good.
He may even be busted, possess not a red;
But he is sure of a supper and also a bed,
And some sort of shelter over his head,
    If only his credit is good.

He may even mix up in social affairs,
    If only his credit is good;
May patronize theatres, lectures and fairs,
    If only his credit is good.
He may dress like a dude, in the finest of clothes,
And wear patent leathers and striped silken hose,
And exhale odorous perfumes wherever he goes,
    If only his credit is good.

The butcher and baker will wait for their pay
    From the fellow whose credit is good,
And the grocer will furnish provisions all day
    To the duffer whose credit is good.
The landlord is never in need of his rent,
And the tailor will trust him to any extent,
And for him new patterns and fashions invent,
    If only his credit is good.

But I somewhere have learned that there's only one way
    Of keeping his credit good,
And that is by strolling in some day
    And paying those to whom his credit is good.
I notice hard cash and nothing else goes
With those who provide shelter, victuals and clothes,
And bottles whose contents I need not disclose
    To you fellows whose credit is good.

The Utility of a Knowledge of Bookkeeping
By J. THORNTON

Official receivers in bankruptcy declare with wearisome iteration in how many instances faulty bookkeeping is the cause of financial disaster, until one is tempted to cry out for a law that no one shall give or take credit who does not keep his books on sound principles.

But the fear of bankruptcy is not the only motive that should impel to a study of this subject. There can be no doubt that ignorance of the principles of bookkeeping has hitherto afforded a wide field for the exercise of the talents of unscrup-

ulous adventurers with a gift for the dexterous manipulation of figures. Figures, it is said, may be made to prove anything. And just as cynics have remarked that the chief use of language is to conceal one's thoughts, so I daresay cynics could be found who would say that the chief use of bookkeeping is to conceal the facts. It is a pity that a science, the primary use of which is to exhibit facts, should ever be used for the very opposite purpose; but this tends to show not that we have too much knowledge of bookkeeping but that we have too little, for it is manifest that if there were none to be duped there would be no dupers, and if every debtor and creditor in the land had a clear idea of the meaning and use of these terms in account keeping, it is probable that designing promoters and scheming directors would not find it so easy a task as at present to delude the public with fraudulent balance sheets. So that on this ground also an increase in the number of students of bookkeeping might in these days be reasonably hoped for.

An Ancient Bill of Sale

That the business men of old Egypt were just as methodical and practical in their proceedings as is the modern merchant, is demonstrated by a curious document which was recently found along with several other fragments of absorbing interest to collectors of antiquities at Oxrhynchus. The document was drawn up in the year 54 A. D., and seems to be the record of a sale of a loom, together with the acknowledgment of receipt of price of same. Those who are familiar with the form such a document would take to-day may find it a matter of interest to compare the same with the wording of this ancient document. Here is the paper in question:

> AMMONIUS. SON OF AMMONIUS. TO TRYPHON. SON OF DIONYSIUS. GREETING. I AGREE THAT I SOLD TO YOU THE WEAVER'S LOOM BELONGING TO ME, MEASURING THREE WEAVERS' CUBITS LESS TWO PALMS, AND CONTAINING TWO ROLLERS AND TWO BEAMS; AND I ACKNOWLEDGE THE RECEIPT FROM YOU THROUGH THE BANK OF SARAPION, SON OF LOCHUS, NEAR THE SERAPEUM OF OXYRHYNCHUS, OF THE PRICE OF IT AGREED BETWEEN US, NAMELY, 20 SILVER DRACHME OF THE IMPERIAL AND PTOLEMAIC COINAGE; AND THAT I WILL GUARANTEE TO YOU THE SALE WITH EVERY GUARANTEE, UNDER PENALTY OF PAYMENT TO YOU OF THE PRICE WHICH I HAVE RECEIVED FROM YOU, INCREASED BY HALF ITS AMOUNT AND BY DAMAGES. THIS NOTE OF HAND IS VALID.

Gaming is a kind of tacit confession that the company engaged therein do in general exceed the bounds of their respective fortunes, and therefore they cast lots to determine upon whom the ruin shall at present fall, that the rest may be saved a little longer.—Blackstone.

Failures During the First Half of 1900

By James G. Cannon

It is true that there has lately been an increase in the number of failures, but this is due to an entirely natural and easily explained cause. In the great business boom of the past two years a large number of small merchants loaded up with merchandise at advancing prices. They overstocked themselves, and when the reaction set in and the abnormally inflated prices began to recede they were unable to carry the load, and were obliged to suspend. There have been many such cases.

The operation is precisely like that of speculators in stocks who follow the bull movement to the top prices, and when the break comes find themselves unable to carry their margined stocks, and are obliged to market them at a loss.

Then there were a number of firms which were on the verge of failure when the business boom struck the country. That saved them from immediate suspension, but some of them, in order to square themselves over, bought in hope of selling on advancing prices. They also have been caught in the recession of prices. For instance, a firm failed the other day that had been marked for failure a long time ago. It managed to keep going as long as prices advanced, but has at last been obliged to suspend.

The business of the country is in a most sound condition. Only those who have overreached themselves in their eagerness for big profits have gone to the wall.

A Contract Payable in Silver

Contracts which by their terms are made payable exclusively in gold coin have frequently come before the courts; but it is seldom indeed that judges are called upon to consider or enforce instruments providing for the payment of silver only. A recent litigation in Baltimore has revealed the existence in that city of a number of leases made forty-eight years ago which stipulate for the payment of ground rent in "lawful silver money of the United States, each dollar weighing 17 pennyweights and 6 grains at least." A purchaser of these ground rents at public auction bid for them at the sale upon the assumption that the rents were payable in current money, silver or gold, no notice to the contrary having been given; and when he discovered that he was bound to receive his rent in silver, he asked to be relieved from his bargain. After the preparation of arguments on both sides the seller consented to a decree releasing the buyer. In the brief for the purchaser his counsel pointed out that 17 pennyweights and 6 grains of silver bullion is now worth less than half a dollar in gold, whereas when the leases were executed, in 1852, just after the enormous output of gold consequent upon the gold discoveries in California, the silver dollar of that weight was at a premium.

Conscience and wealth are not always neighbors.—Massinger.

Brewery Bookkeeping

Brewery Bookkeeping. A practical treatise on brewery accounts and office management. By Edward W. Clarke, Brewery Accountant. 182 pages, large octavo. Published by H. S. Rich & Co. Bound in cloth. $4.00. Morocco, $5.00.

The present is often declared to be an age of specialization, and that it is such is indicated by the technical treatises which are issued from time to time, as well as by the sub-divisions of the trades and professions. The title of the book before us indicates how completely it is individualized. The name of the industry to which it is devoted appears in the general title, in the sub-title and in the designation of the specialty to wh'ch the author has applied himself. In the preface the author says that without desiring to give offence to those who have entered the field of general bookkeeping, candor compels him, after a practical experience of fifteen years, to express the opinion that the vast majority of the business college works on the keeping of accounts are merely bald reproductions of effete treatises on the subject, originally written by men who were entirely ignorant of actual commercial affairs, who never spent an hour in the practical application of the principles of bookkeeping, and whose labor consequently has resulted in the dissemination of obsolete and antiquated theories and methods. With this declaration before us we need have no doubt as to the position which this author occupies in the field, nor his opinion of the usual run of bookkeeping treatises. He has more to say by way of particularization and gives the class to which this paragraph is devoted several stabs, notably on journalizing cash.

Mr. Clarke, as we are informed, was, prior to issuing this work, bookkeeper and auditor for one of the most progressive breweries in the United States, and as we further learn, has set forth in this work much of that which characterized his labor in the office referred to.

The author, apparently in distrust of the elementary treatises on bookkeeping at large which preceded him, commences at the very foundation and describes debit and credit. Following that, he tells how journal entries are to be made. On the first page, in italic type, there is this sweeping direction: "Always post directly from Sales Book, Purchase Book, Cash Book and Journal to Ledger." This direction is fundamental and conveys to the reader's mind at once the fact that however progressive the author may be in various details, he yet clings to books, instead of accepting those modern labor-saving innovations, loose sheets.

The second chapter of the work is devoted to a list of auxiliary books, of which we find there are no less than forty-one. This list should impress the student with the magnitude of the undertaking that is before him, if he has set out to possess himself of all the mysteries of brewery bookkeeping.

The third chapter presents a list of main ledger accounts, of which there are sixty-six. The names of the accounts appear in full face type at the left of the page, whereas at the right of the page, in a parallel column, are designations of the kinds of accounts. The author's analysis will bear a little examination. Advertising Show Cards he has put down as a "loss" account, as are also such items as Allowances and Rebates, Agency Expenses, Brewers' Wages, Collection and Soliciting, Bottle House Expenses, Liability, Insurance, Engine Room Wages, Feed, Freight, Fuel, Insurance, Oil and Grease, United States Revenue, Repairs, Sundry Wages and General Expenses.

This leads us to think that the author fails to discriminate between expenses and losses. The Bank Account is put down as an asset, and so also is Barley, Bills Receivable, Bottles and Cases, Cash, Construction, Mortgages Receivable, Tools, Fixtures and Machinery, Real Estate and Plant. Contrasted with this we find that Sundry Brewing Materials and Rice are Merchandise Accounts. Merchandise, as appears further on, is not regarded as an asset account. Bills Payable, Dividends, Interest Payable, Mortgages Payable, Surplus and Capital Stock are classed as Liability Accounts. Grains and Sprouts are put down as a "gain" account; so also are Merchandise and Rents. In view of the profits that brewers are supposed to make, it would seem that the gain accounts are remarkably small in number. Our author includes in the list a Profit and Loss Account, which he does not attempt to classify, and by the blank that follows it in the column of classification, it would seem to be a law unto itself. Judgment Accounts and Suspended Accounts are described as Contingent Assets.

With this analysis before us, naturally our interest in the balance sheet is excited. Before examining it, however, a question arises as to the working of the system, so far as concerns profit and loss. Under the head of Merchandise Account, we find these directions: "At the close of the fiscal year, hops, malt, rice, grits and sundry brewing materials accounts are to be closed into Merchandise Account by crediting each of the accounts with the stock on hand by red ink, original entry. Then close the balance by journal entry into Merchandise Account. When the accounts are ruled off bring down red ink entry on credit side to debit side in black ink, thus commencing new fiscal year with stock on hand."

Nothing appears in the index under the head of Profit and Loss Statement, and, therefore, we are left to form our own conclusions as to where the profits or losses, as the case may be, are shown.

In the illustration of a complete set of books, the ledger accounts, which occupy twenty odd pages, we find a Profit and Loss Account, but there are no entries in it whatsoever. It is blank. We also find a Surplus Account, likewise blank.

Following this set of books is what purports to be a balance sheet, which is immediately succeeded by what is described as the "Trial Balance." The two exhibits agree in all particulars, save only that inventory values have been brought in to the so-called balance sheet, thus wiping out a credit balance which was in the Merchandise Account, and changing the amounts of the balances in such accounts as malt, hops, grits, rice and sundry brewing materials. A Surplus Account appears in the so-called balance sheet, which does not appear in the trial balance, from which we infer that the author's system does not so far vary from the teachings of the business college works as to bring in a profit and loss statement before making out a balance sheet. Instead he literally follows his own directions of making original entries upon the ledger in red ink, bringing down the balances in black ink. It is to be noted in this connection that the date of the trial balance is one day earlier than the date of the balance sheet.

This work, which evidently has been thoroughly done up to the limit of the author's experience and ability, is chiefly useful to accountants by reason of the blanks and forms which it contains and the foundation that it affords for working out a system of brewery accounts upon the part of those who are required to supervise such accounts.

Our criticism above may be regarded unfair to this extent. We have been measuring the book with the accounting yard stick in our hands, whereas by its title it purports to be nothing but a work on bookkeeping. It is true, the author characterizes himself as a brewery accountant, but all he has promised us in the title page and preface is to give us a treatise on brewery bookkeeping, and this he has done in a way to contribute materially to the general knowledge of the profession. The book abounds in blanks and forms, and is a very satisfactory reflex of what is in use in certain breweries. Different devices which have proved useful in the industry are described, forms of contracts are presented and various features of the techniques of the trade are brought forward in a way to be very serviceable.

Great Men

"So far as I have encountered them," said a citizen of the world, "a characteristic of great men is that they have time. They are not in a hurry; their work doesn't boss them, but they boss their work. They don't act as if every minute you stayed was valuable time lost to them: they don't fret and fidget. What time they do devote to you appears to be time that they can spare, and take things easy in, and be comfortable. The work seems to be incidental, and it seems as though they could turn to it when the time came and get through it with ease; and they always seem, besides, to have strength in reserve. It is a characteristic of the great man that he has time."

All wealth is the product of labor.—Locke.

A Woman Receiver

So short a time have women been active factors in business that surprise continues to be manifested at their success in the field which formerly was exclusively occupied by the other sex. As is well known, there have been occasional women lawyers for some time past, but for non-professional women to discharge special legal and business responsibilities, as in the case of assignments and receiverships, the public is less prepared. The following clipping from a recent issue of the Atlanta "Journal" is interesting in this connection:

Judge E. J. Reagan, of Atlanta, by consent of all parties at interest, has dismissed the case of E. L. Rhodes against S. E. Bowman, discharged the receiver and ordered the assets turned over to the defendant, Bowman, except the accounts of Rhodes & Bowman, which are to be delivered to E. L. Rhodes. The case was instituted several weeks ago by E. L. Rhodes against his former partner, S. E. Bowman. The theory of the suit was that the assets of the business were responsible for the debts of Rhodes & Bowman, that they were being mismanaged by Bowman, and that they were insufficient to meet the partnership debts.

A novel and remarkable feature of the case was the appointment by the court of Mrs. Ida Bowman, wife of the defendant, as permanent receiver. She has since conducted the business profitably, and, having made an inventory and appraised the assets, it appeared that the same were largely in excess of the liabilities. The real situation was developed by the skilful management of the receiver. The plaintiff and defendant soon came together and adjusted all their differences. The final act of a happy agreement was reached in the filing of the petition this morning.

Bankers' Education

The need of the day is the educated business man, or, as it were better stated, the man educated for business. Wherever we turn we find the subject of practical business education receiving attention. The following, bearing upon the point, is an extract from the address of President A. A. Crane, of the Minnesota Bankers' Association, delivered before the eleventh annual convention of that organization:

The Educational Committee, of which Mr. A. C. Anderson is chairman, has begun a work looking to the establishment of a course of study in our State University which shall be of the greatest value to the banks in general, affording the young men desiring to become bankers an opportunity to learn something more than the mere dull, dreary routine of bank work. The banking business is becoming more and more a scientific and exact profession, and the young man who hopes to succeed must have a broader and more liberal education than that afforded by the clerical routine of the office. If we can be instrumental in putting such an opportunity in the way of the ambitious young banker, we shall have accomplished a great good.

And right here I want to call your attention to work along that line which has been taken up by the bank clerks of Minneapolis. Last fall they organized an association for the purpose of taking up lines of study which would benefit them in performing the duties of their positions, and give them a broad, general view of the subjects bearing on their business as a profession. Their work last winter was the study of the law of negotiable instruments, and the course was thorough, practical and comprehensive. Next season they propose to take up other lines. The work they have undertaken is most meritorious and should have our approval. I believe we could do no better thing than to allow that association and similar ones that may be organized to become members of the Minnesota Bankers' Association, and to send to our meetings delegates who shall be privileged to take a part in our proceedings. This would necessitate a slight change in our by-laws, but would be a progressive move and would encourage similar work among bank clerks in towns and cities throughout the State.

The Question of Names and Titles

Every accountant who, by examination or otherwise, has acquired the right to the initials C. P. A., or the name of Certified Public Accountant, has been confronted with the question of how to use the same and in what cases to include the designation of the degree with his signature. Many have decided the question upon the broadest possible rule, namely to use the title everywhere and on all occasions. Others use it in moderation, sometimes employing it and in other cases omitting it entirely. Still others, although they are few in number, make no use of the title at all, modestly preferring to be

known simply as "accountants." The action of one of the prominent accountants' societies in England, wherein the use of initials has been abandoned and the employment of the full name of the title substituted therefor, has been elsewhere referred to in these columns. Whether such action will have any influence on American accountants or not, is an open question, the probabilities of the case being that it will not.

Bearing upon this general question is the action of the superintendent of schools of Manhattan Borough, New York, who has ordered that the names of associate superintendents shall be inscribed on the doors of their offices without the title of "Doctor," and that these officers are to be addressed as "Mister," whether or not they possess the title of LL.D. or Ph.D. It is said that some of these persons object to this change. The "Sun," in commenting upon this, takes the position that the change is a reform and says:

"As a matter of fact the title 'Doctor' is almost as common as that of 'the Hon.,' to which every American citizen is entitled. It is the custom to call all clergymen Doctor, quite irrespective of the fact that they may or may not possess sheepskins. Dentists equally with medical men are so styled, and so designate themselves. The proprietors of drug stores and even the clerks who dispense soda water in their establishments are affectionately greeted as "Doc." by their friends and associates. A "doctor" may be of Divinity or Law, of Music or Medicine, of Science or Philosophy, of Pedagogy or of Christian Science. He may look after the health of dogs, of horses or even cats. The title may even have an ironical sense, as when an old and distinguished practitioner uses it in speaking to a youth just out of the College of Physicians and Surgeons, whose principal occupation is to coax his budding Vandyke beard. So it can be seen that 'Doctor' may mean much or little, or nothing at all. In Great Britain it came to be so much abused that surgeons took to calling themselves 'Mister,' and bitterly resent the coupling of their names with the academic designation.

"Then just think of the number of prominent men who have been 'Doctors,' but who have never been spoken of as such. Colleges have rained degrees on our Presidents. But who ever talks of Dr. Harrison or Dr. McKinley? If somebody spoke of 'Dr. Tom Reed,' the listeners would never think that the ex-Speaker was referred to. When Edinburgh wanted to bestow a scarlet hood on old Tom Carlyle he said that he wouldn't take it because people might get him and his kinsman, Dr. Carlyle, mixed up. And Herbert Spencer, probably the most learned man of his time, has the proud distinction of not writing the letters of a single degree after his name. He has gently but firmly put aside the honors offered him by nearly every university of importance in the world. Sturdy old Sam Johnson was an exception. But he was proud of his LL.D. because it was the evident proof that the alma mater which despised him in his youth honored and respected him in his old age. Although many 'Doctors' are not learned, it is also a fact that many plain 'Misters' are. The second of these is a good plain

title, that is none the worse because everybody has a right to it."

Fortunately for accountants, there is nothing in their degree which can be converted into "Doctor" or any other familiar handle. Therefore, they are not in any way included in the class above described. There is, however, in what precedes an indication of the feeling of the public as well also as of the opinion held by thoughtful persons on this question that may be well taken to heart by accountants as well as others. Plain "Mister" is safe and, therefore, it is generally employed. The initials indicating the accountants' degree are justifiable, and such a method of indicating one's real position in the business community and his qualifications for the work to be undertaken, as using them after his name, should be employed whenever any good is to be derived therefrom.

Statements of Financial Condition

It is so much the rule nowadays for merchants to deposit with their creditors and with the mercantile agencies signed statements of their financial condition, revised from time to time, as their balance sheets are made out, that for the most part it is quite unnecessary to rehearse the reasons for their doing so. There are some merchants, however, who are entirely solvent and abundantly able to submit statements which would secure them far more credit than they are ever likely to ask for, who yet hesitate to comply with the general request which the agencies and merchants in general unite in making. Many young merchants, strong in the belief of the sufficiency of their capital, and in their self-reliance, feel that a demand for a statement is almost an insult, and, therefore, they neglect to make it. To all the business men composing these classes a few reasons why the request for a statement is reasonable and why the debtor should not hesitate to give it will be of advantage.

Sometimes we can see our own position more clearly by attempting to take observations from the other man's point of view. Let every business man, therefore, who is asked for a statement, consider what he would do if he were in the creditor's place and the creditor were occupying his position. The old rule, "Do unto others as you would have others do unto you," is just as applicable in this matter of business as it is in any other direction.

It should not be forgotten that as business activities multiply the dependence of men upon one another correspondingly increase. An injury in a business way to one becomes the concern of many. The mismanagement in business of a single individual hurts numerous others. No business man, irrespective of the amount of capital that he controls, is so independent as to reap alone the results of his administration of his business. It follows, therefore, that all with whom he has transactions are in a greater or lesser degree concerned in his success or lack of success. It is his duty, then, to cheerfully comply with all those business rules which, rigidly enforced, reduce losses and conserve business economics. Even though he knows his capital is so ample and his business ability so great as in a sense to put him beyond the necessity of giving a statement, yet inasmuch as that statement will in no wise be to his disadvantage it should be promptly furnished, first because it will be a good example to others, and second because it will put him in the class of safe and reliable business men, to which he justly belongs.

No honest and fair-minded merchant, who exacts a statement from those to whom he sells will hesitate a moment to cheerfully render a statement of his own financial affairs to those from whom he buys. It is a duty that every man owes to the business community, to be open and fair in all his business transactions. Frankness and absolute fairness are the only sure foundations of a credit. They stimulate confidence and they make business relations more intimate and consequently more advantageous.

The Proof-by-Balance System of Cost Accounts

The very satisfactory and common-sense system of Factory Bookkeeping or Cost Accounts which for several years past has formed an important feature of various specifications of the BALANCE SHEET SYSTEM OF ACCOUNTS, is now offered to manufacturers generally. It is suited to every line of business and to every class of product. The principles are unvarying, but their applications differ from time to time. Adaptations are always intelligently made to meet requirements. The leading features of the system include the following :—

1. The cost value of materials on hand, in gross and in as many subdivisions as may be desired, is shown at all times.

2. The cost value of work in progress, in gross and in whatever detail is required, is indicated at all times.

3. The cost value of goods completed and on hand, in gross and in as fine detail as desired, is shown at all times.

4. The correctness of the figured cost of goods is proven monthly by balancing with total charges to factory.

5. The constant employed for spreading over product the general expenses of factory is corrected monthly in the light of ascertained results to date, thus adjusting recorded costs to actual conditions of output.

6. Inventorying is reduced to the examination of individual departments or classes of materials to verify the corresponding accounts.

7. The cheapest system to install and maintain, and the most efficient and satisfactory in use.

Installations are made upon the specification plan exclusively. Everything is in writing. No oral instruction. No changes in your present system until you have had a chance to study the new, and make sure that all its details please you.

Correspondence solicited.

Account, Audit & Assurance Co., Limited

25 PINE STREET, NEW YORK

Large Results from Small Beginnings

It has been pointed out that both Jay Gould and Collis P. Huntington, says a writer in the "Boston Transcript," began their independent business careers with the peddler's cart. These are striking instances of large results from small beginnings, but if we trace back the careers of a great many whom the world calls successful business men we shall find that they obtained their starts as humble itinerant merchants. It seemed in a former generation to be the early training school for business men, as teaching was, and still is, for those fitting themselves for professional careers. But the peddler's cart, while not yet an altogether obsolete institution, has lost the dignity that once attached to it, and it no longer seems to be the stepladder to larger things that it often in former times proved to be.

The old-time peddler had an exceptional opportunity to study human nature in its various manifestations, and he had need of shrewdness to win success, for, unlike the merchant, he was trading with people on their own ground and not on his. He had his regular line of customers, whereas, in these days of easy communication with trade centers, his successor enjoys only a fitful patronage, dependent upon finding people with unsuspected needs or convincing them of needs of which they were previously unconscious. Moreover, the peddler of fifty years or more ago was, as a rule, a keen-witted fellow, and he was welcomed not alone for his tempting display of merchandise, but for his knowledge of the world. He helped dispel the dullness and the deadness of the isolated community or household. Now he is of ordinary clay, frequently a man who uses the English language imperfectly, and more often than otherwise he encounters a disposition to get rid of him with as little ceremony and loss of time as possible. Moreover, with the daily papers brought to almost every hamlet and with free rural delivery spreading, were he the veriest oracle that ever traveled, he would find his occupation gone.

Settled

In days of old men were not so proficient in the art of writing as they are at the present day. Then, hieroglyphics took the place of written characters, and some of the ancestors of our present over-educated aristocrats were in the habit of dipping their sword points in the ink and making their marks therewith every time their signatures were necessary.

There were once two farmers who were quite deficient in the art of writing, one of whom was indebted to the other for a considerable sum. Over this debt they fell out, with the result that the debtor thought it best to settle his indebtedness without delay. At the same time, suspiciously or shrewdly, he demanded a receipt of his hostile creditor.

The latter, in view of this demand, found himself in quite a dilemma, inasmuch as he was incapable of writing even his name.

He thought over the matter carefully for some time and at last saw a way out of the difficulty. If he could not write, he could at least draw. Very soon he had made a rough sketch of the body of a man "hanged by the neck until he was dead."

"What is that?" inquired the astonished debtor, who had demanded a receipt.

"That," said the artist, triumphantly, "is your receipt."

"What's it mean?" was the next puzzled question.

"Settled."

And the farmer who wanted a receipt looking upon the picture, was obliged to admit that it did spell "settled" as correctly as the proper combination of certain letters of the alphabet. He accepted the receipt.

The Use of "Esq"

The British postmaster-general's instructions as to the proper use of "Esq." in addressing one's male correspondents would seem to show that it is just about as promiscuous a title in Great Britain as it is in this country. Laborers, personal servants and tradesmen are specifically excluded under this official ruling, and in cases of doubt it may be used. It would be interesting to know on what grounds the postmaster-general bases his ruling that depositors in postal savings banks are not entitled to the suffix. Are they of necessity excluded from the gentry of Great Britain?

THE SELF-PROVING ACCOUNTING SYSTEM

A Manual on Higher Accounting With Many Original Features.

By A. O. KITTREDGE, F.I.A., C.P.A., and J. F. BROWN, Merchant.

Large Octavo.   328 Pages.   4 Fac-simile Insets and Numerous Other Illustrations. Good Paper, Excellent Typography and Substantial Binding.

This work describes and illustrates a system of accounts adapted to all lines of business, which has for its foundation a Perpetual Balance Sheet. This balance sheet, in place of being made up at intervals, is an integral and going part of the system and keeps the net results of the business constantly before the eye of the manager. It introduces no new elements, but makes various new applications of old principles. A given business is represented by the smallest possible number of accounts, and each class of accounts is furnished with books adapted to its special requirements.

The ledgers used with the SELF-PROVING ACCOUNTING SYSTEM are so constructed as to be readily sectionalized for purposes of proof. The system subdivides to any extent required by the character and amount of help employed, but always with the work of each clerk and ledger-keeper so arranged as to be capable of proof by itself.

All the secrets of the business are in the Balance Sheet Ledger. This book, which is the central feature of the system, always shows the condition of the business in regard to resources and liabilities, and, in addition, in regard to profits and losses, the same as a balance sheet of ordinary form. It is not neces-

sary to stop the business in order to close or balance the books. The results are always shown. Profits or losses to date may be instantly ascertained at any time and as often as desired.

Postings are from original entries. There is no copying. Modern facilities are used throughout. Several new features of account-book construction and various new ideas in rulings are employed.

By the SELF-PROVING ACCOUNTING SYSTEM all the terrors of the trial balance are fully overcome.

The examples for illustrative purposes used in the MANUAL of the SELF-PROVING ACCOUNTING SYSTEM are taken from the Installment Business, a line of commercial enterprise heretofore sadly neglected by accountants. The Manual, in addition to general features, contains complete exposition of the SELF-PROVING ACCOUNTING SYSTEM applied to the Installment Business, thus making it a hand-book for instant use in that line of trade.

The SELF-PROVING ACCOUNTING SYSTEM makes use of every known satisfactory method of proving ledger-work. At the same time, it is not a secret system, but is explained in full in this volume.

The Self-Proving Accounting System, while double entry in principle, is more than double entry in detail by reason of the methods employed for summarizing and condensing. It is a careful application of the most advanced principles of accounting brought down to date.

The *Accountant's Magazine,* Edinburgh and London, says: "The system is a development of the device of keeping in the general or private ledger, accounts representing the various subsidiary or departmental ledgers. The accounts are classified in separate ledgers corresponding with the form in which they ultimately appear in the Balance Sheet, and an account is opened in the private ledger with each class."

The Self-Proving Accounting System is adapted to any line of business. It is in use in prominent establishments throughout the country covering almost every branch of commerce. The Manual gives complete description of the system so that its application to any required business may readily be made.

Price, $5 carriage paid.   Make remittances to the order of

SELF-PROVING ACCOUNT BOOK CO., 12 Dutch Street, New York

Printed and bound by CPI Group (UK) Ltd, Croydon, CR0 4YY

08/05/2025

01864538-0001